BESTSELLING
BOOK SERIES

Developing eBay® Business Tools For Dummies®

Cheat Sheet

Names and hexadecimal numbers for the basic 16 HTML colors

Although you can specify any color you can imagine by tinkering with the hexadecimal codes below, these 16 colors cover most everything you need on a regular basis. For details about HTML color tags, see Chapter 4. All Web browsers respond to the color names next to the hexadecimal codes below, so you can specify *black* in your HTML statement instead of typing #000000.

Aqua = "#00FFFF"
Black = "#000000"
Blue = "#0000FF"
Fuchsia = "#FF00FF"
Gray = "#808080"
Green = "#008000"
Lime = "#00FF00"
Maroon = "#800000"

Navy = "#000080"
Olive = "#808000"
Purple = "#800080"
Red = "#FF0000"
Silver = "#C0C0C0"
Teal = "#008080"
White = "#FFFFFF"
Yellow = "#FFFF00"

Most useful eBay-specific HTML tags

For full information about the tags (including the options they support), see Chapter 6. Get the most up-to-date listing directly from eBay at pages.ebay.com/help/account/html-tags.html.

`<eBayUserID>`	Displays your User ID with a feedback link
`<eBayUserID NOFEEDBACK>`	Lists your User ID without a link to your feedback
`<eBayUserID EMAIL>`	Shows your User ID with your e-mail address
`<eBayTime>`	Displays the current time, according to eBay's master clocks
`<eBayFeedback>`	Lists your feedback
`<eBayFeedback SIZE="n">`	Displays the most recent *n* items from your feedback
`<eBayFeedback ALTERNATECOLOR="color">`	Adds an alternating color to your feedback listing
`<eBayItemList>`	Lists all items you currently offer for sale
`<eBayItemList SORT="3">`	Makes a list of your auctions sorted by auction end date, with newest auctions listed first
`<eBayItemList SORT="4">`	Shows your auctions sorted by price, in ascending order
`<eBayItemList CAPTION="caption text goes here">`	Displays the text you type as a caption above your item listing
`<eBayItemList TABLEWIDTH="n">`	Specifies how wide to make your item listing, as a percentage of the available space on the page

Generally speaking, you can freely stack options within an individual tag by listing them one after another. (A few of the tags don't work together. See Chapter 6 for those exceptions to the rule.) For example, `<eBayItemList SORT="3" TABLEWIDTH="50" CAPTION="Browse through my auction catalog — save money with combined shipping!">` mixes three options together into a single tag. It sorts the auction list, puts it in a table that takes up 50 percent of the possible width on the screen, and tops the table with a caption advertising my combined shipping.

For Dummies: Bestselling Book Series for Beginners

Developing eBay® Business Tools For Dummies®

Cheat Sheet

Developers Program sites

eBay Developers Program	developer.ebay.com
PayPal Developer Program	developer.paypal.com
USPS developer site	www.uspswebtools.com
FedEx developer site	www.fedex.com/us/solutions/wis/
UPS developer site	www.ups.com/ecommerce/solutions/c1.html

Programming languages for serious eBay development

ASP	msdn.microsoft.com/asp
C#	msdn.microsoft.com/vcsharp
Cold Fusion	www.macromedia.com/software/coldfusion
Java	java.sun.com
Perl	www.perl.org
PHP	www.php.net
Python	www.python.org
Visual Basic	msdn.microsoft.com/vbasic

Software to spruce up your auctions

CoffeeCup Software	www.coffeecup.com
DHTML Menu	www.dhtml-menu.com
DHTML Menu Studio	www.xtreeme.com/dhtml/
Open Cube	www.opencube.com
Soft Complex	www.softcomplex.com
Style Master	www.westciv.com/style_master/
TopStyle	www.bradsoft.com/topstyle/

Finding new JavaScript and DHTML for your Web site

Dynamic Drive	www.dynamicdrive.com
DHTML Central	www.dhtmlcentral.com
CodeToad	www.codetoad.com
Hot Scripts	www.hotscripts.com
Need Scripts	www.needscripts.com
Site Scripts	www.sitescripts.com

Great tools for PHP development

DHTML Central	www.dhtmlcentral.com
Homesite	www.macromedia.com/homesite/
Komodo	www.activestate.com
PrimalScript	www.sapien.com
Zend Studio	www.zend.com

eBay Developer ID entries

DevID	
AppID	
CertID	

For Dummies: Bestselling Book Series for Beginners

Developing eBay® Business Tools

FOR DUMMIES®

Developing eBay® Business Tools

FOR DUMMIES®

by John Kaufeld and Tim Harvey

WILEY

Wiley Publishing, Inc.

Developing eBay® Business Tools For Dummies®

Published by
Wiley Publishing, Inc.
111 River Street
Hoboken, NJ 07030-5774

WILEY

About the Authors

John Kaufeld is a nerdy business geek, but at least he has fun.

John discovered computers in high school instead of girls, and amused himself by laboriously typing BASIC programs into a TRS-80 Model 1 in his high school math lab. During college, he accidentally discovered the profitable world of consulting when he set his hourly tutoring fee at four times the going rate, yet received more clients than all of the other tutors put together. Tying the two fields together made some kind of perverse sense in his mind, so he spent much of his career helping people understand computers (and sometimes helping computers deal with their people).

In addition to writing a bunch of books in the *For Dummies* line, John started several fun businesses with his co-author, Tim Harvey. He spends lots of time at their board game store, More Than Games (www.morethangames.com), particularly during the holiday season. If you look hard enough, you can frequently find him at either Origins or GenCon Indy (www.originsgames.com and www.gencon.com, two of the big summer game conventions). In his copious free time, he enjoys photography, music, and every moment spent with his wonderful wife Jenny and their three children, Joe, Becky, and baby Isaac.

You can find John's auctions on eBay under user ID *linguaplay,* and can reach him via e-mail at jkaufeld@aol.com.

Tim Harvey plunged into the entrepreneurial world as an early teen, invoicing his parents for cleaning up after the family dog. Lured by the exciting pace and flexibility, Tim launched netPoint Design, a Web design and consulting company, while still in college. He has since started two other businesses, More Than Games and ShipperTools (www.shippertools.com) with co-author John Kaufeld. Tim also serves as the Information Systems Supervisor at Grabill Cabinets, a leader in the high-end custom cabinet market. He never wavers in his enthusiasm for new technologies that solve real-world problems.

Having just learned to ride this summer, Tim plans to expand his passion for high-performance motorcycle riding (yes, he owns a "rocket") in the coming season. With an eye toward someday competing in sport-bike racing, he's looking forward to a summer race training course. When he's not tending one of the businesses, you can usually find Tim and his wife Sara looping around clover-leafs or zipping through the winding roads surrounding their home in northern Indiana.

Dedication

John's Dedication:

To Jenny, because I loved you the first moment we met, and every day is like meeting again.

To Critter, Pooz, and The Mighty S-PAL (Sir Poops-a-Lot), for the smiles, the hugs, and the loving way you say "Daddy, is the book done *yet?*"

To my friends and compatriots at John Wiley and Sons, for the opportunity of a lifetime.

Thank you, one and all.

Tim's Dedication:

To Sara, my lovely wife and constant source of joy. Your dedication, sacrifice, and endless enthusiasm made this book a reality. Thanks for challenging me to reach for the sky.

Props to all the friends, family, and customers that endured long hours, frequent schedule changes, and endless talk of eBay. We've got some lost time to make up for!

Special thanks to the folks at John Wiley & Sons, particularly Mark and Kim for their incredible patience and encouragement. You made this project fun.

Authors' Acknowledgments

John's acknowledgements:

First, congrats to you, Tim, on your first-ever book. You survived, but your hair didn't. (Don't worry — we'll have the memorial service soon.)

At John Wiley and Sons, my humble and sincere thanks go to Acquisitions Editors Katie Feltman and Steve Hayes (and Andy Cummings, "the boss"), for giving me a new book when they probably should have run screaming from the building. Major kudos also go to Mark Enochs, our Project Editor, for enduring the task set before him (namely, working with us).

Thank-you's also go out to Kim Darosett and Kyle Holder, our Copy Editor and Technical Editor, respectively. Without them, this book would look like... well... never mind what it would've looked like. Some things are better left unknown.

A special tip o' the hat goes to my wonderful friend Marsha Collier. Marsha is the kind of person that everybody hopes they meet in their life, because she's an energetic dynamo of knowledge and delight. I can't wait to see you again!

Finally, my deepest, most enduring thanks go to Diane Steele. Many years ago, Diane took a chance on an untried geek, carefully watered and cultivated him, and patiently watched me grow into something that kinda-sorta looks like an author, provided you tilt your head at the right angle. Diane, you're awesome.

Tim's acknowledgements:

First and foremost, thanks go out to my coauthor, John Kaufeld. An amazing author, wonderful friend, and talented business partner, John continues to amaze me. Your continual encouragement throughout this book project kept me moving. You guided and coached me along many bumpy roads, always keeping an eye towards growing a stronger Author in me. You rock (verb)!

Mark Enochs, our project editor, made this book happen in a very special way. While we didn't have much phone time, your kind e-mails and thought-provoking questions ensured that my inner-author stayed sane and our readers benefited from a solid title.

Reminding me that I should have paid a bit more attention in English years ago, Kim Darosett turned sometimes bumpy ideas into clear, concise explanations. I thank you, and our readers thank you (trust me, you saved them from a few good ones).

Extra special thanks go to Marsha Collier, author of many eBay "Dummies" titles including eBay for Dummies. Without your partnership and help, we wouldn't be here. Your confidence made one of my dreams a reality. Thanks.

Of course I couldn't have finished this book without the amazing support of the folks at Grabill Cabinets, my wonderful wife Sara, John and Jenny, Mike and Christa and the rest of the gang (Bob, C. Ray, Daniel, Isaac, Jared, Jerad, and Jon — you know who you are). Thank you all.

"Game on!"

Publisher's Acknowledgments

We're proud of this book; please send us your comments through our online registration form located at www.dummies.com/register/.

Some of the people who helped bring this book to market include the following:

Acquisitions, Editorial, and Media Development

Project Editor: Mark Enochs

Acquisitions Editor: Katie Feltman

Senior Copy Editor: Kim Darosett

Technical Editor: Kyle Holder

Editorial Manager: Kevin Kirschner

Permissions Editor: Laura Moss

Media Development Specialist: Kit Malone

Media Development Manager: Laura VanWinkle

Media Development Supervisor: Richard Graves

Editorial Assistant: Amanda M. Foxworth

Cartoons: Rich Tennant (www.the5thwave.com)

Composition Services

Project Coordinator: Nancee Reeves

Layout and Graphics: Andrea Dahl, Lauren Goddard, Joyce Haughey, Stephanie D. Jumper, Barry Offringa, Jacque Roth, Heather Ryan

Proofreaders: John Greenough, Leeann Harney, Jessica Kramer, Carl William Pierce, Rob Springer, TECHBOOKS Production Services

Indexer: TECHBOOKS Production Services

Publishing and Editorial for Technology Dummies

Richard Swadley, Vice President and Executive Group Publisher

Andy Cummings, Vice President and Publisher

Mary Bednarek, Executive Acquisitions Director

Mary C. Corder, Editorial Director

Publishing for Consumer Dummies

Diane Graves Steele, Vice President and Publisher

Joyce Pepple, Acquisitions Director

Composition Services

Gerry Fahey, Vice President of Production Services

Debbie Stailey, Director of Composition Services

Contents at a Glance

Table of Contents

Introduction

*I*f the Great Pyramid qualifies as one of the Seven Wonders of the World, then eBay deserves an honorary award as the Eighth Wonder. Despite its "virtual" existence, eBay rivals the Wonders of old for engineering, size, and impact on society. Granted, those ancient builders figured out how to move tons of stone with little more than rope, rollers, and lots of people power, but the eBay engineers facilitate millions of dollars in sales every day, all across the world. That's gotta count for something.

The similarity doesn't stop there. In a modern reflection of the ancient architects' work, the eBay programmers left many secret passages, mysterious dead ends, and curious clues as they went along. If you hold the skill to explore and navigate through eBay's sometimes strange online realms, you can bring home amazing treasure, just like those intrepid pyramid explorers who unraveled the secrets of the Great Pyramid.

Unfortunately for them, the adventurers of old just picked a spot and kept digging until they found something, You, on the other hand, get a guidebook to help you along the way. That's where the book you hold in your hands comes into play. (Cue the trumpet fanfare as this book enters from stage right.)

Developing eBay Business Tools For Dummies guides you through the gigantic (and often confusing) technical world of eBay. Regardless of your technical adeptness and interest, it offers lots of solid tips and techniques for increasing your profits with some focused dabbling in geeky stuff like HTML, JavaScript, XML, and more. You even discover the legendary hidden machines of the online world, the APIs for eBay, UPS, FedEx, and the U.S. Postal Service.

Strap on your pith helmet, prepare your observation notebook, and get ready to increase your eBay sales. Let the adventure begin!

About This Book

This delightful tome treads a very unique path through the wild digital landscape that eBay calls home. Most eBay books cover the basics of buying, selling, and generally surviving in the online marketplace. They offer advice on topics like why you shouldn't buy a used violin from someone who normally sells frozen fish chunks and why you can't sell your soul online (somebody already tried that, and it didn't work for him, either). Other books explain how to set up your office, establish a shipping system, and make a true business of what started as an eBay hobby.

Put simply, this book doesn't do any of that.

Instead, *Developing eBay Business Tools For Dummies* builds a new Technical Wing onto your existing knowledge of eBay. The book outfits you with tools ranging from easy to geeky, instructs you in some mildly arcane computer topics, and wraps it all up in the friendly *For Dummies* style. Think of it as a book-shaped eBay consultant who wants to increase your profits without driving you insane (or out of business) in the process.

By keeping that machete-like focus on translating technology into profits, this book helps you cut through the technical underbrush. If you want to make more money, save more time, and maybe even change the way you look at geeky tech stuff, then you came to the right place.

Conventions Used in This Book

Some of the technical details in this book look strange enough on their own that they don't need any extra help from the fonts. To tame the technicalities and make them easier to read, the book uses some unique formatting. Here's what awaits you:

✔ **Internet addresses (URLs):** Whenever the book points you toward an online location, the address gets formatted like this:

```
www.ebay.com
```

✔ **Code samples:** No technical book is complete (or at least *helpful*), without a bunch of sample code that demonstrates the arcane things the author talks about. In this book, the code appears in a special font designed for optimal ugliness. Luckily, it also keeps the code lined up nice and neat so it reads as easily as possible. Here's an example:

```html
<h1>Ways to spend your eBay profits</h1>
<ul>
   <li>buy strange and wonderful things to resell</li>
   <li>go on vacation to an exotic land and bring back
       things to resell</li>
   <li>buy a new car and sell the old one in eBay
       Motors</li>
   <li>expand your movie collection through online auc-
       tions</li>
   <li>hire someone to handle your auction shipping</li>
</ul>
<p>The possibilities are <i>endless!</i></p>
```

As an added bonus, a whole group of icons keeps watch over the text to guide you toward useful things, warn you about urgent details, and generally protect you from the stranger and more bizarre content contained herein. For more about the book's ever-present road signs, see the "Icons Used in This Book" section later in this Introduction.

What You're Not to Read

With enough time and effort, you can do everything in this book. *Everything.* The bigger question is whether everything in this book makes sense for you and your business.

There's good news on that topic: It won't. Some topics in this book (such as programming with the eBay API) make more sense for a bigger business than a smaller one. Other things, like adding HTML to your auctions or including a clickable link that stores an auction reminder on your customer's Palm, make sense for just about any business, regardless of the size.

If you look at a chapter and think "Wow — that's way over my head," then stop and ask yourself why. Perhaps you need more information about a particular technology. Maybe that topic simply exists outside what your business really needs.

Much of this material might look new and different (and somewhat strange) the first time you see it. The first time I looked at HTML code, I just about quit and walked away from the whole Web thing right then and there — it looked way too confusing for me! After mustering my courage, I pressed through and discovered that the basic stuff made sense, and that I could make it work. (For the record, some of the more complex HTML tags still throw me back to the reference books.)

Yes, you *can* do everything in this book. You can do it, and you should do it if it makes sense for your business. And this book shows you how.

Foolish Assumptions

What about you? What do you hope to get out of this whole crazy eBay technical development thing? I can't sit down with you and ask a bunch of questions, but I can make some assumptions, based on the folks that I did talk to. Among other things, I think that you . . .

> ✔ Already sell things on eBay. You feel comfortable with the buying and selling process. That's why I left that stuff out of this book.
>
> ✔ May or may not hold a lot of technical knowledge. Whether you regularly create server-based applications or feel faint at the sight of raw HTML, this book is for you. That's why it starts at the basic HTML level and moves onward into more and more technical coverage.
>
> ✔ Like making money and suspect that by adding more technology to your repertoire you can add more bucks to your pocketbook. (You're right, too!)
>
> ✔ Feel comfortable with the basic tools of online life, including the Web browser (Internet Explorer or whatever you choose as your browser du jour).

Most of the techniques in this book don't require any special equipment, software, or Web server access. If you have basic Internet access, a word processor, and the pluck to try something a little geeky, then you're ready to go. The more advanced items demand a bit more — and sometimes *quite* a bit more. Each chapter tells you right up front if it requires anything more than the basic technology available to all eBay sellers.

How This Book Is Organized

All good information gets better when someone makes it sit in order from left to right, up and down, or perhaps in concentric circles. This book breaks down the whole technical world of eBay tools into a few rough groups, mainly based on just how technical and geeky the particular topics are.

In general, the book moves from the most basic information to the most advanced, on a part-by-part basis. The first parts analyze the big questions, like *why you want to do this at all,* while the later ones focus on more technically obscure topics like *things to say to the API on your first date.*

The following sections outline what you can expect, both in topics and geekiness, in each of the book's parts. Feel free to prowl through the Table of Contents for a significantly more detailed content discussion.

Part I: Peering Toward the Technical Side of eBay

This part launches you onto your technical trek. It opens with an overview of what various technologies can do for your eBay appearance, planning, follow-up, and sales. From there, it lays a foundation for evaluating, selecting, and adding all kinds of technological wonders to your online business. The part closes with steps for building a toolbox of software and hardware as well as intangible things like Web server space. If this represents your first step down the road to high tech, then this part eases your concerns.

Part II: Low-Tech Steps to High-Value Returns

Just because something relies on technology doesn't mean it qualifies as *high tech*. This part looks at relatively low-tech ways to start enhancing your eBay business world. It covers the basics of HTML code for dressing up your auctions and making them sell better and offers a bunch of ideas for posting auctions faster and enhancing your online brand with ready-to-use templates. Because eBay provides you with a free mini–Web site known as the About Me page, this part suggests some ways to make the most of the space. (After all, nothing beats *free* when it comes to building your business.) Finally, this part looks at the timesaving tricks contained in your e-mail program and maps out a few simple tools you can create for doing everything from tracking competing auctions to tracking packages as they head toward your auction winners. (And remember to check the CD for ready-to-use templates, anxiously awaiting their opportunity to dress up your auctions!)

Part III: Stepping into Some Programming

If the last chapter of Part II whets your appetite for software development, then think of this part as a gigantic programming buffet. It builds on the basics of HTML by explaining how to add all kinds of nifty *gizmos* — such as in-auction navigation and e-mail links that protect your address from robotic address collectors — to your page. The popular JavaScript language earns some serious coverage here, along with Cascading Style Sheets. For the people handling high volumes of e-mail on a daily basis, the e-mail automation chapter offers steps for creating *very* high-tech mail-processing systems that do things like read incoming messages, pull information out of them, and fire off automated replies.

Part IV: Going API with eBay and More

APIs (application program interfaces) represent ultimate nirvana for business technology tools. If you can imagine an amazing program that will change your eBay business forever, you can probably make it happen with the help of a standard programming language and the eBay API. This part not only introduces and explores the eBay API but also provides insight on the APIs available for PayPal, FedEx, UPS, and the U.S. Postal Service. Sure, this represents a truly geeky bastion of high-tech applications, but the dividends more than pay for the programming effort.

Part V: The Part of Tens

What's a *For Dummies* book without a Part of Tens? (Well, for one thing, it's never going to sneak past the editor — that's what!) This final section of the book puts a slew of resources, handy ideas, nifty tricks, and excellent solutions at your fingertips. The chapters in this part cover a lot of ground and offer many valuable ideas in the process.

Icons Used in This Book

The best communicators use simple landmarks to help their audience stay on topic and remember important points after the meeting. That's why this book scatters these helpful icons throughout. Each one spotlights some seriously helpful information, making your quest for understanding all the easier.

Here's a quick peek at all the icons, along with some explanations of what they mean:

This information might change your whole day (and for the better, too). Always pay attention to items marked with the Tip icon. They point out shortcuts, offer new ideas, give alternate solutions, and offer better ways of doing tasks.

If it's worth doing, then it's worth remembering when it's done. Remember icons mark information *so* important that you simply don't want to miss it. These icons reinforce especially vital instructions.

This friendly *For Dummies* icon normally points out dangerously geeky technical information in a book. But if this *is* a technical book, what can the Technical Stuff icon hope to add? Quite a bit, actually. This icon warns you about topics that require either *very* special technical knowledge or access to specific technology. They mark the most powerful tools in the book (which, as you might expect, demand the most support and require the greatest geeky prowess).

As the name implies, the Warning icon communicates simple but important ideas — ideas like STOP, WHOA, HALT, ACHTUNG, and HEY, YOU IN THE BERMUDA SHORTS! Read the warning information carefully — the code you save could be your own.

After developing and typing all the code in this book, I certainly don't want to make *you* redo all that work on your own. You have other things to do, like make money on eBay. To help you skip the "techno-geek typing" step, the book includes a CD containing all the code examples. Just pop the CD into your computer and then follow the instructions (or just check the CD Appendix, housed in the far back reaches of the book). That's much better than just retyping!

Every *For Dummies* book relies on the same set of icons, so if you ever wander through another title in the line, expect to see some old friends (and probably a few new ones, too).

Where to Go from Here

With the book in your hand and a world of possibility awaiting you, where should you go from here? The answer depends mainly on how much technical background you already possess, what kind of business you run, and just what level of business technology you think that your business needs.

If you're completely new to the technical world of HTML and such, definitely begin in Part I. It helps you get a handle on the whole technology-in-business thing, from the big Chapter 1 overview to the tool-collecting advice in Chapter 3. From there, try your hand at HTML. After you feel comfortable, gently branch into creating some basic personal tools or applying prewritten JavaScript code to your auction listings. Go slow, go easy, and don't worry if something doesn't quite work the way you think it should the first time. That's half the fun of programming. (I don't know exactly what the other half is, but I'm actively seeking it.)

If your belt already has some programming work under it, glance through Part II but focus your attention on Parts III and IV. That's where the real meat of the programming work lives in this book. Don't completely overlook the technologically simpler stuff in the early parts, though. If something helps you make more money in your auctions, then it's worth the time — it doesn't matter whether that "something" is fascinatingly high tech or not.

Are you more of a corporate developer? In that case, you probably need the API information more than anything else. In that case, dive right into Part IV. Make sure you look at *all* the API information because if your company needs the eBay API to make extra money, then it can probably profit handsomely from the proper use of the other APIs, too.

Regardless of what you bring to the table, *Developing eBay Business Tools For Dummies* stands ready to take your business to new profit levels. Good luck — and sell well!

Part I

Peering Toward the Technical Side of eBay

Mr. Patel, when I asked for a look at your merchandise, I kinda thought you'd just link some photos to your site.

In this part . . .

*I*n the beginning, there was technical stuff, and it was, well, *technical.* You suspect that you can increase your profits by plumbing these technical mysteries, but they seem so strange and geeky. What's an eBay seller to do? Pick up this book, that's what!

Part I introduces the world of marginally technical additions to both your eBay auctions and your computerized back office, demonstrating the cool benefits that await the newly high-tech you, including quicker auction postings, better customer information, and, ultimately, more profit from your work.

Chapters 2 and 3 take a look at how these technical tips might (or might not) fit into your business. They help you gauge your current programming-esque abilities, discern how deeply you want to go into the wild world of technical details, and help you assemble the tools that make up your online toolbox. You even find out where to look for great tools that you already own so you don't need to buy new versions. This book is saving you money already!

Don't worry about the strange technical stuff that awaits you out there. You've already conquered eBay itself, divined some great ways to sell your products, and started enjoying the profitable fruits of your labors. With *Developing eBay Business Tools For Dummies* in hand, the possibilities look endless. Good luck!

Chapter 1

Building Big Profits with Little Tools

*F*or some people, hours spent fiddling, tweaking, and generally adjusting some gee-whiz online gizmo is just a way of life. These folks love technology for the sake of the technology, regardless of whether the technology makes money for them. Although these people serve a wonderful purpose in the online world (they often come up with the incredibly cool things that other people ultimately use to make money), their "technology for the sake of technology" perspective doesn't put dineros in the wallet.

For busy eBay businesspeople, time *is* money. You need technology to do something useful and profitable rather than just sit in the corner and look massively cool.

With eBay, properly applied technology makes a huge difference in the following ways:

✔ It makes you more money by helping your auctions stand out from the crowd.

✔ It saves you time by helping to either simplify or actually complete the numerous little tasks that each auction requires from start to finish.

✔ It increases customer satisfaction from the time the person reads your auction listing all the way through to the point where the customer posts positive feedback into your eBay profile.

This chapter gives you a quick overview of the kinds of things that high tech can do for your auctions, your business, your customers, and your cramped schedule. It doesn't go into a lot of details — that's what the rest of the book does. For now, this chapter gives you a foundation, a groundwork, so you can build your own high-tech eBay dreams.

Welcome to the world of business-appropriate geeking. It's a blast in here!

Getting Noticed in the Vast eBay Marketplace

On eBay, image is everything. (Granted, the product and price thing comes into play too, but humor me on this for a moment.) When your prospective customers open up your auction for the first time, they see your product. They *also* get their first glimpse of your company. And based on what they see, they make some snap judgments about the whole package.

Like it or not, those customers make their initial decisions about your firm, your reputation, the quality of your product, and the level of your customer service based on what they see in your auction listing. If they take the time to go into your About Me page, you get a second shot at impressing them with your customer service skills, but that's an iffy proposition. Many buyers never dig that far. If your auction page doesn't convince them right then, they simply move on to the next auction on their search list.

Nope, the best thing you can do is to impress the living daylights out of customers during their first glance at your auction page. Sell them on the benefits of your product. Project your image as a valuable member of the eBay community. Convince them that you're a trustworthy seller who takes good care of buyers in the long run.

Your customers' first stop: The auction page

Shooting good pictures, writing solid text, and including the myriad little details that answer your customers' questions go a long way toward your initial success. But if you apply some technology in the right ways and places, you can build those simple techniques into unstoppable powerhouses of online sales. Your first technical steps toward all of that rest in the formatting and layout of your auction page.

If you need a quick run-through of the basic content of a good online auction (stuff like describing your product, getting a decent digital image of it, and establishing your selling policies), grab a copy of *Starting an eBay Business For Dummies* by the Queen of eBay, Marsha Collier (Wiley). Marsha covers those basics and a lot more. (Plus, she's just fun to read.)

eBay offers several built-in options for dressing up your auctions. On the plus side, these options require no programming on your part, so they make a great place to begin. (Better still, you can use them to *inspire* your own template designs.)

To add these options to your auction, just make a few selections from a handy menu. Suddenly, your auction looks awesome (at least from a layout perspective). What's the downside? All this convenience comes with a monetary price. Although the price stays low for just about everything, even those little amounts add up over time. Still, for a quick-and-dirty solution, it's tough to beat the built-in options that eBay provides.

Simple sprucing with Listing Designer

Chief among these options are the *themes* you can attach to your auctions with the Listing Designer. Each theme incorporates a full frame of graphics around your auction text as well as several options for photo layouts. Using the Listing Designer adds an extra dime to your auction listing fee. Although it isn't a lot on a per-auction basis, those dimes add up over time.

By itself, the Listing Designer reworks your auction with some really slick graphics. Figure 1-1 shows a rather bland and normal-looking auction. You see hundreds (if not thousands) of these every day on eBay. Figure 1-2 shows that same auction with an added boost from the Listing Designer. That's a nice bit of sprucing up for less than a minute's work!

Do a little sprucing of your own

Then again, why bother paying for those nifty dress-ups when, with a little bit of ingenuity, you can achieve most of the same effects on your own? eBay relies on HTML (short for *Hypertext Markup Language,* a term you never again need to read or remember) for all of its formatting. Luckily, you don't need any special degree (or even bizarre programming tools) to add your own HTML to the auction.

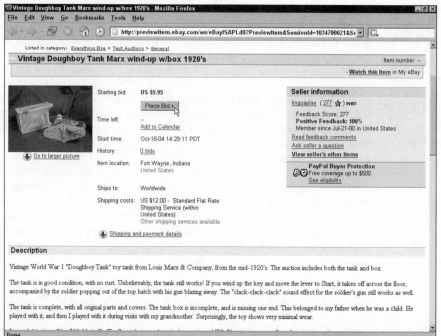

Start with some basic HTML codes that change the size of your auction headline or add color for the things you want to really jump out at the customer. Thanks to eBay's built-in text editor (shown in Figure 1-3), you can flip among fonts, sizes, colors, and settings like bold, italic, and underlined text. The standard text editor even helps you with alignment, bulleted lists, and indentions.

Like any do-it-yourself project, it's easy to get in further than you expected and spend a lot more time than you initially planned to invest. When building your auction layout, keep things simple. (Chapter 4 explains more about your first serious steps in adding HTML to an auction listing.)

To really stir things up with your formatting, fire up your own HTML program (such as Microsoft FrontPage) and design your auction page in that. Figure 1-4 shows my homegrown auction design, nearly ready for its trip into eBay.

By using a dedicated HTML editor, you gain access to all the special coding tricks available through HTML instead of limiting yourself to the basic set of tools built into the eBay system. Moving your sweetly designed auction page from one window to another involves merely copying and pasting. Because eBay understands HTML code, it handles all the important stuff on its own. Figure 1-5 shows the finished project, looking good and ready to start pulling in those bids.

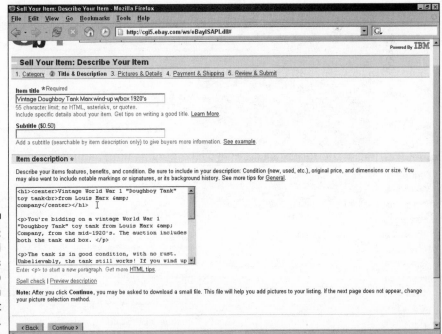

Figure 1-3:
You can add HTML tags directly to your auction in the text editor.

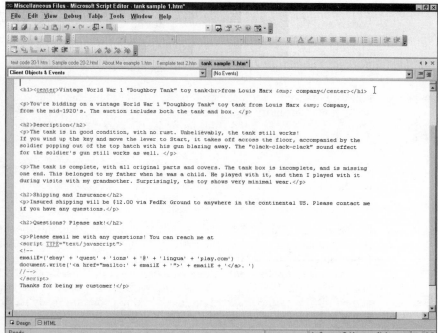

Figure 1-4:
Raw HTML
code looks
a little
daunting
sometimes.

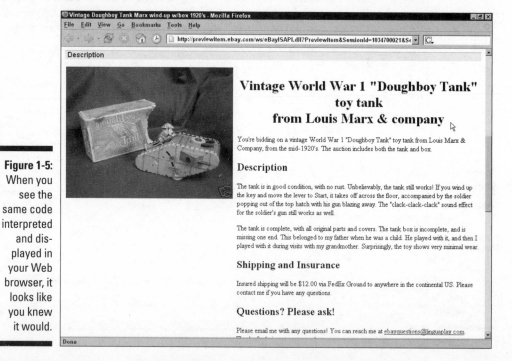

Figure 1-5:
When you
see the
same code
interpreted
and dis-
played in
your Web
browser, it
looks like
you knew
it would.

Don't underestimate the About Me page

The same HTML tricks work in your About Me page, although customizing everything takes a little more effort. As a starting point, eBay helps you build a basic About Me page that includes a title, a couple of paragraphs about your eBay world, a photo (complete with caption), some of your favorite Web links, plus optional listings of your auction items and most recent feedback. eBay also offers three basic layout templates (cleverly named Layout A, Layout B, and Layout C) that organize your information on-screen:

- ✔ **Layout A** puts your text, photo, and Web links at the top of the page, with your current auction list and feedback scores filling in the full width of the bottom section. It focuses customers on your business information first and makes them scroll down to your auctions.

- ✔ **Layout B** creates a more vertical look, with your photo centered, descriptive text on the left, and auctions and feedback in a narrow column on the right. This works great if you included a *lot* of text in your paragraphs but still want to point people to your auctions.

- ✔ **Layout C** looks just like Layout A, except that your Web links shift to the right of the page, directly under the graphic, and your second paragraph of information fills in the space opposite the links. It's okay — a bit odd, but still okay.

Those ready-to-use layouts offer a good place to begin. Still, the most useful About Me pages go far beyond the limitations of those templates.

Creating a killer About Me page means spending some time with your HTML editor, working with everything from font sizes to tables. Thanks to its flexibility, the About Me page makes a great place to sharpen your budding HTML skills. eBay gives you plenty of online storage space to try new approaches, and (unlike auctions) the system never complains if you update the page once, twice, or even 20 times.

If you just started selling on eBay (leaving you with a feedback rating in the single or double digits), your About Me page might well make the difference between getting sales and getting ignored. People *implicitly* want to trust you and buy from you. Give them a reason to by telling your story. Why did you start this eBay business? How did you come by your expertise? What's special about you? Simple things like that soothe customer worries and entice them into buying from you, and that translates into more sales.

Simple tips on attracting customers

Okay, so HTML lets you do amazing things in both your auction text and About Me page, but what *exactly* qualifies as an "amazing thing?" What can you really do with HTML that enhances your money-making prospects? I'm glad you asked:

- **Use different-sized fonts to draw the customer's attention to headlines and other key selling text.** When you get right down to it, auctions work just like advertisements. You promote a product in hopes that a seller reacts favorably to your ad. Advertising folks discovered the value behind steering a customer's eye around the page years ago. HTML font size commands give you the same power in your auctions.

- **Add color to your text to help the reader find the key benefits of your product or service.** Your text sells the product, but color grabs attention. Adding the right colors in the right spots enhances your auction by highlighting important features, benefits, and other information.

- **Place photos wherever you want without paying extra for the enhanced photo gallery settings.** Putting multiple pictures into an eBay auction means either grouping all your photos in one big block near the bottom of the page or paying for one of the prebuilt templates. Either way, you get very little real choice over where your pictures appear. By using some HTML and your own photo-hosting space, you gain complete control over where and how your auction photos land on the page. It's liberating!

- **Make your text and graphics stay where you put them by embedding everything inside tables.** All of this organization needs some kind of behind-the-scenes framework to support it. That's where HTML tables come onto the scene. Tables go way beyond the classic image of neatly arrayed rows and columns (although that's what they do best). By making cells of varying heights and widths, you build the digital cubbyholes to store text, graphics, links, and more. After you master the art of building tables, you can accomplish just about any on-screen appearance you desire.

The first few of the preceding techniques work straight from the eBay formatting window when you enter your auction text. Start there to get a good feeling for how the formatting options work and how best to apply them. After that, get comfy with your HTML-editing program and dive into the deeper stuff, like image alignment and the wild world of tables.

HTML makes the perfect place for you to discover and develop your nascent technical skills. Chapter 4 walks you through the details of everything mentioned here. If you're ready, flip ahead and dive straight in.

Better still, all the skills you develop by enhancing your auction pages translate directly into your efforts to build add-on sales and enhance customer service by creating your own Web site. See Chapter 6 for more about that.

Spoiling Your Customers with Information and Service

We live in an information-driven world. People want everything at their fingertips, whether they really need it or not. Worse yet, if people *don't* get all the information they think they need right up front, they sometimes assume that you're hiding something because you didn't offer it!

Even the smallest omission spawns little feelings of doubt and distrust in the online economy. It's one thing to walk into a retail store where you can look around, get a feel for the place, and ask questions of someone standing right there. The online world demands a completely different level of trust based on information. Fulfilling your customers' informational needs and answering their questions in a complete and proactive way helps you earn their trust.

Trust through presentation

Your presentation says a lot about your professionalism. Your product might look great, with all the bells and whistles imaginable, but if your auction text says "I slapped this puppy together in ten minutes," the buyer might wonder about both you *and* the product. A more professional-looking auction automatically bestows a professional image onto your online business. That image translates into trust, which turns lookers into buyers.

Because establishing trust starts with providing information, give customers everything they could possibly want. Some easy HTML coding lets you go from providing ground-level information (typing everything into a big block of text somewhere in the auction) to easy-to-navigate pages with headings and menus, plus gizmos like shipping calculators and automated reminders. Although some of these might seem like toys or window dressing, from the customers' perspective they say that you care, that you're a pro, and that customers can place their trust in you to deliver a product and experience worthy of their time and money.

Figures 1-6 and 1-7 demonstrate what I mean. In addition to the product information, this auction listing addresses the kinds of things that turn lookers into buyers. How's the condition of the item? This listing not only tells you but also *shows* you. What kind of policies does the seller use? Big headings direct the buyer to everything from shipping information to return policies. The seller doesn't try to slip anything by, but instead makes all the information big, bold, and available.

Figure 1-6:
Headings
help the
buyer find
specific
information
in the listing.

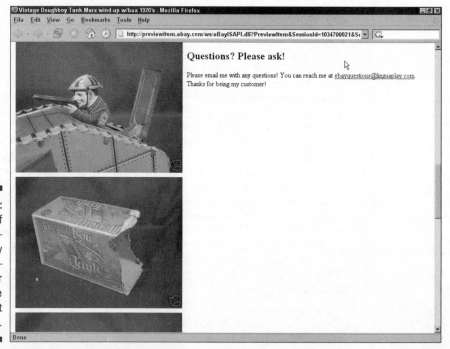

Figure 1-7:
Lots of
pictures —
especially
close-ups —
let the buyer
evaluate the
product
intimately.

Incidentally, your About Me page also is a great place to build your reputation as a solid eBay seller. The more customer-related information you put there — such as your policies, your feedback profile, your knowledge of the product line, and so on — the more comfort you add to your prospective client's decision. When I buy something from sellers who've been "in the business" for years, I feel more comfortable with the idea of buying. Even though I can't see them or haven't met them, the information they provide helps me judge their expertise and experience. But if the seller doesn't tell me those things in either the auction or the About Me page, then I probably won't ever find out. And the less I know about the seller, the less likely I am to buy from him. It's that simple.

When it comes to buying, people don't like surprises. When you flood your prospects with solid information that answers their questions and overcomes their built-in objections, you win their minds along with their hearts.

Communicating with the customer

A little bit of technology helps you with after-the-sale follow-up, too. How many times have you bought from someone who then seemed to disappear off the face of the earth? Every time it happens to me, I worry and fret and finish the transaction with a generally bad taste in my mouth. After-sale communication is almost as important — if not *more* important — than your product presentation when it comes to turning buyers into happy repeat customers.

Use your e-mail program's built-in rules (sometimes called *filters*) to keep a steady flow of communication going with your customer. Depending on the e-mail application, you can build automatic replies, make templates prefilled with standard information that your customers need to know, and manage simple mailing lists that turn a one-time purchase into an ongoing customer relationship.

If you want to get more technical, adding some custom programming to your Web server gives your technology the ability to actually open messages and process them, giving you the ability to automatically generate "thanks for your payment" messages and other customer communications. That level of technology opens entire new vistas of customer service and office automation, which make your company look like a seriously professional enterprise.

Get started with your e-mail application's built-in powers by turning to Chapter 7. For more about in-depth e-mail programming, flip ahead to Chapter 12.

Expanding Sales with Broader Exposure

Happy customers buy more stuff. That's the first rule of selling. (Well, actually the first rule is more like *make a consistent profit,* but I digress.) If you want to build your eBay sales into something terrific, start by delighting your customers. The experience you create through your auction pages and your About Me information lays the groundwork for the process, and your service as you close the sale and deliver the goods puts on the capstone. By delighting your customer, you generate the goodwill to easily get that customer buying from you again.

Every completed transaction gives you not only a happy customer but also that happy customer's contact information, most commonly in the form of an e-mail address. Offer your customers the opportunity to join a mailing list about your products. You can keep in communication with them, tell them about eBay auctions that might interest them, and generally polish your image as *the* expert in your field. Yes, all this stuff takes some time on your part, but it goes with the whole "business for yourself" thing.

On the technology side of life, a mailing list database helps you track who bought what and when they bought it. You can use that information to promote your future auctions or to look for add-on sales that naturally accompany what you already sell. Ask your customers what else they need to go with the items they bought and then consider offering those things. Sometimes, customers just want someone to ask for their business. What started as a good experience with the auction turns into an ongoing business relationship.

If your business has a Web site (and it really, *really* should), promote your business and your eBay sales there as well. List your auctions, complete with links to take your customers directly to pages where they can bid. Add auction links to related information pages on your site. That way, when a customer reads about the wonders of binocular microscopes (for example) on your Web page, they can quickly hop into eBay and buy one from your current selection.

Don't put a link on your eBay auctions that leads to a page where you *sell* the same product outside of eBay. That's a *big* no-no in eBay's world. It's okay to inform customers and give them plenty of information. It's not okay to redirect them to buying opportunities outside of eBay.

A Web page builds professionalism and trust just like a well-designed auction or an informative About Me page. The more that customers learn about your company, the more comfortable they feel buying from you. Your Web page forms another step toward closing today's sale and, at the same time, starting the process on tomorrow's sale.

Saving Time with Office Automation

eBay sure brings customers to your door. That's what it's good at! And those customers turn into buyers, which means money in your pocket. But then there's that last step in the process, where you close the sale with a small flurry of e-mails between you and your buyer and when you actually ship the goods that your customer bought. Those niggling little details can suck the life out of your time, which in turn costs you money because of the time you had to spend. It's a vicious cycle but one that you can break with some smart technology.

Start your timesaving efforts with auction templates, mentioned earlier in the "Do a little sprucing of your own" section. These ready-to-use frameworks ensure that you put a consistent face in front of the customer and that you don't accidentally forget any important information such as the shipping cost or your return policies. Consistency translates into professionalism in the customer's eye and saves time on your end. Life just doesn't get better than that!

Because you spend a lot of time interacting with your customer after the sale, make those exchanges go as smoothly as possible by creating prewritten e-mail messages that you can send at the click of a button. Most transactions require the same basic messages (I received your payment, I posted feedback for you, I will ship your product, I shipped your product, and such). If you still write all those messages by hand, that's a huge time sink.

Instead, automate that process with your e-mail program. Almost every e-mail application on the market includes some kind of boilerplate text option, although they almost never call it that. Eudora refers to it as "stationery," while my AOL client thinks of it as an extra-large signature block. No matter what program you use, it offers a way to implement these pretyped messages. You might need to poke around in the software a bit to find it, but it's there — I promise.

The automated e-mail processing programs described in Chapter 12 take this to a whole new level. Because those programs can easily recognize consistent messages like end-of-auction announcements and PayPal payment notices, you can tell the application to fire off replies to multiple people without touching a single button. When the program receives a PayPal notice, for example, it might send a thank-you note to the customer and a shipping reminder to you, and shove a record into your online auction database noting that the payment for that particular auction came through. When you get into large quantities of online sales, that type of automation significantly expands profits by smoothing out the entire sale process.

Building Serious Business with the eBay API

As you follow conversations on the eBay seller discussion boards (`pages.ebay.com/community/boards/index.html`) or the developer discussion boards (using your Developer Zone ID, sign into `developer.ebay.com` and then follow the Member Forums link), you sometimes get a whiff of something vaguely secret-sounding and just a little mysterious. Someone types something like, "Yeah, we did that, but we used the API." No real explanation, no serious detail, just a note that they expect you to understand. Of course, if you don't know anything about the eBay API, the note means nothing to you. Darn those technical people!

The eBay API isn't anything weird, strange, or mysterious. It's a tool mostly geared toward businesses that move a high volume of products or that have lots of resources available for development. It's also a great way for a budding entrepreneur to develop the Next Big Thing for eBay members around the world.

So just what *is* an API? The term stands for *application program interface*. In short, it's a set of communication tools that helps your program talk directly to eBay. It lists the kinds of questions your program can ask eBay and how eBay sends back the answers. The API doesn't tell you how to use the information, just how to communicate with eBay in order to *get* the information.

For an entrepreneur, the API provides an opportunity to create a program for others to use. If someone comes up with a better way to list and track auctions, for instance, that person can connect the program to the eBay API and talk directly to the eBay computers. Before the API arrived on the scene, programs like this relied on a technique known as *scraping,* where developers anticipated how eBay's screen looked, crossed their fingers, and started pushing information into on-screen fields. Unfortunately, every time eBay redesigned its screens in even the slightest way (which happened about every other week), it broke the program, leaving the programmer to make the requisite changes.

For a big company, access to the eBay API means the ability to do some amazing sales tricks. One company in the eBay Developers Program told about a customer application it created that ties its customer inquiry people directly to eBay. When a customer contacts the company looking to buy a particular item, the inquiry department can launch an auction for that item immediately (complete with all the product information) and then direct the customer to that auction by e-mailing him a link. It's pretty amazing stuff that opens up new realms of selling opportunities.

Small businesses can benefit from the API as well, although they need some reasonable auction volume before it makes sense. Sure, it might *sound* cool to say that your company created a custom application based on the eBay API, but is "cool" worth all the money and development time? (I don't think so, either.)

The eBay Developers Program Web site at `developer.ebay.com` (shown in Figure 1-8) explains all the details about the API, tools for making use of the API, and some inspirational success stories of companies that put the API to work for them. The site also helps you sign up for access to the API and leads you through the rather monstrous licensing agreement you need to sign before gaining access to it. (Think of the agreement like the defenses surrounding a castle — ya know, like a fire-breathing dragon, a moat filled with lava, and gigantic swarms of grumpy killer bees. The agreement is a piece of cake.)

If all this talk about the API piqued your entrepreneurial interest, check out Part IV of this book. It walks you through the basics of working with an API, explores the eBay Developers Program in more detail (and there's plenty of detail to discuss), and then takes you into the eBay API itself. It even introduces you to other related APIs in the world, like the ever-popular PayPal and shipping companies like UPS, FedEx, and even the U.S. Postal Service.

Figure 1-8: eBay thinks so highly of its developers that it built an entire Web site dedicated to the gentle art of building eBay-connected applications.

Chapter 2

Evaluating Your Technical Needs

. . . .

. . . .

During World War II, rationing hit everything from coffee and meat to soft goods and hard goods. It seemed that if a product existed, the government needed it for the war effort. Gasoline ranked high among the rationed items for obvious reasons. To keep the populace from using excess amounts of gas (and tires, oil, and other car-related items), the government advertised a simple slogan: "Is this trip really necessary?"

That slogan lived everywhere. You saw it on billboards. It appeared in newspapers and magazines. Animated characters reinforced it on the silver screen during the prefeature cartoon. And the slogan got people thinking. Was this trip really necessary? Could they combine it with another trip at some other time? The end result: People drove less, saved fuel and other supplies, and then made up for it with lavish consumerism after the war ended. Ah, those decadent 1950s . . . but I digress.

You face the same issues today as you advance your technical skills in eBay. (Well, everything except the lavish consumption part — although hopefully your increased eBay profits allow you to live like that.) As you start thinking about the amazing array of high-tech enhancements available to your eBay business, you need to stop and ask yourself that same question from the WWII days: *Is this trip really necessary?* What technical components enhance your business versus just making it look cool and geeky? What increases your profits instead of simply draining your free time without accomplishing anything useful?

Serious questions like those require serious thought. This chapter helps you evaluate your current eBay business, takes a look at the technical skills you have (or have access to), and ultimately assists you as you figure out what technical tricks make the most sense for growing your eBay business.

Beginning at the Beginning: Assessing Your Current Business

Before you start a journey, you need to assess where you already are. After you know that, it's much easier to figure out a path to your planned destination. Just ask Louis and Clark.

The same holds true in your eBay business. Determining your business needs before applying lots of fascinating technology makes the most sense in terms of both time and money. Sure, many other companies (mostly big companies) like to do things the other way around, but don't let that sway your plans. Just because they're big doesn't necessarily mean they're smart.

Start exploring the needs of your eBay business by asking questions like the ones in the following list. Each question focuses on a different aspect of your business, ranging from the things that *you* see to what your customers think. Feel free to add questions to the list. This isn't some mystical, all-inclusive bunch of ideas but rather a starting point for your brainstorming efforts. You can't ask too many questions when starting a process like this.

The following list gets you started along the path toward profitable brainstorming:

- What doesn't work in your company?
- What do you wish that you could change?
- What frustrates you about your business?
- What wastes your time or your employees' time?
- What are your competitors doing that you aren't?
- What aren't your competitors doing that you could do?
- What frustrates your customers about doing business with you?
- What enchants your customers in general?

With your questions in hand, start brainstorming answers. When doing this, fight the urge to judge your answers before writing them down. Just write! Keep going until you simply run out of things to say. Again, having too many answers works better than not having enough.

Don't rely exclusively on your perspective for answers to these questions. Talk to your employees (assuming you have some). Ask your customers — I know you have those! Some of the best ideas in my business came from employees and customers who wished that we did things just a little differently. By making the appropriate changes to our business, we increased productivity and profits with almost no cost. And *that's* the kind of business enhancement everybody loves!

List the answers in your favorite word processor or spreadsheet (if you feel number friendly). Go through the list again, rearranging the answers by how much of an impact each one would make to your business if you solved it. If something promises a huge payoff, strong savings (because spending *less* money counts the same as making *more* money), or increased customer satisfaction, put that near the top. Little issues that annoy but don't affect the bottom line go near the bottom of the list. Keep going through your whole list. Do it quickly (don't linger long over each item) and don't take anything off the list just yet. For now, focus on the ranking process.

Picking Your eBay Development Goals

With your completed list (the list you made in the last section) in hand, get ready to do something really shocking. Ready? Here goes: Look over the highest-impact items on your list. Can you resolve any of these issues *without* adding new technology?

Facing the toughest question of all

Before starting your big eBay development project, you need to face an uncomfortable question. It's a question you probably don't want to ask because it just might spoil all your fun. Even so, the question demands an answer. Ready? Here's the fateful query: *Are you the best person in your organization to do all of this technical eBay stuff?*

I know, I know — I'm playing the part of Mr. Wet Blanket over here, but I'm really looking out for your business. Stop and think about that question for a moment. Are *you* the best person to handle these tasks? I didn't ask whether you *really, really* wanted to do this stuff or whether you thought that you'd be good at it. Nope, I just want to know one thing: Are you the best person for the job or should you hand the mantle to someone else?

If your time *really* needs to be spent on projects with bigger paybacks for the organization, you should do that and leave the geeking to other folks — at least for now. You can direct them, check in with them, and generally observe their work, but you should focus your attention elsewhere. On the other hand, if you *are* the company, *you* might be the only choice available, particularly if you don't have a lot of money to spend on outside development help. In that case, do the most important stuff first, whether that means creating something wonderful (with this book's help, of course) or something mundane like, oh, keeping the business running.

Either way, now you know. Go with what you know, and your business will thank you.

Yes, you read that right: Before reformatting your auction listings or launching a swell new Web site, figure out what you can accomplish for your business without adding any new technology. Maybe it's something simple, like a process change or a redesigned form. Perhaps it's just a customer phone call or an extra e-mail (yes, that's technology, but because you already own an e-mail program, it counts for this step). Whatever you find, *implement these changes first.*

From a business perspective, you want to put the most effort into the things that provide the most reward. That's straight from Business 101. If nontechnical problems top the list, put this book aside for a while and fix those things first. After that, when your eBay business machine runs even more smoothly than it does now, pick up the book again and start on the technological stuff that you wanted to do in the first place. That way, your technical changes make even *more* of an impact than you thought they would.

With the nontechnical crises out of the way, it's time to turn your attention to the technical side of life. Here's what you need to do next:

1. **Identify the best prospects.**

   Go through the same process you did before, except focus on the things that require some technology (a new application, expanded Web service, custom programming, and so on). Start with the items that you think show the most promise in terms of payback to your business, either through time saved or money made.

2. **Try to anticipate how much technical work each prospective idea requires to bring it to fruition.**

   If you're unfamiliar with the technologies, use this book to guide you on how simple or complex they are. Map your ideas to the relevant book section by using the Table of Contents. Each chapter offers tips that help you develop your estimates.

3. **Optimally, start by implementing the ideas that you can bring into action pretty quickly and that offer the biggest rewards.**

   Large-scale technical projects usually deliver the biggest payback, but they also carry a lot more risk than something you can whip together in a small amount of time. Big projects usually translate into big requirements, and that means big time and big money. You get the idea.

The key words to keep in mind for your first wave of technical innovation include *low cost, low tech, low time,* and *high impact.* Start easy and then build on your success from there. As you gain experience, pick off the progressively more difficult items. In no time at all, the change in your business should amaze you!

Gauging Your Abilities

All of the work on your eBay development project hinges on two important questions:

- **How geeky are you already?** Do you like telling someone else to change your oil, directing someone as they change your oil, or rolling up your sleeves and grabbing a can of 10W30? Those answers direct a lot of what happens next.

- **How geeky do you want to get in your search for the ultimate eBay business tools?** Are you a high-level idea person with a vision of the future or more of a hands-on individual who relishes the challenge of breaking into the unknown and wrestling with something until it works?

There's nothing better or worse about any particular level of technical involvement or prowess. You just need to decide where and how you fit into this process and feel comfortable with that decision as you start the whole thing. As long as you look at this development process from the perspective of always doing the best thing for your business, you'll do fine.

Assessing your technical expertise

Start by answering the easier of the two questions, namely the one about your current level of technical knowledge. It's the easier question because it asks for a more objective answer. You probably know how comfortable (or uncomfortable) you feel with various aspects of online technology. Which of the following characterizations describes you?

- **You're just getting started.** The sight of HTML fills you with dread or at least concern. Although you use Web sites and your Web browser, you never really lifted the hood to see what made it all go.

- **You know a little of this and a little of that.** You created a Web page or perhaps a whole Web site and probably tinkered with things like FTP (file transfer protocol, for moving files between computers on the Internet) along the way. You made it past the basics but not into any heavy programming, although you occasionally copy a clever little on-screen tool, such as a menu system or pop-up message window, written in JavaScript (yet another programming language — they're everywhere) that looks interesting and put it on a page of your own.

- **Web sites fear and obey you.** Nothing gets your heart beating quite like a good romp through some PHP code (a language used in Web and API programming, covered in Chapter 3).

Your particular level of know-how probably sits somewhere among those options. Goodness knows mine does (that's why I snagged a solid technical person as my business partner). Knowing how your current level of technical savvy relates to the problems you want to solve helps you pick and plan your projects. You can fire off the easier ones that you already know how to do while building your skills to tackle the more complex ones.

Often, one project leads naturally into another that requires a higher level of technical skill. For instance, I didn't understand much about database-driven Web pages until I needed to bring up a whole Web site *very* quickly by using a database-driven system. My existing HTML skills got a workout as I became comfortable with the tricks that this new Web site publishing system could do. By the time I finished, I felt confident enough with my new skills that I dove in deeper and learned how the back end of the system worked. My basic HTML experience gave me a leg up when learning the new system, which then gave me the confidence to dig even deeper.

Determining your role

The harder question involves how deeply involved you want to be on this project. It's harder because of that nasty little word *want*. As I say so often to my kids, we all *want* things in life, but that doesn't mean we get them. I want a milkshake and a pony, for instance, but they never show up.

The trick to the whole *want* equation is balancing the personal *wants* (namely getting involved in this way-cool technical project) with the business *needs* of whatever you do with your copious working time. The "Facing the toughest question of all" sidebar, earlier in this chapter, covers precisely this point. It's a tough issue but one that's well worth answering right now before going a single step further. (Yes, I'll wait.)

At this point, you need to decide what kind of role fits you best in this project. Which of the following bullets describes you?

- ✔ **You personally want to make this thing happen.** You're the ultimate hands-on person, ready, willing, and waiting to dive into the depths of code, questions, and answers. It's your baby from start to finish. *Grrrrrrrrrowl!*

- ✔ **You see a vision.** Visionary folks make amazing things happen, but usually those things happen at the hands of unnamed people inspired by the vision and the visionary. If you can elaborate the vision for the design staff (whether they're in-house or outsiders), that's a valuable skill. Every project needs a visionary to see it through.

✔ **You want some involvement, but you're no technical superhero.** Most of us fall into this category. You want to make something happen, but your technical skills only get you far enough to know that you aren't there yet and that you can't get there alone. You must recruit help (yes, this book counts) to leap over those final hurdles that sit between you and the goal.

At this point in the process, you should see some aspects of your project pretty clearly. Specifically, you know whether this project calls for your personal touch or you need to shift the responsibility to someone else. You also have a feeling for how deeply you should go if you decide to dive into the project and how much technical prowess you have toward staying afloat. With this information in hand, put on your decision-making businessperson hat and start rendering judgments.

By asking the hard questions as things get started (particularly the questions about your level of involvement in this fun foray), you build a well-informed foundation for your decisions. That gives your project a much better shot at success than if you just dove straight in, flailed around for a while, and *then* did your research. (Not that I'd know anything about that method of project management from personal experience, of course.)

Getting Help Along the Way

As a budding eBay developer, the best news is that you aren't alone out there in the world. Lots of other folks developed high-tech stuff before you, and many others make the trip by your side. Lots of these folks share their knowledge and resources freely, especially within the eBay community. Everywhere you look, you can find resources about everything from basic HTML all the way to the intricacies of programming with the eBay API. As with most things, the trick to getting this great information involves knowing where to look:

✔ **Discussion boards:** Regardless of your technical level, start at the eBay member discussion boards (`pages.ebay.com/community/boards/index.html`), shown in Figure 2-1. These boards include discussions of basic technical information (particularly using HTML and photographs in auctions), category-specific chats, seller discussions, and myriad other topics for all experience levels. eBay members from the world over manage the boards all day and night, so your questions get answered quickly. Because you're already an eBay member, you already have a membership to the board area. Just go there and take part in the fun!

- **eBay Live:** For face-to-face networking and discovery, take a trip to the annual *eBay Live* program (`www.ebay.com/ebaylive`). Presented by eBay, eBay Live brings together sellers and developers from around the world for a three-day conference on all things eBay. Courses, discussions, and lots of opportunities to trade knowledge abound at these sessions. It's a *must do* event for serious eBayers.

- **eBay Developers Program:** If you plan to go deep into the eBay API, you need the resources in the eBay Developers Program (`developer.ebay.com/DevProgram`). Like the regular eBay discussion groups, the Developers Program costs nothing to join and offers a whole different level of resources and information than the regular discussion boards. Here there be geeks — but geeks who know both the technical world and the run of eBay, too. You rub shoulders with powersellers, corporate technical people, and freelance developers. The Developers Program is a wonderful resource! Chapter 14 tells more about it, including steps for signing up and locations to check for the best information.

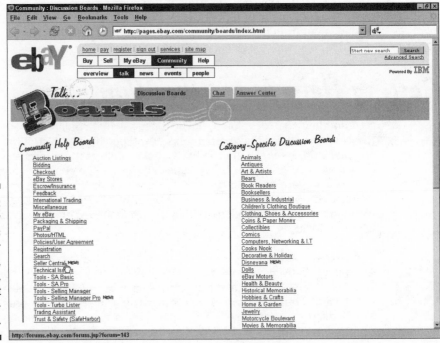

Figure 2-1: The eBay boards cover technology, selling tips, and just about everything else.

Chapter 3

Assembling Your Technical Toolbox

In This Chapter

▶ Determining the tools you will need

▶ Evaluating the stuff you already own

▶ Choosing some new applications

▶ Deciding which programming language fits your technical vocabulary

▶ Selecting a foundation for your Web work

My dad created amazing things from whatever he had on hand. A tire became a swing, an old orange crate turned into a scooter, and a great many things turned into boats, most of which sank almost immediately upon launch. (Thankfully, Dad didn't choose shipbuilding as a profession.)

On one rainy summer afternoon, Dad snagged a couple lengths of 1-x-1-inch wood scraps and, noting my quizzical look, announced that he was going to make a whirligig (more commonly known as a *propeller on a stick*). Over the next hour, I watched him cut, coax, and caress a gorgeous miniature propeller from the smaller length of wood. He carefully drilled the prop and then attached it to the other stick. Turning, he presented me with a handmade, wooden whirligig. I never forgot the "Wow!" of seeing scraps of nothing turn into a wonderful something by skillfully applying some basic tools.

The moral of the story: You don't need a huge professional workshop or massive tool collection to create delightful things. With nothing but a few found items, Dad made an amazing creation. The same goes for you in your technical quest for increasing your eBay profits. Rather than running out to the local software store and plunking down hundreds (if not thousands) of dollars on new software, hardware, and other sundry stuff, look around the office (and the office computer) to see what's already on hand. Thanks to the amazing bundles of software packaged with new computers, you might surprise yourself and save a bunch of money at the same time.

This chapter helps you identify the tools you need to accomplish the technical tasks ahead. Whether you just want to do some cool HTML work or see huge swaths of computer code in your future, the following pages ensure you find the right tools to accomplish the job.

Figuring Out What Tools You Need (And Whether You Really Need Them)

For all the fancy terms and high-falutin' mumbo jumbo that goes along with all things technical, you really need very few resources to start delving into a more technical approach to eBay. The list changes in length depending on what you want to do and what level of technical geekdom you wish to approach, but at its heart, you only require a few basic items — most of which you probably already own.

Some applications come designed for technical work. Others received their somewhat questionable technical prowess as an afterthought, when the programmers said, "Hey, we could make it understand HTML, too!" Keep in mind that just because a program *can* do something technical doesn't mean it does a great job. It works well enough to get you started, but you really should switch to an application designed for the task if you decide to get serious about your development efforts.

Web browsers (yes, that's plural)

First and foremost, you need *at least two Web browsers*. Your machine already includes at least one browser (probably Microsoft Internet Explorer), but because you aim to get more technical, you should install a second one for testing purposes. (Yes, hard as it may seem to believe, not *everybody* uses Microsoft's baby — and because some of those people might troll your auctions, it makes sense to ensure that they can see your amazing technical handiwork.)

The leading alternative Web browsers cost nothing (or very little), so feel free to use them as your testing platform. Your free options include Mozilla (www.mozilla.org) and Netscape (www.netscape.com). The multiplatform Opera browser (www.opera.com), touted as the "fastest browser on Earth," brings up the rear in this list only because it carries a minimal monetary price tag (currently $39).

You gotta have a text editor

For building your programs, you require some kind of *text editor*. Because computers don't care about fancy formatting or cool fonts, text editors focus on the basics like typing, editing, searching, and saving your work. Some editors include extra capabilities that simplify your programming work by proactively reading what you type and looking for obvious errors (more about that later in this section).

You don't need anything so advanced to get started — a nice, basic editor does just fine. Both the Windows and Macintosh operating systems include a basic text editor as part of your standard tools, so you can always use that if you want to keep things cheap. The editor doesn't recognize many fancy keystrokes and performs only the basic search and replacement edits, but it lets you type, and it's free (which should count for something).

If your word processing program knows how to save files in plain text format, you can use it for typing code instead of the operating system's clunky built-in text editor. To see if your word processor fits the bill, follow these steps:

1. **In your word processor, create a new document and then choose File⇨Save As.**

   The Save As dialog box appears.

2. **Look for a drop-down list labeled File Type, Save As Type, or something similar and then click it.**

   This displays a list of all the file types that your word processor recognizes.

3. **If the list contains the options Plain Text or .TXT File, then you're good to go. Otherwise, you need to check the program's installation system to see if you can add a text file option to the system.**

   For more information about that, check your program's documentation or the beloved Help menu.

But wait — it gets even better! Some word processors (notably Microsoft Word) include full-blown HTML programming capabilities built right into the application. To see if your copy of Word can double as a basic HTML editor, open the program and then choose File⇨New from the menu bar. Does Word give you the option of making a new Web page? If so, your HTML editing tools are ready and waiting for you.

If Word doesn't show the HTML editing option right away, get out the installation discs and run the MS Office Setup program to add that capability. Follow these steps:

1. **Run the Office Setup program.**

   This usually runs on its own when you insert the office CD-ROM into the drive. If it doesn't happen automatically, open the CD-ROM drive with Windows Explorer and double-click the Setup program's icon.

2. **Tell the Office Setup program that you want to update your MS Office installation and then find the entry for Office Tools.**

   When the Office Setup program displays a list of installed items, look for the last one on the list. That's usually Office Tools.

3. **Click the plus sign (+) next to Office Tools.**

   A series of little boxes folds out from beneath Office Tools.

4. **Click the HTML Source Editing box. In the pop-up menu, select the Run from My Computer option.**

   This tells the Office Installer that you like the idea of editing HTML code with your MS Office applications, which you do.

5. **Click the Update button to finish this process.**

   Okay, so it doesn't *really* finish the thing, but at least it tells the computer to complete the installation. At this point, you mainly watch the screen (try to look interested) and swap discs if the application complains about anything.

6. **When the installation software finishes, it displays a nice little dialog box informing you that it's done.**

   Congratulations — your Office applications just learned how to understand HTML!

When you finish these steps, you might need to restart your computer. Whether you must do that depends on something slightly akin to the phase of the moon, so there's no predicting what your computer might think about the whole process. Just go with whatever the computer recommends, and everything should work out just fine.

A Web site builder or HTML editor

Many manufacturers include a lot of software with new computers. Somewhere in that mixture, you usually find an application or two dedicated to building a Web site. Now that you actually *want* to do that, it's time to dig around and see what you can find among your preinstalled software.

I can't tell you exactly what to look for, although the odds are good that the program's name includes something to do with either Web sites or HTML code. If your machine came with one of the popular *office* software suites, look among those applications to see if they include a Web site builder.

Two of the more popular preloaded applications are HotDog PageWiz from Sausage Software (www.sausagetools.com) and Microsoft FrontPage (office.microsoft.com/frontpage). Both applications handle the basics (and most of the more advanced stuff) that you want for your eBay business purposes. If your machine includes either of those programs, you're in great shape.

In an effort to save money while still providing free software, some computer makers include *lite* or *express* versions of popular applications. Sadly, those computer industry code words usually translate into "sample software that doesn't really accomplish a lot." Often manufacturers bundle stripped-down versions of Web site building programs with new computers because the manufacturers know that most people don't ever use Web site applications. If you find one of these versions on your computer, don't get frustrated — at least the manufacturer *tried* to help. In that case, flip ahead to the "Adding a New Development Application" section (later in this chapter) for tips about picking up a good development program.

A "cover your assets" backup system

The world contains two kinds of people: those who have lost hopeless amounts of information in a computer crash and those who haven't — yet. Computers fail. It's simply the nature of the things. The bigger question centers on how well you can recover from the failure. You can't prevent a computer failure, but if you keep a good backup, you can recover gracefully from the disaster when it happens.

Thanks to everything from recordable CD drives to USB flash drives to the Internet itself, backup options surround you. You exist in a veritable cloud of data-saving possibilities. You simply need to pick one that works for you, develop a backup plan, and start doing it.

Yes, all of this *do your backups or else* stuff sounds more than a little paranoid, but it's with good reason. Let me say this again: Computers die. It's the nature of such things. They die when you least expect it. They die despite your best and most careful efforts toward keeping them alive. I spend time doing technical support and preventative maintenance, but *my* computers die too! Over the last seven years, three different laptops and two desktops have died on me without warning, and two other laptops graciously provided me with about a week of "I'm not feeling well" behavior. Thankfully, only one of those failures hit when I didn't have a solid backup in place (and even then, my partial backup saved the day).

To perform backups, you need two things: a way to copy the files (some software) and a safe destination for the copies (usually hardware).

Software for backing up

On the software side of the equation, both the Windows and Macintosh operating systems include basic backup software. (See the *Windows For Dummies* or *Macs For Dummies* book for your operating system for details on how those backup packages work.) These applications won't win any awards, but they handle the task of copying your files to somewhere safe. At a really basic level, that's all you need. Heck, you can always just drag and drop files from your hard drive onto your backup device with your computer's file explorer software. Backups don't need to be fancy — they just need to work.

For a more full-featured backup application, run an Internet search on the phrase *backup software* or *computer backup plan*. Most packages out there offer a free downloadable trial version so you can try the software and see if it meets your needs. Pick a program that makes sense to you and that you can operate quickly and easily. Making the task as easy as possible dramatically increases the odds that you'll do it consistently.

A safe storage location

After you decide how you want to handle copying files from one place to another, you need to find a safe destination for those files. Just what does *safe* mean when it comes to backups? Good question.

MSE: The mysterious hidden editor

If your computer includes the Microsoft Office suite of applications (Word, Excel, Access, and such), you also own a full-fledged HTML design environment. (Yup, it was news to me, too.)

Buried away in some file folder deep in your hard drive sits the *Microsoft Script Editor.* To find it, use the Windows Search function. Look for a file named either MSE7.EXE (if you use Office XP/2003) or MSE.EXE (for older Office versions). The program comes as an optional component in the older copies of Office, but Office XP 2003 seems to install it automatically.

If your computer contains Office but doesn't contain the script editor, fire up the Office installation program (on your installation disc) and look in the Office Tools section for an entry called HTML Source Editing. Make sure that it and all entries beneath it (like one called *Web scripting* in the Office 2000 installation program) are set to Run from Hard Drive. With those settings in place, tell the installation program to do its thing. When it finishes, you'll find your copy of the Microsoft Script Editor awaiting you (after looking for it, of course).

In the strange world of computer backups, *safe* means three things:

✔ **Large amount of space:** Worthwhile backups contain lots of files. Lots of files means that your backup device needs lots of space. In the old days, my backups consisted of a few files copied to a floppy disk (and to think that I counted myself as a very advanced computer user . . . sheesh). These days, few of my files would even *fit* onto a floppy disk. Large-scale backups of your entire operating system, software, and data require giga-bytes of space.

✔ **Removable and portable:** Copying your data from one side of the com-puter disk to the other side of the same disk is better than nothing — but only a little. You really need to copy your data to some kind of storage device that lives *outside* of your computer so you can move the backups to a different location, as the next bullet explains.

✔ **Stored somewhere else:** After making your backups on your clever removable data storage product, one last task remains: removing the removable data storage product and storing it somewhere safe. (Yes, there's *that word* again.) Here, *safe* means "somewhere physically away from the computer." Keep your master backups in another building, inside your bank's safe deposit box, or at a friend's house. Regardless of where you put them, they just *can't* live next to your machine. If some terrible misfortune happens to your computer (such as a rampaging delivery truck crashing into your pool, sending a tsunami of chlorinated water and colorful bath toys through your office window), your backups won't float away with the rest of your world. That's why you store the backups far, far away from the computer itself.

Zip drives, recordable CD-ROM drives, external hard drives, and little USB flash drives all make good starting devices when it comes to doing backups. For a basic backup of just your data files, you need something that stores 64MB to 256MB of data. Completely backing up your computer demands a full-fledged external hard drive, a tape backup system, or a recordable DVD drive.

Thanks to the advent of high-speed Internet connections with DSL and cable, a number of companies now offer online backup services aimed at small and home businesses. On the positive side, these services automatically meet all the criteria for a good backup: They offer easy-to-use software, oodles of stor-age space, and secure off-site protection. However, you pay a fair amount every month for the privilege of using the system, and that adds up to serious dollars over time. Still, using an online backup system means putting your backups on *automatic* — you don't ever need to mess with them again. That feature alone makes these systems worth their weight in gold for growing businesses.

Building a backup plan

With all the equipment in place, you now need a backup plan. Here's a simple weekly plan to get you started:

1. **Start with at least three disks (or tapes, or whatever you decide to use). Label them A, B, and C.**

2. **On the very first week (and *only* on the first week), back up your information twice: once on disk A and again on disk C.**

   This creates what the computer people call a *grandfather* backup, which covers you in case your normal backup disk goes bad. (Yes, computer backup people generally feel a little paranoid. Why do you ask?)

3. **On the second week, pull out disk B and perform your backup. On a piece of paper, write down the date you backed up your computer and the fact that you used disk B.**

4. **Continue the process each week, rotating through the disks in order. Always note which disk you used after making each week's backup.**

This system gives you some solid protection for your data. You always have at least two full backups available to you, which gives you a nice feeling of security. If your data changes often (if you process many orders each day, for instance), you should probably switch to a daily backup process.

As your business grows, please take the time to formalize and automate your backup process as well as purchase comprehensive backup software. You can put a very solid backup system (including both software and hardware) into place for well under $200. For more detailed help, consult your favorite local computer guru or do some online searches. The cost of your backup system and the time it takes to make the whole process work pale in comparison to the pain of rebuilding your computer and business records from scratch. Really.

Adding a New Development Application

Adding new applications to your computer is, of course, exactly what the software companies hope you do. They count on that behavior in order to keep the doors open. They *always* want you to own the biggest, newest, fastest, and bestest stuff (preferably in multiple copies). What you actually *need* software-wise depends on your technical goals, what software you already own, and your budget.

It's easy to spend lots (and I mean *lots*) of money on software. To avoid wasting your hard-earned bucks on unnecessary software, take your time and look for recommendations from people already doing what you want to do (and from this book, of course). Then make darned sure that you really need the cool new software *and* that your current software absolutely, positively won't do what you need.

Most applications offer many more features than the average person ever uses. Even so-called *power users* have limits. For instance, I use Microsoft Word every day (sometimes twice a day), yet it's positively embarrassing how few of the program's functions I ever put to work. I'm "an expert" in the program, but I still have many more features to learn about.

Why make a big deal over something small like a software purchase? Because shifting to a new program costs not only money but also time. Getting up to speed on any new program takes days, not hours — particularly when you're dealing with something in-depth like a development tool. Before investing time and money in transitioning to new software, wring the most value from your current software setup. Buy a book or attend a class. Those steps might solve a business problem or two and are much less costly in terms of time and money than migrating you and your applications into a new development platform.

The following sections focus on two types of development tools: straightforward HTML editors and more advanced programming tools. Each type of application addresses a different level of technical need, so they complement each other in addition to overlapping a bit. You might find yourself starting with a nice HTML tool and then moving to one of the more technical tools in the future. Or you might simply stick with one or the other forever. Let your needs and your comfort level with the systems dictate what applications you end up using. If you do that, you can't make a wrong choice.

A simple HTML editor

A good HTML editor looks much like the *What You See Is What You Get* (WYSI-WYG) editing view from your favorite word processing program, except that someone also left the back door of the program open so you can peek behind the screen to see all the strange and wonderful coding that makes a beautiful Web page happen. Flipping back and forth between those two views gives an HTML editing program its edge in the development world. Type and format your stuff in WYSIWYG view and then flip over to HTML view for detailed adjustments or when you need to add some extra programming touches.

Automating your back office

Although this chapter focuses on more technical things like development tools, programming languages, and Web hosting services, another type of program and online service out there can really impact your eBay business. This falls under the category of *back office tools.*

These programs and services represent out-of-the-box solutions designed to make your eBay business run smoother so you make more money. Although you can often create similar tools yourself (and this book even tells you how to do that), sometimes it makes more sense to focus your development efforts on your business's *unique* needs. If you can spend money on software that solves 90 percent of a pressing business problem, you can use the time and money saved to create a ground-up solution that addresses the other 10 percent of the issue.

For expert guidance on existing back office applications — systems and applications that handle everything from auction listings to image hosting to shipping and insurance — check out Marsha Collier's books, *Starting an eBay Business For Dummies* and *eBay For Dummies* (Wiley). Both offer plenty of insight on making your business run smoothly. Also take a look at her Web site, `www.coolebaytools.com`, for up-to-the-minute tips and ideas.

With a little online searching, you can find hundreds of HTML editing programs, and I encourage you to do that if you enjoy playing with software like I do. (I know, I know — I really need to get out more.) For a more direct path to a new HTML authoring application, check out these programs:

- **Microsoft FrontPage** ($199 MSRP from Microsoft, `office.microsoft.com/frontpage`): FrontPage is arguably the most widely available HTML editing program out there but also far and away the most expensive on this list. (Even the discounted upgrade version costs more than its competition!) What it lacks in affordability, it makes up for in features. FrontPage integrates nicely with the other Office applications, putting a friendly and familiar interface onto a somewhat strange development world. If you host your Web site on a Windows-based server with FrontPage extensions (more about that in the "Using a Web site hosting company" section later in this chapter), the software delivers even more automated tools to simplify your life.

- **HotDog PageWiz** ($69 from Sausage Software, `www.sausage.com/hotdog-pagewiz.html`): PageWiz takes the popular HotDog HTML editor into more beginner-oriented territory. The program's Express Mode focuses on helping you quickly develop a Web site from some prebuilt templates. Flip the program into Editor Mode, though, and it turns into a solid entry-level development tool. Its interface really simplifies your life. It lets you easily flip among WYSIWYG development view, HTML code view, an integrated Web browser preview page, and a publishing page that uploads your finished code straight to your Web server.

✔ **CoffeeCup HTML Editor** ($49 from CoffeeCup Software, `www.coffeecup.com/html-editor`): CoffeeCup's first version appeared years ago, back when the Web was young. It has come a long way since then, with many new features and capabilities. Still, CoffeeCup remains easy to use and easy to customize. A built-in *snippets editor* stores often-used HTML code for quick insertion as you work. Don't let the low price fool you: This professional-quality program delivers the goods.

✔ **WebExpress 3.0** ($69 from MicroVision Development, `www.mvd.com/webexpress.htm`): WebExpress covers all the basic HTML editing needs while adding lots of more advanced features in an easy-to-use way. Like HotDog PageWiz, it appeals to beginning Web site designers with its included templates but also provides in-depth coding capabilities and positioning tools so your words and images stay where you want them. It strikes a nice balance between the technically full-featured applications and the more limited entry-level ones.

✔ **Macromedia HomeSite 5.5** ($99 from Macromedia, `www.macromedia.com/software/homesite`): Unlike the other programs on this list, HomeSite focuses exclusively on HTML code. It doesn't offer WYSIWYG editing, preferring to make the more precise "by hand" coding method as easy as possible. Many professional developers rely on HomeSite, although its code-only perspective often looks daunting to beginning HTML developers.

All these manufacturers offer some kind of demonstration version of their programs, ranging from a fully-functional (but time-limited copy) that you can play with at your leisure, to Microsoft's somewhat heavy-handed online demonstration tool (which lets you play with the software at Microsoft's leisure). All these applications cover more than enough HTML coding to handle both your auctions and your accompanying Web site. No matter which tool you choose, it should cover your needs nicely.

Pro-level editing tools

As your programming skills increase, you demand different things from your development tools. All of a sudden, the editor that you knew and loved for years starts showing its limitations. Sure, it understands the statements that your programming language uses (well, at least it knows most of them), and it lets you preview your site in your Web browser (or at least *part* of your site, that is), but overall it just can't handle the type of work that you find yourself doing these days. When you find that happening to you, sigh deeply, smile fondly at your old program, and then start your quest for a new development system.

Software — particularly software development tools — changes more in one or two years than most products change in their lifetime. Because applications change so much in such a small amount of time, look around carefully as you choose development software. The package that you skipped last year because it didn't meet your needs might sport a host of new features this year. Don't automatically spurn something merely because of an earlier incarnation.

The advanced tools in the following list cover quite a span. Some (like HotDog Pro) focus mainly on more complex HTML and Web site development, while others (Zend Studio in particular) provide a whole development environment for designing, testing, and implementing serious online applications. More advanced features also bring a much larger price tag, so you may need to balance what you want against what you can reasonably afford.

Any of these programs make a fine "next step" development tool:

✔ **HotDog Professional** ($99 from Sausage Software, `www.sausage.com/hotdog-professional.html`): Like its little brother, HotDog PageWiz, this program focuses mainly on advanced HTML features instead of supporting broader programming languages. If you plan to work hard on your Web presence, HotDog Pro should do the job very well.

✔ **PrimalScript** ($179 to $208 from Sapien, `www.sapien.com`): Although PrimalScript understands HTML (as shown in Figure 3-1), it goes far beyond that. In addition to HTML, the program also understands and supports over 30 scripting languages, including the popular PHP and XML languages, VBScript (a form of Microsoft Visual BASIC), ColdFusion (from Macromedia), and many others. PrimalScript helps you with everything from getting the statements right in your program to testing the finished application.

✔ **Macromedia Dreamweaver MX 2004** ($399 from Macromedia, `www.macromedia.com/software/dreamweaver`): Another of the most powerful editing tools on the market, Dreamweaver supports Macromedia's ColdFusion language and Microsoft's ASP.NET, as well as JSP, PHP, XML, and more. The new version of Dreamweaver also includes expanded support for Cascading Style Sheets (more about those in Chapter 11).

✔ **Zend Studio** ($249 from Zend, `www.zend.com`): Because Zend Studio comes to you from the folks who created the current version of PHP, it does a really great job of handling PHP coding and testing. Zend also backs up its product (and the PHP language) with an amazing selection of online and classroom-based training. If you decide to develop your eBay tools with PHP, investing in Zend Studio makes a lot of sense.

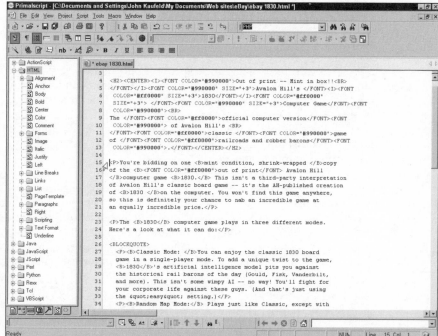

Figure 3-1:
PrimalScript
handles
HTML as
well as
numerous
other pro-
gramming
languages.

As with the HTML editing applications, all these programs offer some kind of demonstration version, so you can give them a try for free. Because these programs have a pretty steep learning curve, pay attention to the training and after-purchase support available from these companies. Their support and course options directly affect your short-term productivity; good training and support shortens your learning curve dramatically!

Picking a Programming Language

Programming languages sit at the heart of the whole technical thing. After all, you can have the coolest idea in the world, work up a complete design of what makes it tick, and assemble the best editor and most perfect Web space, but without a programming language to actually make it happen, the project just lays there, looking at you.

Two broad categories describe all Internet-focused languages: the kind of language (markup language or a true programming language) and where the processing takes place (on the server or on the desktop client). You can tell a lot about a language simply by understanding where it lands in those categories.

Markup vs. full-scale programming language

Markup languages explain how to present information on a page. HTML, the language of Web pages, mainly includes instructions on formatting and placing things within a Web page. Experts don't consider it a true programming language because you can't really *do* anything with it. Sure, you can make a page look absolutely gorgeous and freely mix text with graphics, but you can't make decisions or compute anything in HTML. For tasks like those, you need a real programming language.

Unlike a markup language, a full-scale *programming language* stores, retrieves, and processes data. (Geez, I sound like a first-year programming textbook.) A programming language asks questions, calculates results, and interacts with programs on other servers. It knows how to display results, although it usually leaves those details to a markup language. Internet programming languages usually work with markup languages, using them for the tasks they do best.

Choosing sides: Server vs. client

The other broad category of Internet languages looks at which computer executes the program's code. In a *server-side language,* your Web server runs the program. It sends the results down to the client (your computer and its Web browser). The client computer happily receives and displays the information without any knowledge or understanding of what the server did in order to make the page happen. Because the server does all the hard work, server-side programming languages support pretty much any Web browser, without worries over compatibility.

At the other end of the transaction, you find *client-side programming* (sometimes called *client-side scripting* by technoweenies who care enough to split such hairs). Here, the Web server sends all the code down to the desktop and the Web browser, which execute the program and display the results. Because this process relies heavily on the Web browser, client-side programs often suffer compatibility problems. When creating client-side code, you usually write multiple versions of your program, one for each browser you want to support. When someone visits your Web site, your system queries the visitor's browser to find out what type it is so it knows which version of the program to send.

The client/server and markup/programming language debates don't have any good or bad sides. The choice depends on what you need to accomplish and how technical you feel like getting in the quest for that solution. Although programmers love to argue that their favorite language "works better than that, so there," you don't need to get involved in such arguments. (Nobody ever wins, anyway.)

The likeliest languages to use with eBay

Here's a good starting list of languages to look at as you forge your way into the more technical side of eBay:

- **HTML (client-side markup language):** HTML explains how to format and display information in a Web browser. It can also create interactive forms that collect information, but it can't process the information after collecting it. Instead, it relies on a real programming language to do its hard work.

- **XML (client-side markup language):** This language focuses on storing data inside a Web page and exchanging data between computers. It works with HTML, not as a replacement. XML moves and handles the data, and HTML displays it.

- **XHTML (client-side markup language):** All hail the new, improved HTML! Intended as a replacement for HTML, XHTML formalizes and enforces rules about the proper use of the HTML codes. Although built on HTML, it also includes some XML elements as well.

- **CSS (client-side markup language):** CSS files define (in excruciating detail) every aspect of how the formatting tags work in an HTML document. CSS files help you maintain a consistent look and feel across different Web pages.

- **JavaScript (client-side programming language):** Although it looks similar to the C or Java languages, JavaScript is easier to use and includes lots of features for working with HTML in general (and HTML forms in particular).

- **DHTML (client-side markup and scripting language):** This language borrows tricks from CSS and JavaScript to interactively change items on a Web page. You can do some really neat *on-demand* tricks with DHTML, such as enlarging/reducing an image or changing the appearance of text as the mouse rolls over it.

- **PHP (server-side programming language):** Designed for use with Web pages and SQL databases, PHP pulls information from databases and XML resources and then organizes it for display with HTML statements. It's the language of choice for a lot of server-side Internet programming.

- **ASP (server-side programming language):** Short for *Active Server Pages,* ASP covers much of the same territory as PHP. The difference is that ASP has Microsoft behind it, while PHP lives in the *open source software* category. If you prefer using a Microsoft server with Microsoft software running on it, you'll probably prefer ASP to PHP. (For more about the strange, wonderful, and very inexpensive world of open source software, visit www.opensource.org.)

As you start working with the technical side of eBay auctions, you first need to understand HTML because that drives all your auction descriptions and your About Me page. It also makes Web pages work, so if you plan to make a Web site that supports your business, you need to be comfortable with HTML. Adding gizmos to your auctions requires a more advanced programming language such as JavaScript. Server-side programming languages come into the picture when you begin talking about projects like the ones in Chapter 12 and all of Part IV.

The preceding list barely scratches the surface of languages in the online world. Still, those languages drive a huge number of Web sites, online companies, and (more to the point) eBay auctions. You can always expand your knowledge beyond these basics, but understanding these languages builds a firm foundation for your future development efforts.

To learn a particular language, look for books, online training programs, and classroom training opportunities. Find an avenue that fits your learning style as well as your budget. I highly recommend looking at online training options because they deliver courses directly to your desktop, at whatever pace you choose. A quick romp through Google with the search term `online HTML course` brings up lots of options to explore, including quite a few free courses. (Of course, I could mention that other books in the *For Dummies* line can help you too — including *HTML 4 For Dummies,* 4th Edition, by Ed Tittel and Natanya Pitts, *PHP 5 For Dummies* by Janet Valade, and *XML All-in-One Desk Reference For Dummies* by Richard Wagner and Richard Mansfield [all published by Wiley] — but that might look like somewhat crass marketing. Still, it's an idea.)

Choosing a Web Hosting Company

Although many sellers run their businesses solely through eBay and their e-mail accounts, many of the more advanced tricks covered in this book require a Web site — or even a Web server — of your very own. Staking your claim to cyberspace gives you flexibility and power to increase sales, enhance service, and generally grow your business.

You have two basic types of Web site hosting available: the free kind provided by your ISP, and the more advanced services offered by a third-party Web site hosting company.

Free Web space

Most Internet access accounts include both e-mail and some kind of Web site storage space. It might not be fancy or large (or even particularly easy to use), but it's free, and that makes a fine start for your first bout of Web development.

To find out what kind of Web space you already have (and if, indeed, you actually have some), contact your Internet service provider and ask. If you feel like digging through your provider's online documentation instead of talking to technical support, look in the provider's Web-based support area. Almost every provider on the planet includes step-by-step procedures for accessing and using its built-in Web space.

Free Web space like this comes with one significant drawback: You normally can't use a custom Web address (such as `www.yournamehere.com`) with it. Instead, you get stuck with something memorable like `members.aol.com/yourscreennamehere`, which doesn't exactly roll off the tongue (although it probably falls off the edge of your business card). A custom Web address marks your business as a serious player and automatically instills some trust on the part of your customers.

Still, you can take your first tentative steps into the Webbed world by using free Web space. At the very least, it makes a great spot to hone your HTML-writing skills and try building some custom pages for your own use. Use it as a test center as you develop your super-cool About Me page so you can see what it looks like and how it works without repeatedly slogging through eBay's somewhat long-winded process for posting updates.

Regardless of how you use it, free Web space offers a wonderful starting point for your new technical explorations. Depending on your aspirations, it might do everything you need. On the other hand, if you find yourself wishing for capabilities ranging from a custom Web address to custom programs, check out the following section for tips about getting some serious Web space.

Using a Web site hosting company

Getting Web space for your business sounds like a pretty easy proposition at first blush. After all, thousands of companies offer Web hosting, and lots of them charge only a few bucks per month. But when you look beyond the price, the world of Web space gets very confusing very quickly.

Because you plan to not only host a Web site but also put some custom applications in place, you need more than most garden-variety Web hosting companies offer. Here's a quick checklist of things to look for in a solid business-class Web provider:

✔ Do you want a Microsoft Windows–based server or a Linux-based server?

✔ How much disk space do you need?

✔ What bandwidth limits does the hosting company put on your site? What fees do you incur if you go over the limit?

✔ What support options do you get? Does the company give you a toll-free phone number that leads to a human or to voice mail? Does it guarantee a response within a certain time period?

✔ Do you want to use Microsoft Access databases and ASP (usually available on Windows-based servers) or PHP and MySQL (on Linux-based machines)?

✔ What software add-ons does the company make available? For instance, PHP offers *many* programming options for custom e-mail programming or on-the-fly image manipulation. Ask what the hosting company supports so you know your options up front. (For more about this kind of programming and whether you really care about it, see Chapter 12.)

✔ Does the company offer a Web control panel like Plesk (www.plesk.com) to manage your server space or do you need to do all of that by hand?

You may not need everything on the list right away, but keep these questions in mind anyway. It's a lot easier to add extra features already offered by your Web service provider than to move your Web site from one host to another. (That gives *pain and suffering* a whole new meaning.)

Part II
Low-Tech Steps to High-Value Returns

The 5th Wave

By Rich Tennant

Yes, it's good to turn winning bidders into bigger buyers... when you are the SELLER, not the BUYER, Stuart!

In this part . . .

Just because people call something *technical* doesn't mean that you need a brain larger than the average watermelon simply to comprehend it. No, you just need a little information and a little understanding. Most technical things appear strange and complex from the outside because the technical people *like* things to appear that way. (It makes them feel needed.)

What the techies don't tell you is that *they* didn't understand this stuff the first time they looked at it either.

The chapters in this part guide you gently into the first stages of this new technical world. They focus on things you can do with software you already own (or the stuff that you accumulated back in Part I). Beginning with an indepth look at HTML, you move steadily onward toward understanding and applying this fascinating markup language that holds the Web (and your eBay auctions) together. With the basics of HTML out of the way, this part points out more ways that you can use your new-found knowledge by enhancing your About Me page and developing a Web site to call your own.

Later chapters turn your attention to your e-mail program and resources you can either use or develop on your own. Your e-mail application contains some amazing business powers such as automated mail sorting and replying. Easy-to-make templates within your e-mail application give you a one- or two-click method of writing your customers. And that built-in address book offers a sweet, simple, and fast way to build loyalty among your buyers with repeat contacts. Better still, use your HTML knowledge to create some quick and easy tools of your own, including a personalized search box and even a Web-based template that helps you format and list auctions from anywhere in the world.

All these technical creations and more start with a simple language called HTML. Flip ahead to Chapter 4 and get ready to boost your eBay sales!

Chapter 4

Starting Simple and Cheap: Adding Auction Pizzazz with HTML

*I*magine two stores that carry the same product line. The first store features beige floors, beige walls, beige shelves, and flat fluorescent lighting. As you look around, nothing jumps out at you (at least product-wise, but the salespeople kinda make you wonder). Everything looks plain, mundane, and really boring. The second store uses rich colors in the carpeting and walls, beautiful wooden shelves, and spotlights over various displays. The products practically leap off the shelves into your arms. They look vibrant, exciting, and interesting.

In the online world, those two stores correlate to auctions that feature plain text in the description versus ones that use basic Hypertext Markup Language (also known as HTML) to spruce things up a bit with color, style, size, and organization. Although a basic text auction sells some products, a prettier, better-organized one produces stronger bids, convinces customers that you know your stuff, and says that you approach your online business with an air of professionalism.

This chapter explores the world of HTML coding, with a focus on basic types of coding that every auction uses. It introduces how HTML works, walks you through the concept of HTML tags (the codes that do stuff), and quickly gets you into applying HTML to your auctions. It also supplies some insights into organizing your auction text for maximum readability. After all, you don't want something that looks absolutely amazing but fails to sell the product.

The material in this chapter barely scratches the surface of what HTML can do. For a more complete trip through the language, check out *HTML For Dummies* by Ed Tittel and Natanya Pitts (Wiley), available at your friendly local bookstore (and probably somewhere on eBay, too).

HTML: Programming in a Can

In the great spectrum of programming options, HTML sits somewhere in the middle, with a bit of a lean toward the less complicated but still vaguely geeky side. It's not a true programming language (so don't call it one around any of your geeky friends because they'll shoot you one of those looks). Instead, it inhabits a strange domain called *markup language*.

Unlike a programming language, HTML doesn't really do anything. You can't make a loop or write something to a file or control the input from a joystick. HTML simply tells Web browsers how to format text and pictures in a Web page. It harbors no other secret goals (and that's a good thing, given its limitations). It works *with* programming languages like PHP, but HTML itself doesn't qualify for the *real language* mantle.

Instead, HTML just does its job of making stuff fit in Web browsers, but it handles that task really, really well. To accomplish that, it uses *tags* — pairs of codes that tell the Web browser how to format (and sometimes where to put) the intervening text, image, or whatever it is.

To make HTML tags stand out so your browser can differentiate them from the plain text on the page, you always enclose the HTML tags inside greater-than and less-than symbols, like this:

```
The <b>bold</b> and <i>italic</i> tags work alone (and
          together) to make your text look
          <b><i>really</i></b> cool.
```

When you feed that HTML code to a Web browser, it creates a sentence that looks like this:

> The **bold** and *italic* tags work alone (and together) to make your text look ***really*** cool.

Think of the tags as opposite jaws of a clamp, with their target in the middle. As the example shows, you enclose the target text (the words *bold, italic,* and *really* in the example) with the two tags. The first tag tells the browser where to start applying whatever effect you want. The second tag — the one with the slash mark (/) in it — closes the pair, telling the browser to stop the effect.

If you accidentally forget (or mistype) a closing tag, then the effect goes on throughout the rest of the page. It doesn't hurt anything — it just messes up the formatting. To solve the problem, find the point where that particular formatting starts. Work forward from there, checking each tag to make sure that it has a mate and that the mate looks right (includes a slash with the correct tag code).

You can also nest tags inside each other. (In fact, you end up doing it quite a lot in almost any HTML document.) Two sets of tags surround the word `really` in the preceding example — bold and italic — so it appears in the Web browser in a bold italic font.

When nesting tags, live by HTML's one simple rule: Close the tags in the *opposite* order from the way that you opened them. In the preceding example, the bold tag comes first, followed by the italic tag, and then the text that the tags format. When closing those tags on the other side of the text, you put the italic closing tag first because that's the most recent tag that you opened. After that, close the bold tag because it comes next in line.

Enlisting an Editor for the Boring Work

You can write simple HTML code off the top of your head, right in eBay itself. Adding a few tags to your text doesn't take a lot of extra effort, particularly if you use only the basic formatting tags like bold and italic. Besides, if something goes wrong with one of the few tags you included, you can fix it with relative ease. But when you plan bigger and better things for your auction text and About Me page, using an editor that understands HTML greatly simplifies your life and speeds up both the development and ongoing maintenance.

HTML editors come in two primary flavors, depending on how they present your page as you work with it:

- **WYSIWYG editors** (short for *What You See Is What You Get*) look more like word processing programs than technical development tools. As you work, you see your HTML code as it should appear when customers look at it through their browsers. If you want to make bold text, you highlight the text and click the bold button on the toolbar, just like your favorite word processor. Everything focuses on how the page looks, not on the technical details driving the look.

  WYSIWYG editors generally give you less detailed control over your pages than code-driven editors, but they make up for that with their easy-to-use visual controls. Microsoft FrontPage (`office.microsoft.com/front page`) sits alone at the top of this product class, although a number of other applications desperately want its position.

✔ **Code-driven editors** focus on the HTML code itself — specifically on the detailed task of including the right opening and closing tags throughout your text. These editors watch as you write the HTML code, and automatically type in the second half of any tags you include. You typically use your favorite Web browser to preview your work rather than seeing it directly through your editor. The best products here include the CoffeeCup HTML Editor (www.coffeecup.com, shown in Figure 4-1), HotDog Professional (www.sausage.com), PrimalScript (www.sapien.com, shown in Figure 4-2), and NetObjects Fusion (www.netobjects.com).

You can download trial versions for more of these products directly through the manufacturers' Web sites. I highly recommend giving them a try before making a final selection. As with any tool, pick the one you feel most comfortable with but take the time to give each one a good trial period before either dismissing it or whipping out your checkbook.

As an added bonus, the CD that comes with this book includes trial versions of several great HTML editors. To save yourself some downloading time, check the CD Appendix and see if the editor of your dreams is back there. If this represents your first foray into the world of HTML programming, stick with a WYSIWYG editor like Microsoft FrontPage. It does everything that you need for basic HTML work in a nicely visual way, plus it gives you a "code view" to peer into the inner workings and tweak your work directly.

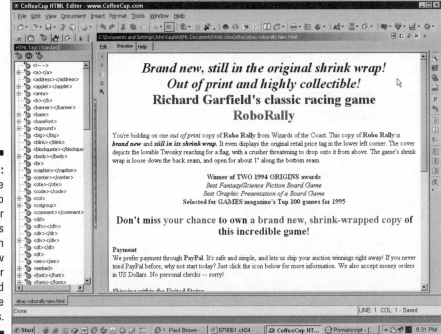

Figure 4-1: The CoffeeCup HTML Editor provides a built-in preview mode for quick and easy code checks.

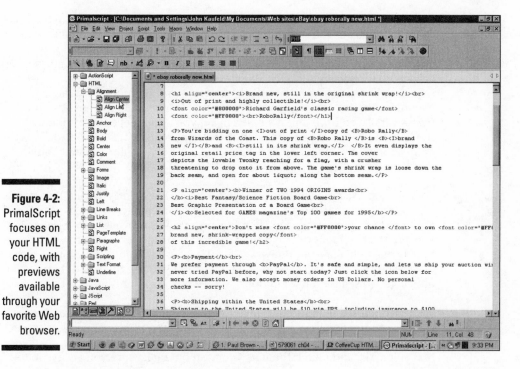

Figure 4-2:
PrimalScript
focuses on
your HTML
code, with
previews
available
through your
favorite Web
browser.

Catching Buyers with Style, Size, and Color

According to people who study such things, color ranks second to sound when it comes to grabbing people's attention. But although you *can* include music and sound effects in your online auctions, most shoppers consider such things the absolute bane of eBay. (And *bane* doesn't translate into *bid*, no matter what language you use.) Wisely ruling out sound for the moment, that leaves your attention-getting efforts focused squarely on the silent options of text style, size, and color. Luckily, HTML makes changing all those things a breeze.

Because HTML's original roots come from a desire to format text on a computer screen, the language gives you a lot of text options, ranging from simple single-purpose tags like *bold* and *heading,* up to complex, multipart tags like *span style* (which puts you in complete command of how your words look on the screen). Best of all, you can freely mix and match HTML tags to create precisely the look you want for your work.

I know that you know what I'm about to say, but it bears repeating all the same (if for no other reason than educating that co-worker in the next cube who borrows your book without asking). Formatting *enhances* the text for your auction — that's all it does. Formatting doesn't sell products by itself. No amount of formatting replaces a well-written description, clearly expressed sales policies, a cool auction title, and a great product photo. Adding a lot of cool formatting to a badly written auction is like swabbing lipstick onto a pig — it looks colorful, but it's still a pig. If you don't feel comfortable with the how-to's of writing a solid auction description, set this book aside for the moment and dive into *eBay For Dummies* by Marcia Collier (Wiley). You'll thank me later — really.

To make the most of your formatting efforts, use it sparingly. Formatting stands out the most when you daub it here and there. For instance, if you use bold text for just a few things on a page, your buyer's eye gets drawn to those items first because the text looks different than the rest of the page. Turning a whole page bold doesn't enhance your message at all because nothing stands out. Go easy on these formatting tags the first few times that you use them and then reevaluate your work after a few auctions. Keep what works and replace the rest.

With those words of wisdom scrawled across your mental chalkboard, it's time to dive into the details of basic text formatting with HTML. The following sections look at basic stylistic tags, heading tags, and your options for changing text color. Mix and match them as you wish but make sure you always follow HTML's one simple rule for making tags work: *Close tags in the opposite order that you opened them* — from the inside of a series of tags to the outside.

Simple text styling

Most of the basic tasks for formatting auction text rely on just three simple tags: bold, italic, and underline. As I mention earlier, these tags work by themselves or as a team to change the formatting of your text on the fly. Table 4-1 shows the code for these three tags, along with a sample of the tags in action. As an added bonus, the table also includes samples of the tags mixed together (all with the proper closing techniques, too).

Table 4-1		HTML Formatting Tags	
Name	*HTML Tag Set*	*Sample*	*Results*
Bold	`<b>text</b>`	`Bold <b>this</b>`	Bold **this**
Italic	`<i>text</i>`	`Italicize <i>that</i>`	Italicize *that*
Underline	`<u>text</u>`	`Underline <u>what</u>?`	Underline <u>what</u>?

Name	HTML Tag Set	Sample	Results
Bold italic	`<b><i>text</i></b>`	`<b><i>Wow!</i></b>`	***Wow!***
Bold underline	`<b><u>text</u></b>`	`<b><u>Wild!</u></b>`	**<u>Wild!</u>**
Italic underline	`<i><u>text</u></i>`	`<i><u>For sale</u></i>`	*<u>For Sale</u>*

eBay lets you use any of these tags at will in your auction text or About Me page but not in the auction title or subtitle. To get bold text in the title, you must add the Bold Title option when you set up your auction (and pay the minimal extra fee eBay charges for it). You can't cheat the system by putting a bold tag in your title text. (Sorry — the eBay technical wizards already thought of that one.)

Adding headings

In addition to basic formatting options, HTML also includes special tags that make *headings* in your text. Headings help your customers quickly find the information that they want in your auction listing because they stand out from the rest of the document, not just by size but also by vertical spacing. Web browsers automatically throw in a little extra leading and trailing spaces around the text in a heading tag to give the heading some breathing room. That white space breaks the monotony of the page, which helps your design by making it look more airy and open, so your auction wins twice with both organizational benefits and design kudos. (Life just doesn't get much better than this.)

Heading tags work with every browser on the planet, so compatibility isn't a problem. However, all that compatibility comes at a price. Heading tags do *not* guarantee consistency across different browsers. The tags promise only that the browser will recognize that you want the text formatted as a heading. Unfortunately, the browser ultimately decides what that means in terms of font, size, and spacing.

One customer's browser might display headings in the Arial font, while another decides to use Times New Roman or even (gasp!) Courier. As a designer, you can't control that behavior with the heading tag itself, although you can override it with Cascading Style Sheets. (See Chapter 11 for more about CSS.)

A heading tag has two parts: The heading tag itself and a number from 1 to 6 that specifies the heading size. Smaller numbers generally mean larger headings, so an `<h1>` tag makes a big headline, and an `<h6>` tag barely differentiates itself from plain text.

Figure 4-3 shows the outcome of the following HTML code in the Firefox browser (www.mozilla.org). Figure 4-4 shows the same code displayed by Microsoft Internet Explorer. Although both browsers use their default settings, small differences still occur. Firefox spreads things out on the page by adding more white space, whereas Internet Explorer goes for a more compact presentation. Both browsers select the same fonts for both the headings and the body text, with the exception of the size 3 and 6 headings. On those, Internet Explorer crunches the text together more than Firefox does.

```
<h1>Heading 1 -- biggest and most eye-catching; use for main
        headings</h1>
<p>This normal-sized text gives you an easy comparison to the
        various headings. Since the browser controls the
        details of both headings and "normal" text, you
        never know exactly what your customer might see
        unless you enforce the settings with a style sheet
        or <I>span style</I> tag.</p>
<h2>Heading 2 -- still solid; great for sub-sections within a
        main heading</h2>
<p>This normal-sized text gives you an easy comparison to the
        various headings. Since the browser controls the
        details of both headings and "normal" text, you
        never know exactly what your customer might see
        unless you enforce the settings with a style sheet
        or <I>span style</I> tag.</p>
<h3>Heading 3 -- still bigger and bolder than plain text</h3>
<p>This normal-sized text gives you an easy comparison to the
        various headings. Since the browser controls the
        details of both headings and "normal" text, you
        never know exactly what your customer might see
        unless you enforce the settings with a style sheet
        or <I>span style</I> tag.</p>
<h4>Heading 4 -- barely more than bold text, but the white
        space sets it apart</h4>
<p>This normal-sized text gives you an easy comparison to the
        various headings. Since the browser controls the
        details of both headings and "normal" text, you
        never know exactly what your customer might see
        unless you enforce the settings with a style sheet
        or <I>span style</I> tag.</p>
<h5>Heading 5 -- shrinking, shrinking still</h5>
<p>This normal-sized text gives you an easy comparison to the
        various headings. Since the browser controls the
        details of both headings and "normal" text, you
        never know exactly what your customer might see
        unless you enforce the settings with a style sheet
        or <I>span style</I> tag.</p>
<h6>Heading 6 -- Hello up there! Can you see me at all?</h6>
<p>This normal-sized text gives you an easy comparison to the
        various headings. Since the browser controls the
        details of both headings and "normal" text, you
        never know exactly what your customer might see
        unless you enforce the settings with a style sheet
        or <I>span style</I> tag.</p>
```

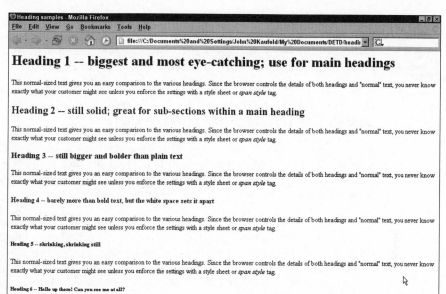

Figure 4-3:
Mozilla
Firefox adds
plenty of
white space
before
and after
headings.

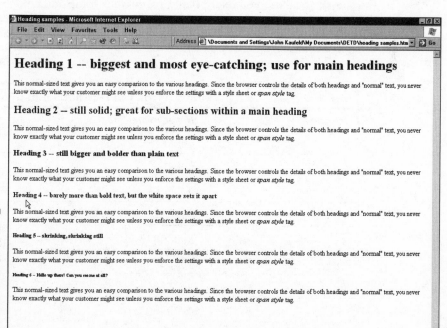

Figure 4-4:
Microsoft
Internet
Explorer
crunches
things
together
a bit.

Notice that the plain text parts of the code use paragraph tags (<p>), but the headings don't. When a Web browser sees a heading tag, the browser automatically plows in a carriage return character and plenty of white space to make the heading stand out on its own.

Spicing things up with color

All that formatting still leaves you with a big problem — your auction still lives in a black-and-white world. Your black text sits on a white background, just like licorice jellybeans on copier paper. It says "Yuck" (both visually and from a taste perspective).

You need — or more specifically, your auction needs — some color in its world! In addition to the nifty styling tags described earlier in this chapter, HTML also gives you quick and easy ways to splash color throughout your auction text. It even lets you pick precisely which color you want from a gigantic palette of, well, just about any color you can imagine.

HTML understands its basic colors in two ways: by name and by the color's arcane hexadecimal code. The code tells your browser how to mix 256 shades of red, green, and blue to make any color you want. Of course, the name *red* flows much easier from your memory than #FF0000 (the *hexadecimal code* for the color), so unless you really, really, *really* want some odd color, stick with the 16 standard colors listed in Table 4-2. (The table includes the hexadecimal equivalents for each color name, in case you feel like flexing your geek muscles to impress your significant other.)

Table 4-2	Standard HTML Color Names and Codes
Color Name	*Hexadecimal Code*
aqua	#00FFFF
black	#000000
blue	#0000FF
fuchsia	#FF00FF
gray	#808080
green	#008000
lime	#00FF00
maroon	#800000
navy	#000080
olive	#808000

Color Name	Hexadecimal Code
purple	#800080
red	#FF0000
silver	#C0C0C0
teal	#008080
white	#FFFFFF
yellow	#FFFF00

By the way, if you mistype the name of a color or don't include all six digits in a hexadecimal number, the Web browser ignores whatever color instructions it doesn't understand and substitutes its default setting instead. In the previous example, if I accidentally typed wite when I meant to put in white, the browser would render my text in the default color (probably black) instead of whatever color I hoped — and planned — to use instead. Oops.

To connect the color you want with the text on your page, HTML uses a special tag called span style (<span style>). By including different attributes in your code, the span style tag gives you an amazing amount of control over formatting your text, but it also demands more effort and attention to detail than the simpler tags do. Still, the benefits make the extra work well worth it. With a bit of experimenting, you might amaze yourself with what you put together!

In the name of pure technical accuracy (because you might find this important one day as your programming prowess increases), what I refer to as the *span style tag* actually is the *span tag* with the *style* attribute added to it. However, because you see <span style=...> as you browse through your code, it makes more sense to refer to it as the *span style tag*. Despite that, your favorite HTML reference guide probably lists it as the *span tag* with the *style attribute*. (Besides, now you can impress your geeky friends at parties by pointing out the difference between the tag itself and the tag's associated attribute. Woot!)

Although you *can* change text colors with the font tag (<font>), the technical experts of the world say that's a bad idea these days. Granted, the font tag still works fine, but the span style tag does a lot more for you. Besides, you use the same commands and options with the span style tag that you do with Cascading Style Sheets, so your knowledge carries over quite nicely. For your auction text, I suggest going with whichever tag works best for you. For large-scale Web site development work, stick with either Cascading Style Sheets or span style tags.

The span style tag lets you turn on a particular group of settings (specifically color, for this example) across any amount of text, from a single word up to multiple paragraphs. You can also use other tags inside span style, like bold, italic, and such.

To format an area with span style, you begin with the opening portion of the tag (`<span`) and then follow that with a `style=` entry to specify the details that you want. For instance, the following code displays the phrase *this amazing antique* in a bright red color:

```
Don't miss <span style="color: red;">this amazing
           antique</span>. Bid now!
Don't miss <span style="color: #FF0000;">this amazing
           antique</span>. Bid now!
```

The first example uses the color name (`red`), and the second uses the hexadecimal equivalent (#FF0000). The pound sign in front of the number tells the Web browser to recognize that strange combination of letters and numbers as a hexadecimal number. By sticking with the color name instead of the number whenever you can, you make the HTML code easier to understand and less sensitive to typing mistakes.

Because the span style tag works just fine with other HTML tags, you can make the text stand out even more by adding a bold tag along with the color instructions:

```
Don't miss <span style="color: red;"><b>this amazing
           antique</b></span>. Bid now!
```

This combination makes the text thicker *and* more colorful at the same time, so it really leaps off the page at your customer.

Combining a text color with a complementary background color also brings your text to life. To fiddle with the background color:

```
You'll love the way <span style="color: white; background-
           color: black">this amazing antique</span> looks
           in your living room or den.
```

You can stack multiple text attributes inside a single span style tag by separating each one with a semicolon and enclosing the whole group of attributes in quotation marks. In the preceding code, the first instruction in the `style=` clause changes the text color to white, and the second flips the background color to black. The two together create a nice "reverse video" effect with white text on a black background, as the top section of Figure 4-5 shows.

The sample at the top of the figure also uses a pair of *nonbreaking spaces* ( ) to pad the text just a little bit on each end and round out the background color effect. Without the nonbreaking space tags, the color just chops off either exactly at the edge of the reverse-colored text or right next to the normal-colored text. Unfortunately, it looks bad both ways. Make sure you include a couple of nonbreaking spaces to bring your color effect in for a perfect landing.

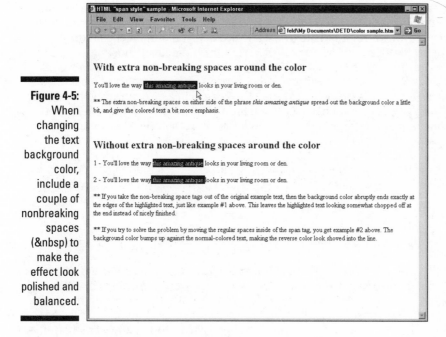

Figure 4-5:
When
changing
the text
background
color,
include a
couple of
nonbreaking
spaces
( ) to
make the
effect look
polished and
balanced.

Adding Extra Photos for Free

"What people see is what they buy" — at least it works that way on eBay. Adding images to your listing increases sales and decreases complaints, both of which rank high on every seller's wish list. eBay knows the importance of photos, so that's why it gives you a free picture in every listing (and provides a variety of additional low-cost image options as well). Unfortunately, eBay shoves all its images — even the very cool, tricky ones — down at the bottom of your auction text. Your auction ends up looking like a digital stovepipe hat, with the text balanced high on top of the image.

For a stronger visual presentation, include the images with the text — right next to it — so they form part of the description itself. That way, your auction mimics the design of a paper-based catalog, which your buyers already understand and feel comfortable using.

Before trying this, you need a place to store your images online. Any Web server space works just fine (even AOL). You don't need tons of space, either. Good eBay product images take up only a few thousand bytes of space each, so it would take a lot of work to run out of space in even the smallest storage space out there.

After arranging for the online storage space, copy your auction images onto the server through your favorite FTP (File Transfer Protocol) program or the server's own Web-based file transfer system. If you don't feel comfortable moving files between servers with FTP, look up the image hosting information in Marsha Collier's bestselling *Starting an eBay Business For Dummies* book (Wiley). For easy organization (and because some geeky part of me always makes *me* do this), I suggest storing the images in a directory called `images`. By doing that, it simplifies your life later if you decide to do any Web development or store other files out there for some reason (like for doing easy backups, perhaps).

With your files safely tucked away on your server, it's time to add code into your auction text that pulls the images into position. You do this by tweaking the `<img src>` tag to add some further instructions for the Web browser. In its most basic form, the `<img src>` tag looks like this:

```
<img src="http://www.linguaplay.com/images/mcpoker1.jpg">
```

This HTML code tells the Web browser where to find the image and that it should display the image on your Web page. However, the tag includes no instructions on how to align the image with the other elements on the page. Lacking that information, the Web browser shrugs its shoulders and mindlessly shoves the image onto the page. Because it doesn't know any better, the browser assumes that you want *nothing* next to your beautiful image. If it finds text after the image tag, the browser simply inserts the text at the end of the image (the image's lower side) and lets the words flow from there on down the page. The results don't look too good.

To fix the problem, give the browser some formatting information. In this case, adding an alignment tag solves the problem nicely:

```
<img src="http://www.linguaplay.com/images/mcpoker1.jpg "
         align=left>
```

This code tells the browser to place the image on the left side of the screen. That doesn't seem like much information, but it makes a big difference to the browser. Now that it knows (in the barest sense) how to handle the image in relation to the other things on the page, the browser gleefully flows the remaining text on the page beautifully around the image. It looks awesome — and all you added was one little instruction!

Of course, you can get a lot more detailed than that. Try adding a couple more codes, like this:

```
<img src="http://www.linguaplay.com/images/mcpoker1.jpg "
          align=left border=5 hspace=15>
```

If all goes as planned, your image now sits framed in a crisp black border next to the text, courtesy of the `border` attribute. Your text still flows next to the image, but now it stands off a bit from the picture thanks to a touch of white space (and the horizontal space attribute, `hspace`).

Making Your Auctions Look Professional with Tables

HTML draws its roots from the scientific community. Yes, just like the Internet itself, this whole crazy Web thing started because a bunch of scientists wanted a better way to share information. Little did they know that their system for storing and accessing intensely technical documentation would lead to developments like `www.neopets.com`. (I'm sure some nuclear engineer out there feels proud.)

Because of its scientific roots, HTML includes several tags that format information in very, well, scientific ways. Some of these tags retain all the real-world usefulness of most undergraduate college courses, but one group in particular stands out because it adds a lot of functionality to every Web designer's world. I refer, of course, to the set of tags that help you build *tables* on your page.

In their simplest form, table tags create a standard-issue table for displaying columnar information. With just a few steps, you get neat, tidy rows and columns filled with identical little cells, just like a spreadsheet.

Of course, it didn't take Web designers long to begin playing with tables in some very nonscientific ways. They started shifting columns, merging cells, and generally treating tables more like storage compartments than, well, tables. Ultimately, they figured out that by jiggering with the table tags, they could create frameworks for laying out text and graphics on a Web page. Their results turned simple tables into powerful development tools.

Unfortunately, tables were never really meant to fulfill the job of *multifunctional support grid supporting Web design elements*. Building large-scale tables that support an intricate Web design takes time, energy, and more hair than most people can sacrifice. (Did you ever wonder why so many cutting-edge Web designers go bald? Well, now you know the truth.)

That being said, tables still make a lot of sense in their development role, particularly when it comes to smaller applications like eBay auction text. You don't need a huge, complex table to show off a cool headline, some pictures, and a bit of body text. However, you *do* need a good development tool because hand-coding tables takes more patience and attention to detail than most people want to give (me included).

Take a look at the basic table structure in Figure 4-6, for instance. It contains space for a title and body text, plus four product images, a graphical border, and some sort of purchase-inspiring message below the body text. It appears pretty simple and straightforward, right?

Now look at the code in Listing 4-1, which makes the simple and straightforward table in the figure:

Listing 4-1: Creating a Basic Table

```
<TABLE width="100%" bgcolor="#ffffff" border=1 cellpadding=2
         cellspacing=2>

 <TR valign=top>
  <TD colspan=5 width=518 valign=center>
   Title to invoke desire and amazement
  </TD>
 </TR>

 <TR valign=top>
  <TD rowspan=3 width=24>
    
  </TD>
  <TD width=241 height=211 valign=center>
     Photo 1 displaying item's beauty
  </TD>
  <TD rowspan=2 width=460 height=416 valign=center>
   Body text to impress and amuse
  </TD>
  <TD width=211 height=211 valign=center>
   Photo 3 evoking item's delicacy
  </TD>
  <TD rowspan=3 width=22>
    
  </TD>
 </TR>

 <TR valign=top>
  <TD rowspan=2 width=241 height=127 valign=center>
   Photo 2 promoting item's functionality
  </TD>
```

```
   <TD rowspan=2 width=211 valign=center>
    Photo 4 depicting item's uniqueness
   </TD>
  </TR>

  <TR valign=top>
   <TD width=460 height=22 valign=center>
   Eloquent message to inspire purchase</DIV>
   </TD>
  </TR>

  <TR valign=top>
   <TD colspan=5 width=518>
    Splendid graphical border to close off the package
   </TD>
  </TR>
 </TABLE>
```

The `<table>` tags tell the browser that you want to build a table, but that merely begins the process by defining the boundaries of the table itself. It's like ordering a dresser for your bedroom but not saying anything about the drawers that go into it.

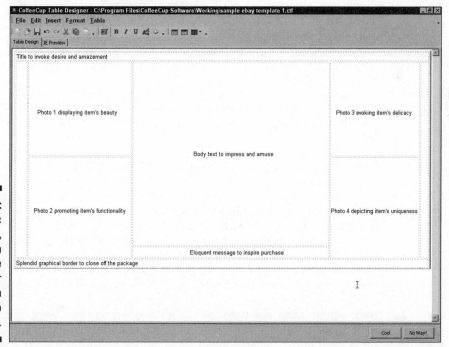

Figure 4-6:
A basic
table layout,
shown in
the Table
Designer
from
CoffeeCup
Software.

A look through eBay's linking rules

Because many of your linking activities take place inside eBay, you need to play by eBay's rules on the subject. (You knew this was coming, didn't you?)

Although eBay generally doesn't mind links, it gets a little sensitive about links placed in your auction text. According to the official eBay policy on such things, you can't place a link in an auction listing that leads a customer to an off-site sale for the same item. You can, however, use off-site links that lead to more product information or customer service information. In general, you can link to anything that helps buyers complete their transactions *inside eBay*. You can also add a link to your About Me page, but don't go overboard — eBay lets you put in one link of your own to the About Me page (in addition to the one eBay includes automatically at the top of your auction). You can also promote your

eBay store as much as you want because eBay gets a cut of sales over there as well.

The rules get a lot more relaxed when you turn to the About Me page. You can't sell products on your About Me page (that's why auctions and eBay Stores exist, after all), but you can do almost anything else. You can link to your online store, to your Web site, and (frankly) to just about anywhere you want, provided you don't tell people that they shouldn't buy through eBay. (Do you see a common theme developing here?)

If you do any business on eBay, take the time to read and understand the linking rules. They don't take that long to work through (and they aren't terribly boring — a little boring, yes, but not terribly boring). To see the complete eBay rules and regulations on linking, visit `pages.ebay.com/help/policies/listing-links-faq.html`.

You populate a table with rows (`<tr>`) and then populate each row with cells (`<td>`). When you finally dig your way down to this smallest level of the table, you also start plugging in text or image tags to actually put content into your framework.

Rather than fighting with all these tags and their myriad settings, focus your attention on your favorite HTML editing tool. They all include some sort of automated assistance when it comes to building tables. Some give you an interactive tool for building them, such as the Quick Table feature in the CoffeeCup HTML Editor or the Draw a Table option in Microsoft FrontPage. Others offer a complete tool for the task, such as CoffeeCup's Table Designer. Get to know the tools, including their features and limitations. Make strangely shaped tables and see how your editor thinks they should look versus how your favorite browsers interpret them. The difference might surprise you!

Although the table reigned supreme as the method of choice for laying out a Web page a few years ago, Cascading Style Sheets essentially replaced them for large-scale Web development. See Chapter 11 for more about the surprising power (and moderate complexity) of using style sheets in your world.

Linking Here, Linking There (And Doing It the Right Way)

Links — those wonderful clickable connections between documents scattered throughout the planet — form the basis of the Web itself. Even eBay relies on links for everything from navigation to leaving feedback. But links serve a much more important function in your eBay auctions — namely, to make more money for you!

These tools come in very handy for navigating inside your auction listings, cross-promoting your related auctions, and connecting people to customer service information (and still more products) on your company Web site.

All links start with the same HTML tag: the anchor (<a>). Anchor tags tell your Web browser to create an area on the page that responds to a click of the mouse button. (Anchor tags also identify sections of a Web page, letting you link not only to a particular page but also to a certain point on that page. Look for more about that a little later in this section.)

When a user clicks the link, the Web browser recognizes the click and acts on it, based on the instructions stored in the anchor tag. The following example opens the home page of a Web site:

```
<a href="http://www.linguaplay.com">Visit the LinguaPlay Web
         site</a>
```

This anchor tag contains four unique sections. First, the anchor tag tells the Web browser that you want to insert a link here. The href portion identifies the address that the link points to — in this case, a Web site. After that, the link includes some plain text Visit the LinguaPlay Web site. When a browser interprets this tag, it displays the plain text part as *link text,* which usually gets formatted with a different color and an underline. The closing tag (</a>) brings up the rear of the code.

Although most links point to Web pages, links can do other things as well. The specific action depends on the URL that you put into the href section of the anchor tag; the rest of the HTML remains the same.

For example, the following code tells the browser to make a new e-mail message and address it to ebay@linguaplay.com:

```
<a href="mailto:ebay@linguaplay.com">E-mail me a question</a>
```

This link code contains all the same pieces as the previous example (the one that sent the user to a new Web page). Only the quoted information in the `href` section changed. Instead of putting in a Web address (with a URL that starts with `http://`), this one uses a `mailto:` URL instead. When the browser sees that, it automatically knows to start the user's default e-mail program, create a new message, and shove the address you specify into the message's recipient section. Pretty cool, eh?

Links can also tell Web sites to execute scripts or run programs. This great little piece of code instructs eBay to add your user ID to someone's Favorite Sellers list inside eBay:

```
<a href="http://cgi1.ebay.com/aw-
        cgi/eBayISAPI.dll?AcceptSavedSeller&sellerid=yourI
        Dhere&sspageName=DB:FavList">Add me</a> to your
        Favorite Sellers list!
```

To use this code, replace the text *yourIDhere* with your eBay user ID. When the customer clicks the link, the Web browser feeds the `AcceptSavedSeller` command to one of eBay's servers, which puts your ID on the customer's list. You can add this link to your auctions, your About Me page, and even your Web site. It's a great example of how to make eBay's existing tools work for you.

Anchor tags also help you build a navigation system *inside* your auction or About Me page by creating links that go to specific positions on a Web page. This trick requires a two-step approach, as the following example shows. The first bit of code creates a marker on the Web page; the second bit of code creates a link leading to that marker:

```
<a name="destination_name"></a> (creates the marker)
<a href="#destination_name">Destination link text</a> (goes
        to the marker)
```

To make the marker, you write an anchor tag with the `name` option. This tells the browser that if it runs across a link somewhere pointing to this destination name, it should come to this point in the HTML code and display the rest of the page.

The anchor tag that makes a link to a marker looks exactly like a normal Web page link, except that you use a pound sign (#) in the URL position. The pound sign tells the browser that it should look for a marker of that name on the current page instead of going to some other Web page.

Listing 4-2 puts anchor tags into action. The first part of the code creates a menu of places to go on the current page. A pair of *horizontal rule tags* (`<hr>`) make the menu stand out a bit from the headings. Before each heading, the code creates an appropriately named marker with an anchor tag. The links in the menu refer to each marker name in the rest of the text.

Listing 4-2:   Inserting Anchor Tags

```
<hr align=center>
<center><b><A href="#description">Description</A> -- <A
          href="#payment">Payment</A>
-- <A href="#shippingus">US Shipping</A> -- <A
          href="#shippingint">International
shipping</A> -- <A
          href="#questions">Questions?</A></b></center>
<hr align=center>

<a name="description"></a>
<h1>Description</h1>
<p><i>Product description goes here.</i></p>

<a name="payment"></a>
<h1>Payment</h1>
<p><i>Payment information goes here.</i><P>

<a name="shippingus"></a>
<h2>Shipping within the United States</h2>
<p><i>US shipping information goes here.</i></p>

<a name="shippingint"></a>
<h2>International Shipping</h2>
<p><i>International shipping information goes here.</i></P>

<a name="questions"></a>
<HR ALIGN=center>
<center><b>Got a question? E-mail us and ask!!</b>
<A
          HREF="mailto:ebay@linguaplay.com"><B>ebay@linguapl
          ay.com</B></A></center>
<HR ALIGN=center>
```

All these examples move to markers on the current Web page, but you can use the same technique to create a link to a marker on a completely *different* Web page. To do that, just alter the link a little by adding the Web address to it:

```
<A href="http://www.linguaplay.com#shipping">See our complete
          shipping terms and information.</A>
```

The anchor tag starts with a regular Web address (the `http://www.lingua play.com` part) and adds the pound sign and marker stuff to it. The result says to a Web browser, "Go to this Web page and then find this marker tag on it." The browser opens up the new page, scans through it for the appropriate marker tag, and then starts displaying the page. If it fails to find the tag, it just displays the Web page normally.

Organizing Your Presentation

Selling products through an online auction works just like selling things face to face in real life. As the seller, you need to connect with the customer, entice and interest the person in your product, provide information, answer questions, overcome objections, and close the sale — or, in this case, get the bid. Because you sell on eBay, you rarely get to interact directly with the customer (except through the occasional e-mail, phone conversation, or local product pickup). Instead, you need to accomplish all these selling techniques through your auction listing, turning it from a passive communicator into a high-powered selling machine.

As an added bonus, a well-organized auction looks a lot better than a slapped-together one, giving you yet another edge over less professional sellers when it comes to winning your customer's trust. A consistent design also builds your eBay brand in the eyes of your customers, which enhances your professional stature among the buyers and browsers and encourages new (as well as repeat) sales at the same time. That's a pretty good payoff for a little bit of work.

What makes a well-organized auction? It starts with the basics: complete, descriptive auction text and plenty of pictures that flatteringly (and fully) show off your product. Atop that foundation, add headings for each major section of your auction text — namely the description, payment, and shipping information blocks.

If you want to go all-out, use the anchor link trick discussed in the preceding section to build a menu that moves your customer back and forth to the key sections on the auction page. Granted, a menu system like that makes the most sense for a listing with a *lot* of text, but those listings usually translate into high dollar amounts. I follow a simple, general rule: The more money I want from my customer, the more information and service I supply, and that starts with the auction description.

Nobody will ever e-mail you to complain that your auction included *too much* information, but you can expect comments if your auctions don't say enough. By organizing your creation with headings (and maybe even a built-in menu system), you show your customers that you care about your business — and that you care about them.

Chapter 5

Using Templates to Create Listings Quickly

*P*erusing eBay, you'll notice that the most successful folks (or at least the folks who have a lot of feedback) use a consistent and customized description in their auctions. Their auctions have a similar look and feel. Quite simply, an attractive auction generates more bids and higher sales. By staying consistent, you also save yourself the time of creating a new layout for each auction as well as build customer confidence.

Just as every McDonald's restaurant has a similar look and feel, your auctions should use a consistent design. That way, your customers will begin to identify your auctions by the look of the page. As you build your eBay reputation, using an auction design that connects the item on the screen with your business makes buyers more confident. They're more likely to buy the item when they realize that a trusted seller put it up for auction. This chapter introduces you to reusable auction designs that save you time and give your auctions a unique look.

Building a Framework for Your Auctions

To give your auctions a consistent look and feel, you create a *template* (or pattern) that each auction follows. Just like a stencil that you'd use to paint a repeated pattern, an auction template makes it easy to create many similar-looking auctions.

Thankfully, you don't have to sell identical items to use an auction template. Just as a stencil allows you to use different colors while painting the same shape, your auction template gives each auction the same look and general layout while still making it easy for you to customize it for individual items. Some parts of your template will be the same in every auction, and others will need to be tweaked for the product that you're selling.

Although you may not know it, you may already be using an auction template. Figure 5-1 shows a simple template, like many that you have run across in your eBay travels. Most eBay sellers stumble onto auction templates by accident. Any time you use the same HTML code, shipping details, or return policy in all your auctions, you're using a template. Even if you don't need to tweak the template for each auction, you're still saving yourself time by reusing the same information or HTML code for all your auctions. This chapter helps you take your existing templates to the next level and shows you how to make more complicated and useful templates.

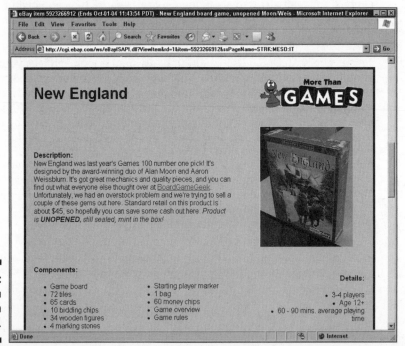

Figure 5-1:
A custom
auction
design.

Creating an auction template doesn't have to result in sleep deprivation or an extended time locked away in your office. Templates are actually easy to create. In a nutshell, you take an auction description you've already created and then start removing the text and photos specific to the individual item you're selling. But rather than simply deleting the item description, product condition explanation, and item-specific shipping details, you replace them with *placeholders.*

Rather than create all your code by hand, use an HTML editor when creating templates. They make it easy to replace sections in your template, saving you time. Figure 5-2 shows Macromedia Dreamweaver MX, an excellent HTML editing tool. For more information on HTML editing applications, check out Chapter 3.

For example, in place of your explanation of the item's condition, add a note to remind you to insert the item condition. Consider using something like this:

```
[[ PUT ITEM CONDITION HERE ]]
```

This text makes it easy to find all the sections in your template that you want to replace with item-specific details. When you go back to update your template, you can search for `[[` and quickly find the sections you planned to change. But before you dive into one of your current auctions to create your shiny new template, consider sprucing it up a bit first, as described in the next section.

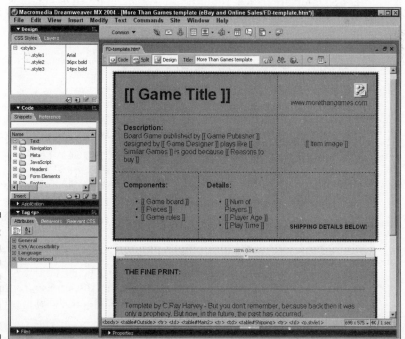

Figure 5-2:
A custom auction design transformed into a template.

Creating a Look That's Uniquely You

Creating an auction template that looks snazzy should rank high on your priority list. Sure, you can create a template that reduces your auction setup time and gives you a consistent look, but if the template doesn't make you look good, then it's all for naught.

Chapter 4 delves into the mystery of HTML and gives you some great tips for making your auctions look their best. If you've spent some quality time with your HTML editor or WYSIWYG design tool, you're ready to begin transforming it into a boilerplate auction design. However, if you're like most of us, you don't have time to create your own template from scratch. Have no fear! Many online vendors offer an array of templates that should fit your needs.

When deciding whether to create your own template or find a prebuilt one, consider how much control you want to have over the design. If you're comfortable using a template that other sellers are using and can live with designs that don't allow much customization, then a prebuilt template may be for you. However, if you want to create a truly unique design and don't want to have any limitations placed on your creativity, it's time to dig into HTML and create your own!

A quick search on Google (`www.google.com`) for `eBay auction templates` yields over 100,000 results! Within the first few pages of the results, you'll find numerous sites that offer hundreds of custom templates. Although some sites offer free templates, most require you to sign up for their services. They typically charge a monthly fee in return for access to their template libraries and other services.

Rather than make you wade through all the numerous possibilities, here are a few sites for you to check out first:

- ✔ **Aucgen.com** (`www.aucgen.com`): After you select one of the over 100 templates, Aucgen.com's simple system fills in your item's details. At $7.99 a month, you also receive 100MB of image hosting.

- ✔ **Auction-Resources.com** (`www.auction-resources.com/templates.html`): You can buy over 100 auction templates for $12.95, no monthly fee attached. Although many of the templates look similar, you may find something for you.

- ✔ **auctionSupplies.com** (`www.auctionsupplies.com`): This personal Web site includes several simple (and more importantly, free) templates.

- ✔ **BidBoosters** (`www.bidboosters.com`): For just $6.95, you can dig into BidBoosters' growing template gallery as well as use its image hosting services to store your item's photos. You can try the site for free for 30 days, or you can take advantage of the custom template design service.

- ✔ **Seller Sourcebook** (`www.sellersourcebook.com`): This site offers over 300 auction templates and image hosting, starting at $5.80 per month.

Like anything else, you'll want to protect yourself when you consider signing up for an eBay service or purchasing auction templates. You may run into shady Web sites offering hundreds of eBay templates for next to nothing. Be particularly wary of sites that offer to sell you templates that you can turn around and resell. You have to ask yourself, "What kind of honest sellers would want you to turn around and compete with them?"

In addition to simple HTML templates that you download, you also find sites that offer WYSIWYG tools to insert your item's details into the template automatically. Although the built-in template editor is nice when you first get started, you may outgrow it as you need more flexibility.

If your favorite template doesn't include a built-in editor, you get to do some modification of your own. But don't worry; your HTML editor or WYSIWYG design tool makes the job easy. If you haven't picked up an HTML design program, take a look at Chapter 3. If you're new to editing HTML, you'll probably want to use an editor to update the template for each auction item. To make life even easier, Chapter 8 introduces a free tool, Template Filler (www.template filler.com), that automatically picks out the spots in your template you need to fill in and replaces them for you.

If you decide to use an automated template system that automatically fills in your item's details, then you're just about finished. All you need to do to use your template is to fill in the blanks and then paste the template into your auction. The template system will likely have documentation to help you insert it into your auctions. If your template doesn't have an automatic system for filling in the blanks, the next section tells you what you need to do.

Transforming Your Auction Description into a Template

Armed with an auction design you want to use for all your auctions, you're ready to customize the template so that it will fit any of your auction items. Even if you purchased or downloaded a template from an online auction site, you'll still want to add special text and make room for the details you typically include with each auction. By creating a customized template, you eliminate much of the busywork that comes with creating an auction description.

Before loading up an auction design to create your template, make a backup. Nothing is worse than ruining your glorious auction design during the template process and then discovering that you don't have a copy of the original to go back to. Take a hint from those that have gone before you and learned this the hard way: Back up your work before you change anything. That way, when you get into the template and find you've made a serious mistake, you can go back to the original.

To create an effective template that saves you time, you need to make room for all your item's details, photos, and generic auction text (shipping details, payment terms, return policy, and so on). You add placeholders or actual text (and images) for as much information as possible to make the template easy to use. Do you include PayPal logos on your auctions? Add them to the template. Include a blurb about your return policy? Put that in, too.

Remember that the more you add to the auction template, the less time you must spend later. However, be careful not to go too far. If you're too specific, your template may not fit all your items. Your items may have different return policies, or you may store images in different places. Like many things, you want to strike a balance between making the template so specific that it fits only a small subset of your auctions (making item descriptions for those items a snap) and making the template too generic (and not saving much time).

Consider the simple auction design shown in Figure 5-3. Listing 5-1 shows the necessary HTML used in the figure.

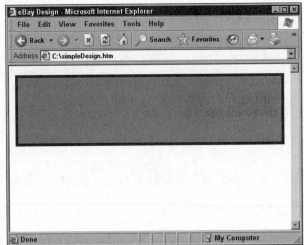

Figure 5-3:
A simple
auction
design.

Listing 5-1:   A Simple Auction Design

```
<table width="100%" cellpadding="5">
<tr>
  <td bgcolor="#000000">
    <table width="100%"  border="0" cellpadding="20"
           bgcolor="#999999">
    <tr>
      <td>
        <!-- An empty box -->
```

```
          <br>
          <br>
          <br>
          <br>
        </td>
      </tr>
      </table>
    </td>
  </tr>
</table>
```

This chapter walks you through transforming this HTML code into a functional template. First, you create a place in your auction design for all the important details you include in your auctions. To help you remember which details go in the placeholders, type in a simple description, such as Item Image Name. Then to make it easy to see your auction placeholders, surround them with special characters or markings. You can use double brackets ([[and]]) because standard HTML doesn't use brackets. Listing 5-2 shows the code from Listing 5-1 reworked to include placeholders:

Listing 5-2:   Adding Placeholders to the Auction Design

```
<table width="100%"  cellpadding="5">
<tr>
  <td bgcolor="#000000">
    <table width="100%"  border="0" cellpadding="20"
          bgcolor="#999999">
    <tr>
      <td>
        <p><img src="http://www.yourwebsite.com/images/[[
          Item Image Name ]].jpg" alt="" width="200"
          height="200" border="1" align="right">
        <strong>[[ Insert Item Title here ]]</strong></p>

        <p>[[ Item Description goes here ]]</p>
      </td>
    </tr>
    </table>
  </td>
</tr>
</table>
```

Listing 5-2 shows the three key item details: the title, description, and photo name, replaced with double brackets and a short explanation of the information to include. Note that rather than remove the entire image HTML tag, the example replaced only the item image name, shown in bold as follows:

```
src="http://www.yourwebsite.com/images/[[ Item Image Name
          ]].jpg"
```

The URL for the image hosting site and folder (`http://www.yourwebsite.com/images/` in the example) and the `.jpg` file type stay the same because those most likely will be constant in all your auctions. The image filename changes most often, so the example includes a placeholder for it. When using this template, you type in only the image name, saving you the time of typing the URL, folder, and file type.

If you're using a WYSIWYG Web page design tool, you can create placeholders in your auction design as you preview the result rather than editing pure HTML code. The template will work just as easily. Plus, you'll have an idea how the design will look in its generic template form.

Now that you've seen how you can save time entering your image tags, here are a few other things you may want to leave room for in your template:

- ✔ **Lists:** You'll probably benefit from using a bulleted list in your auctions. Lists make it easy for potential bidders to scan your auctions to quickly find out as much information as possible. If you want to include a bulleted (or numbered) list in your auction, be sure to leave at least one bullet in your template. That way, you can copy the first bullet as you add more.

- ✔ **Images:** The earlier example shows you how you can save time by changing only the image filename (you don't even have to reenter the file extension). However, the example works only if you always store your images in the same place and they're all the same size; that may or may not work for you.

  When making room for your images in the template, decide how specific you want (or can afford) to get. Consider whether to include the Web site and folder in which you store images (if you use the same location for your images) and the image extension (if you always use JPEG files). If you use the same size image in every auction (which gives your auctions a more consistent look), feel free to include the size attributes in the image tag. If they change, you can easily leave them out because the browser will automatically figure out the image size.

- ✔ **Generic item terms:** If you regularly include shipping details, a return policy, or some description of your business in your auctions, include that information in your template. What do you do if those details aren't the same for every auction you run? No problem; you can include all your return policies in the template, for example, and then remove the policies that don't apply to the particular auction you're creating.

With your auction design transformed into a generic template, be sure to save your work. Name the HTML file something you'll remember because you'll be using it frequently. You may even want to create a shortcut on your desktop so it's right at your fingertips.

Listing 5-3 shows the revised template now with item-specific information in each box (*table cell* for those into HTML). The template also uses Cascading Style Sheets (covered in Chapter 11) to improve the text formatting.

Listing 5-3:   The Auction Design Template with Item-Specific Info and Improved Text Formatting

```
<style type="text/css">
<!--
p {
  font-family: Arial, Helvetica, sans-serif
}
.itemTitle {
        font-size: 36px;
        font-weight: bold;
}
.myHeading {
        font-size: 14pt;
        font-weight: bold;
}
-->
</style>

<table width="100%" border="0" cellpadding="5">
<tr>
  <td bgcolor="#000000">
    <table bgcolor="#999999" width="100%" border="0"
           cellpadding="20">
    <tr>
      <td colspan="2"><p class="itemTitle">[[ Game Title
        ]]</p></td>
      <td width="30%" align="right"><img
          src="http://www.morethangames.com/layout/More_Than
          _Games/images/logo.gif"><br>www.morethangames.com<
          /td>
    </tr>
    <tr valign="top">
      <td colspan="2"><p><span
          class="myHeading">Description</span><br>
        Board Game published by [[ Game Publisher ]] designed
          by [[ Game Designer ]] plays like [[ Similar Games
          ]]. You'll want to bid on it because [[ Reasons to
          buy ]]</p>
        </td>
      <td align="center"><img
          src="http://www.morethangames.com/eBayImages/[[
          Item image ]].jpg" alt="" border="0" width="200"
          height="200"></td>
    </tr>
```

(continued)

Listing 5-3 *(continued)*

```
    <tr valign="top">
      <td width="34%"><p class="myHeading">Components</p>
        <ul>
          <li>[[ Game board ]]</li>
          <li>[[ Pieces ]]</li>
          <li>[[ Game rules ]]<strong><br>
          </strong></li>
        </ul></td>
      <td width="36%"><p class="myHeading">Details</p>
        <ul>
          <li>[[ Number of Players ]]</li>
          <li>[[ Player Age ]]</li>
          <li>[[ Playing Time ]]</li>
        </ul></td>
      <td align="center" valign="bottom"><p
          class="myHeading">SHIPPING INSTRUCTIONS
          BELOW!</p></td>
    </tr>
    </table>
  </td>
</tr>
</table>
```

Figure 5-4 shows the finished template after breaking it up into smaller pieces with Macromedia Dreamweaver MX.

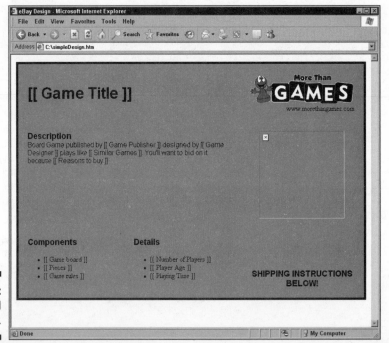

Figure 5-4:
The finished
product.

Sending Your Template into Action

Armed with your new template customized to fit your needs (and auctions), you'll save countless hours and develop an image as an online seller. Buyers will begin to relate your auction design with you. Does that mean you should never change the template again? Heavens no! Keep an eye out for simple modifications you can make to improve your design. Simple updates will make your template more effective and won't compromise your seller image.

You've got an auction to post and want to put your new template to use, but how do you do it? Here's the general process:

1. **Open the template file (which isn't your only copy, right?) and then use the Save As command in your HTML editor to make a copy.**

   Pick a filename for your new auction item. After you've created a copy, you're ready to customize the template for the auction at hand.

2. **Item by item, go through your template and replace the generic place-holders with the details for this item.**

   It helps to work from the top down, adding as you go. Keep an eye out as you go so you don't miss an entry! You'll kick yourself if you post an auction that includes [[Put item condition here]] right in the middle of the item description (and don't ask why I know that).

3. **Go through the auction template twice to make sure you replaced every entry and then give the item description a whirl on eBay.**

   The item listing process includes an item description preview. Pay special attention to your images because changing images in your template will probably give you the most trouble the first few times. It can take a few tries to get used to entering only an image name instead of the whole address. It's also easy to leave an extra space where it doesn't belong.

After clicking that final, fateful button and listing your auction, always, always, *always* take a moment to click your auction link and look at your finished work. Despite eBay's preview system and the fact that HTML code works just like you think it will *most* of the time, occasionally the technology gremlins conspire to deliver a rude surprise. The only way to know for sure is to take a look at what your customers see. If everything looks great, smile and continue with the next auction. If things appear, well, *odd,* then avail yourself of the Revise Your Item link in your auction listing to make things right again.

Chapter 6

Driving Sales and Satisfaction with Your About Me Page and Web Site

*P*romotion, promotion, promotion — the three keys to most successful small businesses. In the real world (the one with automobile emissions, fast-food wrappers, and physical storefronts), promotion means getting your business name and products in front of people as much as possible. Whether you do it by advertising on the radio and TV, placing articles in newspapers and magazines, plastering flyers to telephone poles, or handing out business cards like crazy, you need to do it every day, like clockwork. Promotion gives your company and your products the "top of mind" awareness that keeps people thinking of you.

In the online auction and business world, promotion works a bit differently. You still need to get your products and your company in front of potential buyers, but you do things a bit differently. You hone the title text for your auction listing so it informs and entices, all in the space of 55 characters. You craft an About Me page that sells customers not only on your products but also on your company as an ideal trading partner. You build a Web presence that enhances your image as a premier business in the field, while offering opportunities for add-on sales as you develop first-time customers into long-term ones.

Although the techniques differ a bit, the goal remains the same: Polish the image of your products and your business so that people find you, know you, trust you, and buy from you.

The image you present to the customer counts for a lot in the online world. Most of the time, your customers can't meet you face to face, can't visit your business, and can't physically touch the product before buying it. Instead, the entire transaction sits squarely on a foundation of information that you offer to the customers. If your auction text, About Me page, and Web site work together right, customers feel like they know you and can trust you. This results in better bids on your auctions (we all want that) and more money in your pocket.

This chapter explores some ways you can use your About Me page and your Web site to not only capture first-time sales but also retain customers for second, third, and fourth sales. It looks at promotion, proactively answering your customers' questions and building a truly cool (and useful) About Me page. You also find out how to start a sideline business making money with the eBay Affiliate Program (because the money all spends the same, regardless of whether they bought something *from* you or *through* you).

Promoting Your Auctions, Your Products, and Yourself

Start the promotion process with your auction listings. A good listing not only sells the product but also sells you as the best possible supplier. To do that, your auctions should include the following information:

- **Full product information with multiple photos:** Use the inline photo trick discussed in Chapter 4 to create a professional-looking catalog layout inside your auctions.

- **Complete terms of the sale:** Educate customers about doing business with you. Tell them your shipping costs, satisfaction guarantee, return policy, and everything else you can think of relating to customer service and policies. Make the information easy to find and clear to read.

- **A link to your About Me page:** This begins the process of moving your customers from *one-up purchasers* into *long-term buyers*. By connecting them to your About Me page, you draw them further into interaction with your product lines and your company.

- **An invitation to purchase:** Selling doesn't get more *old school* than this. Invite the customer to purchase your item. Say it right there in your auction text:

    Place your bid now! Our product, our quality, and our service make this a great deal for your money. We guarantee it!

For most of your customers, your auction text represents their doorway into your business. They find your auction as they prowl the mall-like halls of eBay. After they go into your auction, it's as if they paused to look into the front window of a store. If what they see catches their interest, they go into the store — or in your case, they click your View Seller's Other Items link to see the rest of your products or click your About Me link to find out more about your company. At each step, you want to continue drawing customers in by giving them more information and directing them to links leading to still *more* about you, your company, and your products. The more that the customers know about you, the more comfortable they feel about trusting your word on the product and entrusting you with their money.

Your About Me page forms the second stage of promotion and information for your customer. Because eBay provides the space for this page, eBay obviously hopes that you use it. To encourage that behavior on your part, eBay promotes the About Me page as a tool for buyers to learn more about sellers.

As part of that promotion, after you create an About Me page, eBay automatically adds a nifty little *Me* icon link next to your user ID. The icon link appears with your user ID in all your auctions as well as on your member profile page. Thanks to eBay's end-user training, most eBay members who see the icon know that they can click it to take a look at your About Me page. You might as well take advantage of that training by putting together a solid, informative About Me page that sells your customers on the idea of buying from you.

At least they *mostly* speak the same language

Both the About Me page and your Web site speak the same basic language: HTML. That means you can get double duty from your development work by making code that functions in both environments. It takes some careful planning, but the extra functionality of making your About Me page work like your Web site certainly offers a lot of benefits for both you and your customers.

If you compare the About Me page to a normal Web site, you quickly find that the About Me page represents the tougher of the two development environments. That only makes sense because eBay gives you the server space and bandwidth for your About Me page as a free part of your account. Of course eBay wants some say in what you do there! However, because that page lives inside eBay's virtual walls, the company can also give you some extra freebies that your Web site can't match.

For instance, your About Me page knows a bunch of special HTML tags that only work there — you can't use them anywhere else. On the flip side, eBay limits the amount and type of JavaScript code that you can embed into an About Me page. Keep that in mind if you plan to do a lot of extensive JavaScript work on your Web site — it probably won't migrate well to the other environment.

By planning and developing both your Web site and your About Me page to work with each other, you create a seamless sales and support environment for your customers. That shows professionalism, which in turn builds customer confidence in you and your products. And confidence means dollars in your auctions.

People love stories, so use your About Me page to tell the story behind you and your business. Include anything that helps weave the tale, such as the following:

- **General information about your business:** What would you tell people you just met if they asked about your business? Well, you would probably start talking about your products and services. If they didn't know much about your field, you might take a moment to outline your industry and then help them see how you fit into that picture. That makes sense, right? Use that same line of reasoning as you approach the About Me page. Tell customers something about your industry, your products, and your company.

- **Tell your story, too:** One of the best business introductions I ever read explained how George Rohrbacher invented *The Farming Game.* The tale of how he came up with his game idea, how he marketed the finished game from the back of his truck during its first years of production, and how the game ultimately spread throughout the United States — and even to the former Soviet Union, thanks to the World Bank — just makes you smile. You *want* to like this guy and his game. You can't help yourself. Your business has a story like that, too. Even if it's just a few words about how you decided that you could do a better job selling phone accessories than the other guys, that's a start. Personalizing yourself to your customer helps build a simple trading relationship.

- **Promote your products:** Tell your prospective customers about your products — how you found them, why you chose them, and the quality your customers can expect when using them. Don't just toss out a raw list of your open auctions — tell customers why *your* poker chips or *your* antiques stand out from someone else's offerings. Tell about the lengths you go in order to find the products you sell. If you do something exotic or over-the-top, tell that, too! I read a fascinating story about a junkyard owner who flew a helicopter from auto auction to auto auction so he could find the most cars possible on each sale day. The amazing selection at his junkyard reflected his efforts. The story underscores his business's focus on its product. Tales like that put customers on your side from the start, so the task of selling them on your products becomes even easier.

- **Give them something interesting:** Give your customers a reason to go to the About Me page the first time and come back over and over. Perhaps you include some ongoing content, such as product reviews or industry news. (Yes, it's that story thing again.) If people see you as an expert, they trust you more. The more they trust you, the more they trust your judgment when it comes to products. By offering some sort of ongoing information, you get the opportunity to sell to the customer again and again and turn that person into a raving fan (albeit an online one).

Because the products in your online auctions all connect to your About Me page, then your About Me page needs to return the favor by providing easy links back to the auctions. It should also include a direct connection to your company's Web site (and vice versa — make sure the Web site leads to the About Me page). All these tools should seamlessly link together, letting the customer move between them at will, looking at products, learning about your firm, checking out your policies, and making purchases without ever finding themselves led into a dead end. Always provide a way to wherever your customer wants to go within your world.

Your Web site represents the third leg supporting your promotional efforts. Like the About Me page, the Web site needs a broad collection of information:

- ✔ **Background information:** You covered this ground on the About Me page, but it costs nothing to reproduce it — and maybe even expand on it some more — here. The more that you tell your customers about you, the better for your sales. Pour on the info!

- ✔ **Detailed product descriptions:** Create a simple online catalog of your regular offerings, with links back to your auction listing on the About Me page. Use plenty of pictures because online customers like to *see* what they're buying. Keep the menus simple — plain text links work great — so the search engine robots can traverse them easily and index your Web site.

- ✔ **All the appropriate customer service links:** You might think it odd, but the more opportunities you give people to contact you, the more confident they feel about buying from you. On more than one occasion, I crossed sellers off my buying list because their Web sites and auction text didn't identify the company and give me simple, straightforward ways to contact them.

- ✔ **Customer testimonials:** When your customers say nice things about you, tell the world! Nothing works better than when customers sell *each other* on the benefits of doing business with you. As the compliments roll in, ask the customers if it's okay to use their comments on your Web site. It's okay with just about everybody, but you still should ask. Who knows? You might run into that one odd person in a thousand who only wanted *you* to know how he felt.

For its information, your Web site should stand on its own. At the same time, your site *needs* links to your About Me page. The more seamlessly you integrate your Web site and your About Me page, the more powerful each one becomes. Integration should include visual style (so that both sites look and behave similarly), ease of use, and rules for online content.

Answering the Questions Customers Always Ask

Customers always have questions. It's the nature of things. Whenever you get involved with a transaction where you're parting someone from their money and giving something in return, the party giving up the money always wants to know some detail or other. And who can blame them? Like our grade school teachers told us, the only dumb question is the one you don't ask.

Online buyers want to ask questions, too, but they also want to finish their transactions quickly and efficiently. That gives you, the seller, a unique opportunity to delight your customers by answering their concerns *and* providing the answers in an easy-to-access way. A simple *frequently asked questions* document (or FAQ) does the job perfectly.

Although it doesn't take too much time to create an FAQ, it does take thought. Write your FAQ from the customer's perspective and with the customer's concerns in mind. Answer real questions — the kind of questions that you want answers to when you buy things. An FAQ populated with pointless entries like *How Does Your Company Offer Great Products at Such Low Prices?* just irritates customers. Your customers get more than enough irritation every day without adding more of it from an online seller. You want to please your customers, not drive them away.

The best FAQs use a simple "heading and question" layout. Again, you don't need an amazing-*looking* FAQ — you need an FAQ with amazing *content*. Figure 6-1 shows a basic FAQ in the making. It clearly identifies its purpose in the world, includes a basic navigation bar and company branding at the top, and invites customers to browse through the page contents and see if their question is answered in there. It also gives customers two easy ways to ask a question that's not covered: the *Ask Us Something* navigation bar item and the *Ask Us* link in the text. The questions themselves come from real experiences with real customers.

Notice that the FAQ lists some of the questions two or three times, with slightly different wording (see the first few lines in the About Payments section next to the mouse pointer at the bottom of Figure 6-1). By posing a question in different ways, you make the answer accessible to the broadest possible audience. In this case, an experienced online buyer might ask if the company accepts payments via PayPal, but someone new to the online world just wants to know how to pay for stuff in general. By including both questions in the FAQ (*Do You Accept PayPal* and *How Should I Pay for My Purchase*), you make the information easy for both people to find.

Figure 6-1:
Your FAQ document needs to focus on things from the customer's perspective.

Make your FAQ a living document by consistently adding to it. When customer questions come through your e-mail, think about adding the answer to the FAQ. Or if the FAQ already contains the answer, try to figure out why the customer didn't find it there. Did she look in the FAQ and fail to find the answer, or did she miss the FAQ in the first place? Use what you discover to make your FAQ as complete, useful, and available as possible. Your customers will thank you!

Building Repeat Business

After a customer decides to buy from you, it puts you in a great position to do even more business with that customer in the future. People like consistency — they like doing things the same way, over and over. After they get a chance to use your product and experience your service, that builds a great foundation for the next sale and maybe even the one after that.

Not all products lend themselves to repeat business from the same group of clients. If I hire an exterminator to get rid of ants in my house, I don't *want* to call the person again for the same problem, because the job wasn't done right in the first place! If you sell a single-purchase type of product or service, focus your efforts on building referral business instead of repeat business. This uses many of the same techniques as the repeat business model, except that it looks for ways to help your customers tell other people about the joys of doing business with you. E-mail newsletters and referral reward programs (things like *Refer a Friend and Get a $10 eBay Gift Certificate,* for example) make great tools for encouraging happy customers to sell — er, *tell* — your service to their friends and family.

To create repeat business, you need two things: a communication link with your buyer and ongoing things to say. Your Web site and About Me pages both count (they're both communication connections between you and your buyer), but e-mail makes the whole process work a bit easier.

Although you get your buyers' e-mail addresses when they buy something in your auction or through your eBay store, eBay's rules say *specifically* that you can't use those addresses for anything other than completing business with those buyers. However, it's completely within eBay's rules to *invite* customers to join your company's e-mail list by putting a link in your regular e-mails to them or by including a Join the Mailing List box on your About Me page or Web site.

You *cannot* put people's e-mail addresses onto your mailing list and then *invite* them to take themselves off the list if they aren't interested. Nope — no can do. eBay rules require that customers do some sort of "positive action" to express their interest in joining your customer list, like clicking a link or sending an e-mail message. That directly outlaws the old *you automatically joined our list but here's how to remove yourself* method of customer acquisition.

Many programs out there help you manage mailing lists and newsletters. To find one that works for you, feed your favorite search engine the term `newsletter software` and prowl through the results. Also check with your Web hosting service because it might offer that functionality for a small extra monthly fee (or maybe even for free with your hosting package). To get started on the cheap (as they say in the Old Country), Chapter 7 gives you some ideas on handling the whole mailing list process with your standard issue e-mail program.

With your mailing list in hand and some kind of tool for sending messages, now you just need something to say each month (because a monthly newsletter hits a nice balance between keeping your company name in front of customers and annoying them with nonstop messages). Among other things, you can tell them about

- ✔ New items that you listed on eBay

- ✔ Announcements of upcoming special events or anticipated products

- ✔ Usage tips for the products you sell

- ✔ Reminders about buying consumable items (such as rolls of shrink-wrap or score pads for a game) from you

- ✔ New ways they can use their product

- ✔ Other interesting newsy tidbits about your company and your industry

If this sounds like a lot of work, well, it is. Actually, it's not a *lot* of work, but it certainly demands a fair amount of time, energy, and effort. Promotion pays huge dividends, though, because it's a lot easier to retain a customer than to grow a new one.

Learning the Secret Language of eBay's Special Tags

Like any self-respecting Web space, your About Me page understands most types of HTML tags. You can use any of the basic formatting tags, plus headings, tables, lists of all sorts, and even some JavaScript (provided it fits into eBay's narrowly defined limitations on what's okay for such things). But the About Me page speaks a secret second language as well, which only it understands — the language of special eBay HTML tags. Pull out your spy shades and get ready for some undercover action.

As part of their ongoing efforts to help you promote your eBay auctions, the eBay programmers created a group of special HTML tags especially for use on the About Me page. They give you quick and easy ways to create custom displays of information about your auctions, your feedback, and other uniquely eBay things.

These tags *only* work on your About Me page. That's a shame because I'd love to plop some of this information straight into my auction listings instead of redirecting people to the About Me page all the time. Perhaps eBay might allow this flexibility in the future, but for now, you're stuck with using these little gems *only* on the About Me page. Such is life, I guess.

All the tags present some kind of eBay-specific information. Most of them include some formatting or display options as well, although not all the options work as described in eBay's documentation (pages.ebay.com/help/account/html-tags.html). In fact, some of the options don't work at all. Still, the tags give you more than enough options to do some amazingly useful and sale-promoting things with your About Me page.

You can dress up any of these tags with other HTML options, such as headings, bold, italic, underline, fonts, and colors. Your browser treats the tags just like any other HTML command because eBay's servers feed the *results* of the tag to your browser, not the tag itself. Thus, the browser doesn't need to understand the tags at all because it never even sees them.

<eBayUserID> tag

<eBayUserID>: Displays your user ID and feedback rating as links to your member profile page.

<eBayUserID BOLD>: Puts your user ID and feedback rating in bold text as well as makes them into member profile page links.

<eBayUserID NOFEEDBACK>: Shows the user ID only, without your feedback rating.

<eBayUserID EMAIL>: Displays your user ID, feedback score, and e-mail address and makes all of them links. The user ID and feedback rating both lead to the member profile page, whereas the e-mail address link uses the mailto tag to help people send you e-mail with a single click.

<eBayUserID NOMASK>: Displays your user ID but omits the icon that appears if you recently changed your user ID, making the display look exactly like the one with the <eBayUserID> tag by itself. Why eBay even *offers* this option makes no sense to me because it seems to "legally" avoid eBay's standards. (Perhaps one of the programmers felt especially rebellious and freethinking that day.) Using this tag on your About Me page doesn't prevent the user ID change icon from appearing on your auction text or at the top of your About Me page; it just suppresses it for the odd moment that you use the tag.

<eBayUserID NOLINK>: Avoid using this tag. It's another tag that makes me wonder what the eBay programmers had in mind. This one displays only your feedback rating number and the appropriate little star but doesn't include your user ID. Stranger still, it formats the rating number as a link (just like it normally does), but it deliberately leaves your user ID *out* of the link. You end up with your numeric feedback rating and your star, displayed in parentheses and formatted as a nonfunctioning link. If customers click the link, they get an error from eBay saying User ID invalid. I don't know about you, but that kind of error doesn't exactly say "friendly, trustworthy, and technically competent seller" to me.

<eBayFeedback> tag

<eBayFeedback>: Recalls, formats, and presents a table containing the three most recent pieces of feedback in your history. It also automatically inserts a link to your full feedback listing at the bottom of the table.

`<eBayFeedback SIZE ="`*n*`">`: This lets you show more (or less) of your feedback entries. The option displays the most recent feedback items in your profile. Just replace the *n* with the number of items you want to show (whole numbers only, please), and eBay automatically handles the rest. It also includes a link to your full feedback listing.

`<eBayFeedback COLOR="`*specified color*`">`: For the artistic sellers in the crowd, this tag changes the color of the *lower line* in each feedback entry. It leaves the upper line as a faint blue-silver. It adds the link to your full feedback listing. The tag responds to the standard 16 HTML color names and the hexadecimal color codes.

`<eBayFeedback ALTERNATECOLOR="`*specified color*`">`: Similar to its other half (described in the preceding bullet), this option lets you replace the color in the *upper line* of the feedback listing. Use both tags to totally revamp the feedback table's color scheme. Like its brother, the tag understands the standard 16 HTML color names and all the myriad hexadecimal color codes.

`<eBayFeedback BORDER="`*n*`">`: This sets the thickness of the gray beveled frame surrounding the feedback table. The default is 0, which displays no frame at all. Put a 1 in there to give you a hairline border. A 5 shows about ½₂ of an inch of gray frame, and a 20 looks like someone went after your page with a broad tip marker. The between-cell borders always stay the same, regardless of the number you enter for this option.

`<eBayFeedback CAPTION="`*specified text*`">`: Displays whatever text you enter as a caption at the top of your feedback table. Unfortunately, eBay gets to pick the font, size, and style, none of which look very nice by default. Instead of using this option, I recommend putting your caption into a heading 1 tag (`<h1>`) immediately before the `eBayFeedback` tag. It just looks nicer.

`<eBayFeedback TABLEWIDTH="`*n*`">`: Sets the width of the feedback table to *n*, where *n* is the width of the feedback table as a percentage of the available space. The command defaults to 90%. If you embed the `eBayFeedback` tag inside a table (an easy way to control both the size and position of the results), set this option to 100. That tells eBay's system to fill the whole width of the table cell with the feedback listing. From there, tweak the table settings to fine-tune the listing's exact size. It works *much* easier that way.

`<eBayFeedback CELLPADDING="`*n*`">`: Sets the amount of space around and between individual feedback comments. The default setting (0) scrunches everything together, whereas 5 or more makes a noticeable frame around each comment block. Stick with lower numbers like 2 or 3 for simple border effects.

<eBayItemList> tag

`<eBayItemList>`: Creates a basic list of the items you're currently offering for sale on eBay.

`<eBayItemList SORT="`*n*`">`: Builds your item list and then sorts it according to the obscure number you put into the SORT option. Your sorting choices include by date with newest first (option 8), by date with oldest first (option 2), by auction end date with newest first (option 3), and by price in ascending order (option 4). The strange numeric progression of the options makes you wonder if other as-yet-unreleased sorting possibilities might exist at some point.

`<eBayItemList SINCE="`*n*`">`: Normally, the `eBayItemList` tag displays only your current, unsold auctions — you know, the ones you hope people might bid on and purchase. However, in the interest of giving customers everything they could possibly want, the eBay programmers created this option so you can show off several days of *closed* auction listings along with the current ones. The number you put into the option represents how many days into the past you want to show, so `since=7` shows your last week of closed auctions plus all your current open auctions. This option doesn't work with the BIDS setting described in a minute. To show only your current items, either omit this setting or put in `-1` for the value.

`<eBayItemList BORDER="`*n*`">`: This works *almost* exactly like the BORDER option in the `eBayFeedback` tag. The setting puts a beveled gray border around the whole table and draws border lines around each of the table's cells. The size of the outside border depends on the number you put into this option, but the inside cell borders don't ever change. If you like a beveled outside border, set this to 5 or so. If you don't want any outside border, set the option to 0. However, if you remove the outside border, you also remove the cell borders *inside* the table. That leaves your text floating in loose columns on the page background. It still looks nice, but it's a much different outcome than you get from setting the BORDER option to 0 in the `eBayFeedback` tag.

`<eBayItemList CAPTION="`*specified text*`">`: Use this tag to display your "specified text" (whatever it says) in a particularly ugly font atop the item list table. Instead of using this option (because the font looks *really* ugly), just put a regular HTML heading right before the table. Text surrounded by Heading 1 or Heading 2 tags (`<h1>` and `<h2>`) looks particularly spiffy.

`<eBayItemList CELLPADDING="`*n*`">`: Shoves "*n*" extra horizontal spaces into the cells of your table. The default is 0, but the tables look a lot less crammed, jammed, and generally shoved together if you set this between 5 and 10. That tosses in just enough white space to make the table quite attractive, in a technical sort of way.

`<eBayItemList BIDS>`: I can't imagine why anyone would ever want to use this option on an About Me page. No, really — I can't. This setting lists all the open items that you placed a bid on. Why you want to show the world your "buy" list is your business, but don't look for this setting on my About Me page. (By the way, this option doesn't work with the `SINCE` option, described earlier. No, I don't know why.)

`<eBayItemList CATEGORY="`*n*`">`: *Theoretically,* this tag should make a list containing only the items you currently offer for sale within some category number or another. In actuality, the tag doesn't do anything (or at least it didn't do anything when I tried it). You can try it yourself sometime. For a list of all category numbers, click the Buy link at the top of the main eBay window and then click the All Categories link near the bottom of the window. In the All Categories page, click the Show Category Numbers option button near the top of the page and then click Show.

`<eBayItemList TABLEWIDTH="`*n*`">`: Although this *should* set the width of the Items table to *n*% of the available space on the screen, it doesn't. In fact, like some of its brethren (notably the `CATEGORY` option), this option doesn't seem to *do* anything at all. Regardless of the setting, the table always takes up exactly the same amount of space. If you want to make an item list table thinner on the page, put it inside an HTML table (maybe even a table with just one cell) and then shrink the cell width. The item list table automatically adjusts to fill the full width of the cell.

`<eBayTime>` tag

`<eBayTime>`: This simple little tag does one thing and one thing only: It lists the current eBay time in month-day-year hh:mm:ss PDT format, such as *Dec-25-05 20:11:19 PDT.* Nothing more, nothing less.

`<eBayMemberSince>` tag

`<eBayMemberSince>`: Like a few other options that the eBay programmers make available to you, I don't fully know why you should care about this. It displays the day and date that you created your eBay account, formatted to show the day of the week first, followed by the date, with an abbreviated month — *Friday, Jul 21, 2000* for example. Although it definitely resolves arguments over who joined eBay before whom, it doesn't offer any functionality beyond that. I guess you could make an online marquee like the old McDonald's signs, saying *Serving You Since <eBayMemberSince>,* but do you really need one?

You can also stack most any of these options by shoving them together into a tag and separating each option with a space, as the following example shows:

```
<eBayItemList BORDER="1" CELLPADDING="5" SORT="4">
```

This tag whips up a visually stunning, beautifully sorted, and nicely padded list of your eBay items. The BORDER option puts a hairline border around the table, and the CELLPADDING option throws in a few extra spaces so the table cells look nice. The final option, SHORT, puts your items in order by price, from cheapest to most expensive.

Adding Profits with the Affiliate Program

Everybody wants more money, right? It's practically a national pastime here in the United States. Companies want to expand their profits, and the folks at home could always use a few extra bucks to pay off the mortgage, buy the RV of their dreams, or take off for one of those sparsely populated islands in the South Seas. You already know about making money by selling things on eBay, but what if you could enhance your bank account by *not* selling things?

No, it's not some kind of weird government program where you get paid for sitting around (although if you know about one of those, please e-mail me the details). I'm talking about the *eBay Affiliate Program,* a program where eBay pays you to help it get new members and drive traffic to *other* people's auctions.

It might sound strange at first blush, but think about this for a moment. You don't handle any products, you don't answer any e-mails, you don't pay for any auctions, and you never worry about when the next 18 cubic feet of packing peanuts might arrive. Instead, you spend time doing what you love: building Web pages, developing keyword campaigns, and creating amazing new eBay API systems. And if you do it right, you make money — potentially *lots* of money.

Before you go into some kind of multilevel marketing *imagine the possibilities* hyperventilation attack, let me clarify some things about the eBay Affiliate Program:

✔ **It takes work. Lots of work.** You need to research eBay buying patterns (eBay provides you with lots of monthly information for free), find ways to reach the target buying audience, and create content that turns window-shoppers into bidders, buyers, and active eBay participants.

✔ **The potential looks stunning, but nobody gives you any guarantees.** You might put in a lot of work but get nothing serious back from it. Heck, you might put in *months* of work with no payday. Then again, with the help of eBay's various affiliate tools and *best practices* ideas, you might strike a mother lode. It all depends on how much you want to put into it and how cleverly you approach the problem.

Joining the Affiliate Program costs nothing at the standard level. If you decide to join the Affiliate API program at `developer.ebay.com/devprogram/membership/affiliate.asp` (for people and companies who plan to develop their own online applications that drive business to eBay), you pay a $250 start-up cost, plus some possible extra fees if your application makes too many API calls without generating enough bids. (Read the Affiliate API Membership terms agreement *very* carefully if you plan to give affiliate application development a try. You'll thank me later.)

The Affiliate Program does have one important limitation: You can't promote your own auctions through Affiliate Program links. Sorry, that just won't do. Because you already make money (at least hopefully) from selling stuff, you can't double dip by getting an affiliate bonus as well. (But you *do* get bonus points for creative thinking. Good job.)

eBay pays for two things: new members and bids or Buy It Now purchases. You get the most money for bringing a new member into the system, but you get the payoff only if the person comes to eBay directly through one of your affiliate links *and* makes a bid or Buy It Now purchase within the first 30 days after signing up. In that case, you get between $10 and $20 for your efforts, depending on how many people sign up through your links that month. If a current member goes through one of your links and places a bid or uses a Buy It Now link, eBay tosses between a dime and a quarter into your affiliate account, again depending on your total production for the month.

Like many performance-based programs, you make more money as you generate more business. Both the active registration and the monthly bid/BIN payment systems use a tiered system based on your total activity for the month, so more production means higher payments for *every* one of your affiliate link hits.

To get started in the Affiliate Program, you need a regular eBay user ID (no surprises there). To sign up for the program, follow these steps:

1. **Start with a visit to** `affiliates.ebay.com/join-program`.

   This brings up the Join the Program page, which (as you probably guessed) outlines the steps involved in joining the affiliates program. Read over the information so you understand what's going to happen and then go on to the next step.

   For an overview of the program itself, visit the main Affiliate Program site at `affiliates.ebay.com`. It includes links leading to details on program payments, current success stories, and lots of tips for increasing your profits and building a strong affiliate business.

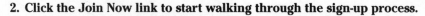

   2. Click the Join Now link to start walking through the sign-up process.

   That link takes you to Commission Junction, eBay's affiliate system part-ner. Commission Junction handles the details of tracking and counting clicks and disbursing money to program members.

   You must join Commission Junction in order to play in eBay's affiliate pool.

   3. It takes a few minutes to wade through all the Commission Junction signup forms, but eventually you emerge from the other side.

   A few minutes after completing the process, your new affiliate package arrives via e-mail. That's it — you can start doing your affiliate thing!

At this point, spend some serious time getting to know the Affiliate Toolbox (affiliates.ebay.com/tools) as well as the Best Practices section (affiliates.ebay.com/best-practices). You need to know your options in both areas before getting too far into planning your affiliate business.

Chapter 7

Uncovering Your E-Mail Program's Timesaving Powers

. . . .

In This Chapter

▶ Looking for e-mail in a variety of programs

▶ Take that, you filthy spam!

▶ Saving your fingers with pretyped text

▶ Adding some automation

▶ Turning your AOL e-mail account into a lean, mean mailing machine

. . . .

*I*n the beginning, there was e-mail. It looked dull but worked well enough. After the explosion of love and interest in the Web, it looked like e-mail might decline a bit, but that prediction was almost as inaccurate as the whole thing about the paperless office. Instead, e-mail turned into one of the most-used features on the Internet, with almost too many messages to count flowing around the world in a constant stream.

Just as your online auction text, About Me page, and Web site represent your place of business to an online customer, your e-mail communications take the place of talking with your customer face-to-face. For most purchases, e-mail conversations are the only direct communication that you and the customer have. Thus, providing good customer communication means keeping up with your e-mail.

If you sell a lot of stuff online, that means sifting through a deluge of incoming messages: eBay auction reports, PayPal receipts, presale questions from potential customers, postsale questions from buyers — not to mention the hundreds of spam messages that pour into your box, offering everything from free cable channels to infections of the latest Internet worm. The volume of real business messages combined with the ever-increasing amount of junk mail threaten to overwhelm your time, turning your customer communication tool into a black hole that sucks hours from your daily routine.

Thankfully, you *can* beat the e-mail beast into submission and wrest control of your mailbox. By cleverly using the tools built into your e-mail program, you can simplify — and even automate — common replies, sift through the spam to find the messages that you don't want to miss, and generally organize things to quickly track down any message you want to find.

This chapter explores those topics, giving you hints and tips for accomplishing more in less time with your e-mail, regardless of which e-mail program you use. It starts with a look at the e-mail program options out there (because, frankly, Microsoft Outlook *isn't* one of the world's best mail clients) and presses onward from there.

If you can, work through this chapter at your computer, with your e-mail program running. Because each program names its features a little differently, you might need to poke through your program's online documentation to figure out how to accomplish some of these tricks in your application.

Matching Your E-Mail System and Software to Your Business Needs

E-mail on the Internet comes in three basic types:

- ✔ Web-based mail through your browser (such as Hotmail or Yahoo! Mail)
- ✔ AOL (hey — no snickering)
- ✔ Client/server mail (commonly known as POP3 and IMAP) that works with a Net-connected server and a local e-mail program

Sure, the technical folks out there might get nit-picky and name a few other specific technologies, but these three cover the bulk of the Internet e-mail world.

Web-based e-mail

Web-based e-mail systems usually offer the most limited set of features and flexibility (although, goodness knows, AOL used to practically fight them for the trophy — more about that in a moment). You get the interface they give you and the tools they give you, and that's that. You can't hang a new interface on a Web-based system because you access the system only through your browser. Its servers control everything about your interaction with your messages.

If you use Web-based e-mail for your online business, I *highly* recommend replacing it with a client/server mail solution instead. There's no comparison between a Web-based mail interface and the power of an e-mail program on your computer desktop. As your business grows, your e-mail handling abilities *must* grow with it. Web-based mail systems just can't do what your online business needs.

AOL

Lots and lots of people use AOL for both Internet access and e-mail communication. AOL offers some of the benefits you get with a full client/server mail system (such as flexible mail processing), but it also inflicts many of the limitations imposed by Web-based systems (such as a limited selection of tools). Thankfully, the old prejudice against AOL e-mail addresses has largely faded away because so many people out there use AOL because they like the system and it does what they need.

Picking your perfect e-mail program

You can try most of the programs listed in this chapter for free. To do that, just visit the appropriate Web sites, download a few of them, and take them for a test drive.

Like every program on the planet, each one features its own unique interface and operation quirks. You might completely bond with one package or find yourself wooed by the features in another, but you won't know which one works best for your business until you try them. (That's why developers invented the whole *try before you buy* thing.)

If you prefer the most flexible and customizable client possible (and you're willing to poke, prod, and program your way toward that goal), look to Marlin, Pegasus Mail, and PocoMail. These programs give you tons of options and lots of flexibility but occasionally require some techno-weenie skills in order to do what you want.

Pegasus Mail leads the way with its extensive filtering options (it can even add and delete addresses automatically from mailing lists). Nothing stands up to Marlin's capabilities with templates — that program almost gives you too many options. On top of all its regular e-mail features (like filters and templates), PocoMail adds a full-fledged internal scripting language, letting a dedicated developer create almost anything.

For a more work-a-day application, go with Eudora. It has years of development and widespread use under its belt, rock-solid performance, and solid documentation that explains how to do what you want. Eudora's spam filters work like a dream, but you get them with only the paid version of the software. Its filters and templates definitely do the job but without the extra (and sometimes confusing) options available in the other programs.

From a business perspective, AOL works reasonably well, although you probably want to expand its capabilities with either AOL Communicator (AOL's stand-alone e-mail application) or a third-party program that lets standard e-mail applications like Eudora and Outlook send and receive AOL e-mail messages. You can find out more about both of those options in the section "Adding Much-Needed Power to AOL E-Mail," later in this chapter.

Client/server mail

When it comes to business e-mail, client/server e-mail processing with POP3 or IMAP really shines. You get a lot of power to control your incoming and outgoing messages, plus you can choose your own client application from among any number of commercial e-mail programs. Out of the myriad Windows e-mail applications available, a few really stand out above the rest. In alphabetical order (because otherwise I might irk somebody), they are as follows:

✔ **Eudora (**www.eudora.com**):** Eudora got an early start in the e-mail race and has been running strong ever since. It comes in three versions: Light (free, but limited features), Sponsored (free, but with ads), and paid (same as Sponsored but with SpamWatch automated spam filtering). Eudora features a strong filtering system for automating tasks, plus support for checking multiple mailboxes and sending with multiple e-mail addresses.

✔ **Marlin (**www.marlin-mail.com**):** This little application focuses on usability and user protection but packs in a bunch of great features at the same time. On its Web site, you can get a freeware version (minus the automated spam-filtering system and a few minor features) or purchase a full Pro version. Both versions offer everything that you need for basic e-mail processing, including filters and multiple mailboxes. If your mail service includes spam blocking, try starting with Marlin's free version. It might cover everything you need — and you sure can't beat the price!

✔ **Outlook and Outlook Express (**www.microsoft.com/outlook**):** The basic version of Microsoft's flagship e-mail package, Outlook Express, comes free with every copy of Internet Explorer — which means the software lives on pretty much every Windows machine in the world. The full version of the software comes with Microsoft Office, so it gets a pretty wide distribution as well. Both packages include a lot of bang for the buck, but because of their wide distribution, malevolent software developers also target both programs for e-mail viruses, worms, and other dangerous coding tricks. (Sadly, there's a real reason that the techies nicknamed this software *Microsoft Outbreak.*) Due to the overwhelming number of attacks specifically directed at these packages, I recommend *not* relying on them for your business. Unless you have some sort of driving need to use Outlook, pick one of the other packages instead. They do most everything that Outlook does but without the near-constant vulnerability to viruses and such.

✔ **Pegasus Mail** (`www.pmail.com`): Like Eudora, Pegasus Mail dates back many years. It started out as a free application, and it still proudly wears that mantle today. You can download the full version — yes, you read that right, the *full version* — for free directly from its Web site. The software includes a basic help system to assist you in learning the ropes, but if you want a manual, you have to pay for it. (Because you got the software for free, it's only fair that the company makes money somewhere.) Pegasus Mail offers everything you could possibly want in an e-mail program, including one of the most flexible and powerful filtering systems out there.

✔ **PocoMail** (`www.pocomail.com`): A relative newcomer to the e-mail business, this delightful little program comes in several versions, all of which cost money (although you can try them for free). The two main versions, PocoMail and PocoMail PE, cover a lot of features:

- **PocoMail:** This program certainly equals the power of the other applications here, plus the developers made it immune to attacks focused on Microsoft Outlook.

- **PocoMail PE:** If you need to take your e-mail with you as you travel, consider PocoMail PE, a truly unique innovation in e-mail applications. You can install this program onto a standard USB storage device and then carry the whole e-mail program with you wherever you go. When you want to check your e-mail, just plug your USB storage device into an Internet-connected computer, start PocoMail PE, and do your thing. That innovation alone makes it worth the registration fee for folks who spend their days migrating from machine to machine.

All the preceding programs include some kind of spam blocking (at least in their registered versions) as well as customizable features like filters, stationery, address books, and more. Apart from the warning about Microsoft Outlook and Outlook Express, any of these packages should do a great job handling your business e-mail.

Defeating (Or at Least Inhibiting) Spam

Believe it or not, junk e-mail — or, as most people in the world (except those working at Hormel) call it, *spam e-mail* — makes up over 75 percent of the Internet's e-mail traffic at any particular time of the day. And, depending on the season, that number might go as high as *90 percent of all messages!* On most days, one peek into your inbox usually confirms the depth of the problem.

As you do more business online, the amount of junk e-mail pouring into your account usually increases. Why? Because your customer service e-mail address gets posted here and there on your Web site, your auctions, and your About Me page. You *need* to do that, of course, to help your customers. Unfortunately, robot software endlessly scans Web pages and eBay auctions to find that unique combination of characters that make up e-mail addresses. When it finds one, it copies the address into its database, and voilà — oy vey, do you have mail.

You can fight spam at several different levels. If your current eBay customer service address gets overwhelmed with junk e-mail messages, you might start with a *new* e-mail address instead of fending off attacks on the old one. When I started selling on eBay back in July of 2000, I naively put a mailto link for ebay@linguaplay.com into all my auction text. It didn't take long for what seemed like every spammer in the world to find that address. In the interest of cutting down spam, I recently abandoned the address in favor of ebayquestions@linguaplay.com. To protect the new address, I used a nifty little JavaScript trick described in Chapter 10 that obscures the mailto link so that robot software can't find it. The trick's really easy, and it works *great!*

Most e-mail software now includes varying degrees of spam filtering as part of their feature packages. Although you need to spend time training the filters to get the most out of them, they nail a clear majority of junk e-mail messages right from the start. As time goes on, they get better and better.

Unfortunately, filtering your e-mail software still means that you download all those junk messages, which can take a lot of time. For the ultimate attack on junk mail, turn to a server-based solution like the popular (and free) SpamAssassin software (spamassassin.apache.org). SpamAssassin runs on your mail server and applies a whole range of tests to incoming e-mail messages. Some spam messages might fool the individual tests by themselves, but because SpamAssassin combines the results of the tests together into a single score, junk e-mail has a much harder time sneaking through.

After adding SpamAssassin to our company's e-mail server, our junk e-mail count went from over 400 messages per day down to a paltry 15 or less, without a single false positive yet. That's what I call a successful implementation. Check with your company's Web hosting service about adding SpamAssassin to your server. It's worth the time and money.

Typing Less with Prebuilt Messages

Hopefully you make a lot of sales on eBay, because if you do things right, that translates into some great income for your business. But a big sales volume means lots of communication with both prospective customers and bona fide buyers. Unless you type really fast (or simply love writing), answering a deluge of e-mail gets old pretty fast, particularly when you find yourself typing the same boring things over and over again. *Yes, we combine auctions. No, we can't mark your international shipment as a gift. Yes, we stock other colors as well.* It just wastes your time.

Thank goodness your software doesn't care if it does the same stupid task all day long. In fact, it actually *excels* at performing mundane, repetitive jobs that no self-respecting human wants to do (or at least nobody with satellite TV access because there's always something interesting on). All e-mail programs handle repetitive text messages quite nicely. Even the basic AOL client covers this one (although you do it somewhat nonintuitively by creating a new signature, but more about that in a moment).

The e-mail applications usually call this feature a *template* or *stationery*. Regardless of the name, this function lets you enter a bunch of standard text that automatically pops into an e-mail message when you call for it.

Figure 7-1 shows a prebuilt letter ready to go in Eudora. This particular message answers questions about international shipping. When someone writes to ask for an international shipping quote on an auction, they not only need to know the shipping amount but also the seller's policies on handling the shipment. Rather than risk forgetting to include something in a hand-typed reply, this prebuilt message covers all the common stuff at the bottom — things like handling fees, insurance, and customs forms.

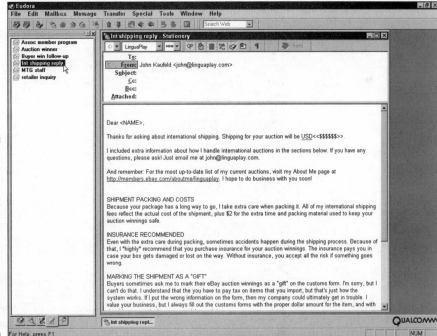

Figure 7-1: A mostly written letter about international shipping appears in Eudora, ready to send with just a couple of clicks.

At the top of the message, I added simple text markers (the things inside *greater than* and *less than* symbols) to stand for stuff that I plan to type into the message. Sadly, Eudora doesn't replace the markers with real text automatically. I do the replacing by hand. The markers help me remember where to put information when I use this template for replies. (When I get in a hurry, I'm *such* an airhead.)

Just like the difference in naming the tool, each program uses a slightly different series of steps when putting the template message into action. Because these templates are included in order to make your life a little easier, using the templates never takes a *lot* of effort.

To use the prebuilt message in Eudora (it calls these messages *stationery*), you first open the customer's message and then right-click on the piece of stationery you want to send. In the pop-up menu, select Reply With. Eudora builds a new message from the stationery and inserts the e-mail address, subject, and body text from the original message. Figure 7-2 displays the finished reply, after a little bit of manual editing to include the recipient's e-mail address in the greeting, the shipping cost, and a quick note to answer the person's question. The rest of the message came straight from the stationery without any extra typing or editing. That's a serious timesaver.

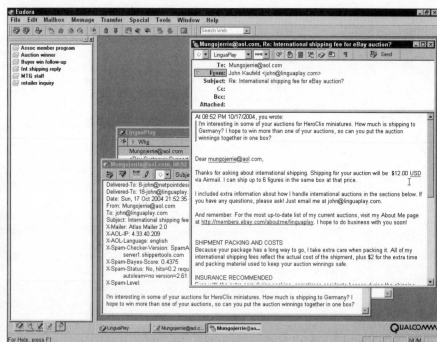

Figure 7-2:
The customer reply message hops onto the screen, ready to finish and send.

Templates in other e-mail applications give you quite a lot of automated customization features, such as special fields that automatically bring information from the original message into the reply. Marlin, for instance, takes the whole process several steps further by letting you customize just about everything in a template — right down to which information gets copied from the original message and where the program puts the cursor when it displays the template-based reply. Talk about customization!

Turning Up the Power with Rules and Filters

For all their differences, e-mail applications all agree on one thing: Rules make a difference. They don't mean rules that limit your world by telling you what you can and can't do — your e-mail program doesn't want a job as a part-time parent. No, when e-mail applications think of *rules,* they mean guidelines for how to automatically process incoming messages. With rules (or *filters* or *filtering rules,* as various packages call them; this section uses the terms interchangeably), your e-mail program can sort mail by itself and prepare replies. The rule systems in some e-mail programs (notably Pegasus Mail) can even handle simple mailing list management tasks.

With the ever-increasing deluge of mail, adding even a *little* bit of automated message processing saves you quite a lot of time and money. Although it requires some time investment to start the process, building mail rules pays back huge dividends almost immediately. Every time your e-mail program files messages away into various folders by itself, you save time. A minute here and a minute there add up quickly into serious amounts of time — and that translates into immediate monetary savings, just from teaching your e-mail program to do something that you hate.

In their most basic form, mail filters scan the text in a message and act on key words they find in there. To make a filter, you tell the e-mail program three things:

✔ **Where to look in the message:** Filters can scan text anywhere in the message, but they work better if you point them in the right vicinity for the information you need to check. Most of the time, you set filters to look for things in the message header, which includes the To, From, and CC (carbon copy) e-mail addresses and the Subject. A few odd tasks call for filters that search through the entire message (including both the headers and message body text), but most of the time, you need to mess only with the headers.

✔ **What to look for:** Here, you identify precisely what you want the filter to find. You might tell it to look for a particular domain (such as `linguaplay.com`) or an exact e-mail address (such as `ebay@linguaplay.com`). You can also seek out certain combinations of words (such as *question about combined shipping,* the subject line generated by one of the options behind eBay's Ask Seller a Question link). Most packages give you some basic logic tools to create combined filters — things that look for both an e-mail address *and* certain text in the message body, for instance.

✔ **What to do about it:** When your software finds a matching message, you can tell it to take action. Here, your options depend entirely on your program. Most packages focus their efforts on basic processing, such as moving messages from one folder to another, creating a reply, or perhaps just notifying you in some creative way that the message arrived. A few programs (notably Pegasus Mail and PocoMail) provide extensive filtering options that come close to full-scale programming.

Before setting a bunch of filters to handle your e-mail, make some folders in your e-mail program to store and organize everything. Precisely how you do it depends on how retentive you feel about organization as well as how much e-mail wanders through your box every day.

TIP

After a lot of experimentation, I settled on a group of seven folders for my eBay messages, and this same setup might work well for you. The folders include: New Messages, New Auction Mail, Working Messages, Working Auction Mail, Action, Archive Messages, and Archive Auctions. My filters primarily parcel out mail among the New and Action folders, and I manually file things into the archives. (Because my e-mail program sorts the mailboxes by name, starting both of the Archive folders with the word *archive* keeps them together on the list.)

The automatic filters throw auction questions sent through the Ask Seller a Question link and requests for shipping totals into the Action folder, eBay and PayPal notifications about my auctions into the New Auction Mail folder, and any other inbound communications into the New Messages folder. While something is in process, I move it from the New folder to the appropriate Working folder and eventually drop it into one of the Archives. At first, it felt like too many folders (and a little too much organization) for my taste, but thanks to the filters, this setup works really well.

Filtering all those messages means knowing what text to look for in the headers. Table 7-1 takes care of that problem for you by listing the basic header text used in the most common automated eBay communications. Most of the entries cover messages arriving on the seller's side of the process, but the table includes a few buyer-side subjects as well. Although the headers arrive in mixed upper- and lowercase, you don't need to worry about that. Focus on getting the right words into your filters and then tell the filters to ignore the case. (Most filters do that by default, although you can optionally force them to pay attention if it really matters.)

Every now and then, eBay changes the wording in its Subject lines. Test and correct these entries as you discover messages slipping through your filters and landing in strange and unusual mailboxes.

Table 7-1	Common E-Mail Headings for eBay Seller Messages
Header Text	**Message Arrives When . . .**
question about combined shipping	A customer clicks the Ask Seller a Question link.
question about shipping for item	A customer clicks the Ask Seller a Question link.
question about payment	A customer clicks the Ask Seller a Question link.
question for item	A customer clicks the Ask Seller a Question link.
eBay listing confirmed	You list a new auction.
eBay item purchase	Your auction closes successfully.
eBay item not sold	Your auction closes unsuccessfully.
please send me total amount	Your customer requests a payment amount through the links on the auction page.
your invoice for eBay purchase	You send an invoice to a customer or receive an invoice as a buyer.
notification of an instant payment received	Your customer pays via Instant Payment through the auction page.
notification of instant payment received for multiple items	Your customer pays for multiple items at once through Instant Payment on the auction page.
notification of payment received	A customer manually sends a payment via PayPal.
you created a shipping label with PayPal shipping	You use PayPal to generate a label.

(continued)

Table 7-1 *(continued)*

`PayPal electronic funds transfer`	You move funds from your PayPal account to your bank account (always a moment for rejoicing).
`eBay end of transaction`	You buy something through Buy It Now.
`receipt for your payment`	You manually send a PayPal payment.

With the header information in hand, you can quickly whip up filters for just about every occasion. Figure 7-3 shows an auto-reply filter created in PocoMail. The filter watches incoming e-mail messages for the heading `question for item`. When it finds that heading, the filter moves the message to the Action folder and sends a standard reply message that's built into a template. That completes the job with this type of message, so it tells PocoMail to stop processing that particular message and go on to the next one.

Although every mail application can handle processing like this, you usually need to do a bit of tweaking to get things working right. For instance, Figure 7-4 displays the same filter inside the Marlin e-mail program. Marlin uses a cleaner interface, so you can more quickly tell what's going on. If you look closely, you also notice that the rule in Marlin *doesn't* include a "stop processing" statement like the one in PocoMail does. That's because Marlin automatically stops processing a message after it triggers a single rule. If you want it to keep going, you distinctly say that in the filter by adding a `continue processing` option at the end.

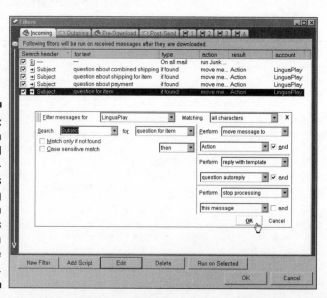

Figure 7-3:
This filter in PocoMail automatically files incoming auction questions and sends a reply to the customer.

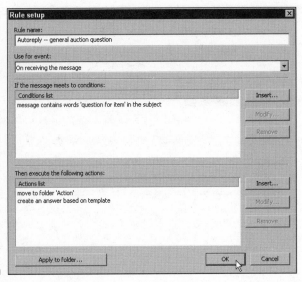

Figure 7-4:
Here's the same filter in the Marlin mail client. Although Marlin uses the term *rule,* it covers the same features and does the same thing as the Poco-Mail filter.

Adding Much-Needed Power to AOL E-Mail

Although America Online (AOL) pioneered the way for millions of people to join the online world, it sometimes suffers because of its focus on basic home customers. Its proprietary e-mail system includes all kinds of formatting features but provides almost nothing that helps you save time when it comes to handling incoming messages — and don't even *think* about automating anything with the basic AOL client program. AOL users asked the development staff to add e-mail rules to the main software for years, but to no avail.

To be kind, AOL is a big company, and big companies often take a while to even hear, let alone *respond,* to issues like this. And, after waiting for many a year, the development staff inside AOL finally came up with some interesting solutions aimed at people who use their AOL accounts for more than merely corresponding with Grandmother Mimi in Cincinnati.

First, AOL added a flexible signature system to its main program. Figure 7-5 shows the Edit Signature dialog box in action. Because AOL gives you plenty of room in each signature, you can include a whole lot more than a mere three or four lines of your name and address. I use the signature shown in this figure when replying to eBay questions. When a question comes in, I create a reply and then use this signature block in it. The signature automatically fills in the bottom of the message with all the extra information that I want to include, just like the templates do in the stand-alone e-mail programs. I type my specific reply at the top of the message and then send it on its way. Granted, it doesn't work like Eudora, but it's a lot better than nothing.

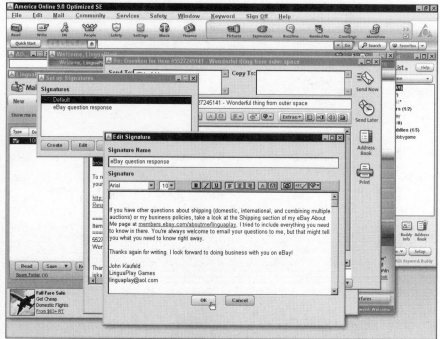

Figure 7-5:
The main AOL software doesn't offer much in the way of timesaving e-mail tools, but at least the signature tool behaves a bit like a ready-made template.

Adding full-fledged filters to an AOL account takes a bit more effort. You have two options, depending on how badly you want this capability: Get a copy of the free AOL Communicator software directly from AOL or use a commercial application like eMail2Pop (from PorkChup Solutions, `www.e-mail2pop.com`).

AOL Communicator

AOL Communicator walks a rather strange path. Overall, it looks like a stripped-down version of the main AOL software, but at the same time, it includes a few features that the main package doesn't have, such as rudimentary e-mail filters for sorting incoming mail. Sadly, Communicator can't handle anything more complex than that (it can't generate replies automatically, for instance), but *some* filtering works better than none.

You can get full information about AOL Communicator and download a copy for free by signing onto AOL with your regular software and then going to keyword **AOL Communicator**. The site offers a nice visual demonstration of the software, tosses out some answers to the most-asked questions, and gives you an easy downloading link.

eMail2Pop

For a more flexible and full-powered approach, take a look at eMail2Pop, from the folks at PorkChup Solutions (see Figure 7-6). This program acts like a bridge between AOL's proprietary e-mail system and standard e-mail programs like the ones discussed earlier in this chapter. From AOL's side of the transfer, eMail2Pop pretends to be just another regular AOL application, requesting e-mail for you. After it gets the messages, the program starts speaking its Internet e-mail dialect and passes the messages to your favorite e-mail application. The e-mail program doesn't know the difference — it thinks that it's talking to a normal e-mail server somewhere on the Net.

Believe it or not, the whole process works so cleanly that it's almost a little unsettling. The first time you fire up Marlin and watch it fill with messages from your AOL account feels just a little bit weird. The weirdness quickly dissolves into glee as the message processing rules start running, some automated replies go out, and your messages flow smoothly into various file folders. It's the functionality that high-end AOL users always wanted, and you can get it today!

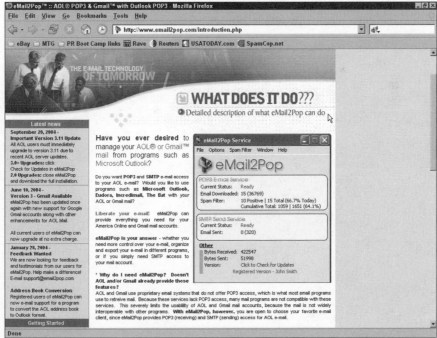

Figure 7-6: The add-on program eMail2Pop connects your AOL e-mail account with a full-fledged e-mail program like Eudora, Microsoft Outlook, or PocoMail.

Of course, anything that incredibly cool practically *begs* for a disclaimer of some kind. With eMail2Pop, the problem is AOL itself. If AOL makes changes to its e-mail software systems, eMail2Pop might stop working for a day or so. The developers at PorkChup Solutions take their work very seriously, though, so if eMail2Pop suddenly breaks for no apparent reason, they hop right onto the problem and post an updated version of the software pretty quickly — usually within 24 hours. Still, you should keep a regular copy of the AOL software around as a backup, in case eMail2Pop stops working right in the middle of your biggest selling season ever.

Chapter 8

Building Some Basic Timesaving eBay Tools

In This Chapter

▶ Enabling customers to track their packages

▶ Simplifying communication with your customers

▶ Finding an easier way to make templates

*T*o grow your business, you must value your time. Every unnecessary minute you spend posting auctions and completing transactions sucks money from your bottom line. The less time you spend performing repetitive tasks, the more efficient your operations.

Thankfully, PCs excel at performing repetitive operations and offer many tools to save you time. To decide which tools to pursue first, you need to evaluate your business. Look at where you spend your time. If possible, map out an entire week, recording every 15-minute block of time. When you're done, you'll have a map of how you spend your time.

With your time map in hand, see what tasks take the most time from your business. For example, suppose that answering customer inquiries takes the biggest percentage of your time. Armed with that information, take a look at which questions come up most often and figure out a way to answer them. Then you may want to add a Frequently Asked Questions (FAQ) section on your Web site. Be creative in your solutions.

As you surf the Web, keep an eye out for software or systems that reduce your busywork and save you time. However, be careful to invest in tools that will have the greatest impact on your business. You don't want to spend a lot of time and money solving small problems. To help get you started, this chapter introduces several simple computer tools that utilize a bit of geekiness to save you time — and, in turn, money.

Generating Easy Package Tracking Links with ShipperTools.com

Dealing with customer inquiries saps more time than almost any other task in online sales. Seemingly, the most common question you'll receive is, "Where's my stuff?" Unfortunately, every customer feels that his or her question should make its way to the top of your to-do list. The customer doesn't want to wait long for an answer and typically takes on an agitated tone with the request for more information.

Thankfully, you can reduce the number of inquiries you receive by helping customers answer their own questions! Answering the common "Where's my stuff?" question doesn't pose any challenges. Most eBay sellers realize that sending a package tracking number offers customers a sense of security and a way to answer their own questions. Unfortunately, many customers aren't familiar with the various shipping service Web sites and how to utilize their newfound tracking number.

Here's where a little bit of geeky know-how comes in handy. Rather than send your customers a simple tracking number, why not include a link to the latest tracking information? It's easier than you might think and makes a world of difference. Your customers will thank you when they open your package-shipped e-mail and find that it takes just one click to get the latest information about their newly purchased goodies.

Although it'd be nice if FedEx, UPS, and the USPS offered a nice simple way to create package tracking links, they don't. A few years ago, you could add the tracking number to the end of a special Web link, and you'd give your customers an easy link to their tracking information. However, the big shipping companies have since made it harder to create tracking links. They prefer to see you use their shipping programming tools (covered in Chapter 17) for tracking requests, reducing the traffic to their home pages. Although the programming tools make sense for larger online sellers, they leave the little guys with few alternatives.

ShipperTools.com (`www.shippertools.com`, a site envisioned, created, and operated by your friendly neighborhood authors — namely us), shown in Figure 8-1, takes the frustration out of giving your customers a quick, easy package tracking link. We've taken the time to work through all the programming headaches necessary to integrate with FedEx, UPS, and the USPS. Just append a tracking number to the Web address from ShipperTools.com, and you've got your tracking link. In the following examples, replace *tracking number* with the package tracking number from your shipper:

✔ **UPS link:** `www.shippertools.com/trackups/`*trackingnumber*

✔ **FedEx link:** `www.shippertools.com/trackfedex/`*tracking number*

✔ **USPS link:** `www.shippertools.com/trackusps/`*tracking number*

That's all there is to it! ShipperTools.com offers its package tracking link service free of charge. All you have to do is use its links, along with your package tracking numbers, to offer your customers a quick, easy way to get the latest information on their packages. You won't have to answer the infamous "Where's my stuff?" question anywhere near as often.

Figure 8-1:
Shipper
Tools.com
Tracking
Links home
page.

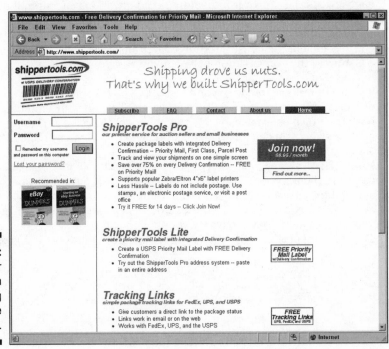

Managing the Flood of Questions with a Customer Service Help Desk

Although answering customer inquiries by e-mail may work when you're small, the inevitable avalanche of e-mail that follows eBay success will quickly bury you. You can easily lose track of which customers you've answered and what you've told them. Add an employee or two to your operation, and you have the makings of a communication nightmare.

Computer software comes to the rescue. Online automated help desk software organizes myriad questions and e-mails from your customers and maintains a history of requests. While traditional help desks offer phone support, auto-mated help desk software organizes e-mail support requests. Many solutions also offer a self-service knowledge base feature that compiles responses to your most common questions, giving customers an opportunity to help them-selves, which saves you time.

An online *help desk* offers a single point of contact for your customers. They can view answers to your frequently asked questions and submit questions of their own. The software prompts your visitors for the necessary contact details and, best of all, logs every question into a database. When you log in, you see a list of the latest questions. After answering each question, you have a history of the conversation between you and your customer.

If your operation extends beyond just you, you'll appreciate the additional organization that most help desk software offers. All your employees can have their own usernames inside the help desk. Receive a question that you can't answer? You can forward the inquiry to one of your employees.

Many help desk programs can pick up e-mails out of a mailbox and automati-cally add them to your help desk database. By setting aside a special e-mail account for customer inquiries (something like support@yourdomain.com or ebay@yourdomain.com), your customers can still e-mail their questions to you, but you don't have to worry about checking your help e-mail account. The software periodically imports all the messages into the help system.

Now that you're convinced that you absolutely must have a Web-based help desk, you get to pick one out! Help desk software has grown over the last few years, so many solutions exist. Web-based help desk software comes in two basic flavors:

✔ **Hosted:** With a hosted solution, the software company takes on all the headaches associated with installing and maintaining the software. It even leases you the software and provides Web space for the help desk. Even if you don't have a Web site, you can take advantage of the power-ful help desk software available. For beginners, this is the way to go.

✔ **Purchased:** If you're technically proficient, you can purchase the software and install it on your Web site. You save money and don't have to rely on another company for your help desk hosting. You typically have more customization options with a purchased help desk solution. Unfortunately, you need to be well versed on Web sites, Web programming, and Web-based software setup.

For most people, the hosted option makes the most sense for the following reasons:

✔ You don't have to take time to install or test the software on your site or worry about server requirements. You just sign up, and you're ready to go.

✔ You're more likely to receive technical support with a hosted help desk.

✔ The software developer can automatically update your software as soon as bug fixes or updates come out. You don't have to worry about performing the upgrades yourself.

Selecting a hosted Web-based help desk

Selecting a help desk solution may require some research time. You want to choose a software vendor that offers the features that best fit your business needs. Many vendors offer a help desk solution, so you're likely to find one that offers the mix of features you need.

Feel free to try a few different help desk programs before settling on one. Many of the hosted help desks offer free trials. If not, they frequently provide a demo help desk that you can log into and try out the interface and features.

When selecting a Web-based help desk, you want to evaluate several key details:

✔ **Fees:** Most companies offer their software for a monthly fee, although some charge per year. Some software vendors vary their monthly fee based on the number of help desk technicians who access the help desk.

✔ **Technician count:** How many people need access to the help desk? If you're a one-person shop, you don't need to worry about the technician count. However, if you have five employees that you'd like to answer customer inquiries, keep an eye on the cost per technician accounts. You also need to consider how the software vendor tracks technician accounts. Vendors typically count either the number of technicians registered or the number of technicians currently logged in. If your five employees all work different shifts, you can probably get along fine with single technician software that counts logged-in technicians.

✔ **Support and upgrades included:** Typically, Web-based software you pay for periodically (monthly, yearly, and so on) includes free updates.

Double-check the availability and cost of the software's support and upgrade options *before* you sign up; that way, you'll avoid frustration down the road. Take a look at what support is included and whether the vendor charges for support.

✔ **E-mail submission availability:** If possible, select a help desk that allows you to set up an e-mail account that customers can use to submit a help request. Otherwise, you'll get a fancy help desk setup only to find that some customers still insist on sending e-mail (you'll be stuck adding the inquiries to the help desk manually). With automatic e-mail submission, the software grabs any new e-mails and adds them to the help desk.

To help choose among the available options, HelpDesks.com (www.helpdesks. com) offers an extensive listing of help desk software vendors. The company has contacted many of the software companies and has compiled charts of features and pricing for each. You can compare the different help desk solutions to find the best one for your business.

Setting up a help desk with HelpDesk Connect

To give you an idea of how easily you can set up your own help desk, this section walks you through the process of setting up and using the HelpDesk Connect Web-based help desk software at www.helpdeskconnect.com (see Figure 8-2). An inexpensive help desk solution, HelpDesk Connect offers all of the most important features mentioned in the preceding section:

✔ **Free trial period:** You can use the software free for 30 days or 20 help desk requests, whichever comes first.

✔ **Low $9.95 monthly fee for each technician:** Technician pricing is based on the number of concurrent users, so unless you need multiple help desk technicians logged in at once, you're covered under the basic price. With such a low price, you can afford to add a few more technicians without breaking the bank.

✔ **Customizable help ticket fields:** You can change the help tickets to include the information you need (eBay item number, PayPal account ID, and so on).

✔ **Automated e-mail ticket submission:** Set up an e-mail address to forward to HelpDesk Connect's special submission e-mail address, and your e-mails instantly transform into help tickets.

✔ **Frequently Asked Questions (FAQ) tools:** Answering the same question over and over doesn't make sense for a serious business. With the FAQ feature, you can publish a help ticket response into the permanent FAQ. As the HelpDesk Connection Web site says, "Do not force your customers to waste their time asking questions answered before!"

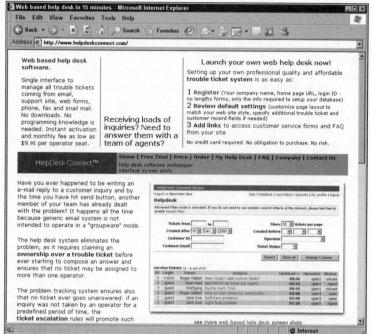

Figure 8-2:
HelpDesk
Connect
home page.

Registering

Registering with HelpDesk Connect takes only a few minutes. The system activates your new help desk within 15 minutes. To get started with your help desk, follow these steps:

1. **Visit the HelpDesk Connect home page at** www.helpdeskconnect.com **and then click the Register link (at the top right of the home page).**

2. **Complete the HelpDesk Setup form.**

   The setup screen takes only a moment to fill out. You may want to select a HelpDesk ID that matches your eBay username.

3. **When you're finished completing the form, click Continue.**

   The software automatically sets up your help desk. After registering, you find yourself at the System Setup screen.

4. **On the System Setup screen, you can modify the help desk settings if you want.**

   The initial settings are pretty generic, so you don't need to rush in to change anything in particular. After working with the help desk, you may consider changing the various e-mail and screen templates, but the starter templates should serve you well for now.

5. **When you're finished, click the Logout link.**

Creating a help desk request

After you've completed the registration process, it's time to try out your help desk. The following steps walk you through the process of creating a help desk request:

1. **If you're logged into the help desk, log out by clicking the Logout link at the top of the help desk control panel.**

   Your help desk *dashboard* appears. The dashboard is the support home page that your customers see. You can customize the look and content later to suit your needs.

2. **Click the Contact Customer Service link to create a new help desk ticket.**

3. **Complete the help desk ticket.**

   Although you can register, you don't need to for this test.

4. **When you're finished filling out the ticket, click Send.**

   You've entered a new ticket into the help desk system. See the completed help desk ticket in Figure 8-3.

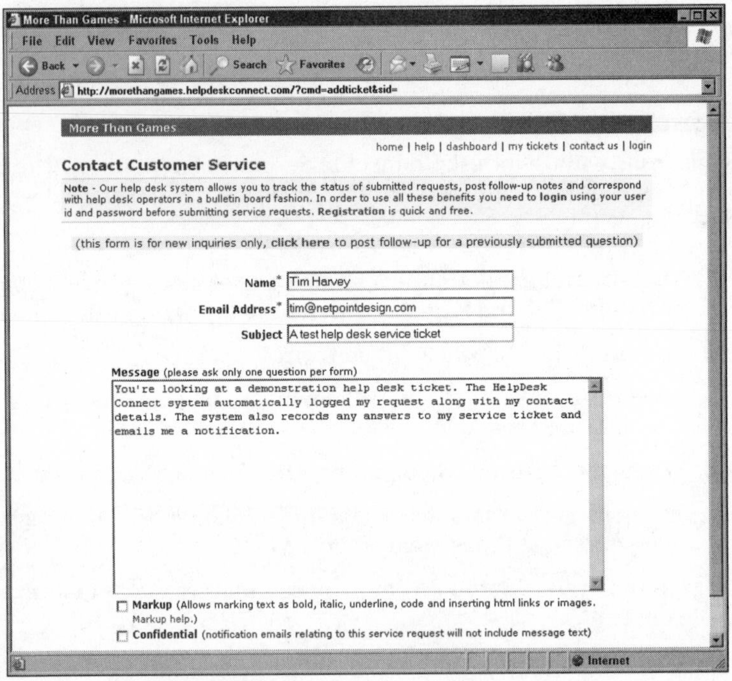

Figure 8-3:
A HelpDesk Connect service ticket entry.

Answering a help desk response

After you've entered a help ticket into the system, you're ready to try out the help desk response system. Answering help desk requests takes only a moment, and the system maintains a complete history of customer communications. You also have the opportunity to add your response to the permanent FAQ. (Down the road, you'll even have an opportunity to answer a customer inquiry by using a response from the FAQ.) To answer your test help desk request, follow these steps:

1. **Click the Login link at the top of the help desk page, fill in your user-name and password (the details you entered when you registered your new help desk), and then click the Login button.**

   You see a list of service tickets.

2. **Click the subject of your service ticket to open the message.**

3. **Click the Compose an Answer link to begin your response.**

4. **Enter your response to the service ticket in the Message box. If you want to make notes readable only by your internal staff, select the Internal check box.**

5. **After you've answered the service ticket fully, select the Solved check box to close the service ticket. Then click the Send button to record your response.**

   The individual who submitted the help desk ticket receives a copy of your response via e-mail.

Incorporating your help desk in your auctions

After you've tried out the help desk, you're ready to begin utilizing your help desk. Add a link to your help desk in your e-mails and Web site. The link you use is *helpdeskid*.helpdeskconnect.com where you replace *helpdeskid* with the HelpDesk ID you chose when you signed up. If you can't remember your ID, it's included in the welcome message that HelpDesk Connect sent when you registered.

Be sure to include the address of your help desk in as many customer communications as possible. The more your customers use the help desk, the more benefit you'll realize. For the customers who don't want to use an online form, you can accept service tickets by e-mail. HelpDesk Connect offers an e-mail address that automatically imports every e-mail as a service ticket. To create a help desk service ticket by e-mail, your customers simply send an e-mail to *helpdeskid*@helpdeskconnect.com where *helpdeskid* is your HelpDesk ID.

If you want to get really clever, you can talk with the company that handles your e-mail to create a special e-mail account that forwards to your help desk. You can create a `customerservice@yourdomain.com` e-mail address that automatically forwards to the `helpdeskid@helpdeskconnect.com` address. That way, your customer service e-mail address still has your domain in it.

To further organize your help desk operations, HelpDesk Connect offers three levels (called *tiers* in the software) for service tickets. The service ticket tiers make it easy to assign certain staff members to simpler, less urgent questions while reducing the load on more experienced employees. The system automatically escalates service tickets that sit without a response after a set period of time (configurable in the help desk settings).

Creating Auction Text on the Go with TemplateFiller.com

Chapter 5 introduces you to the power of HTML templates. By using templates, you can give your auctions a more consistent look, and you don't have to worry about formatting your auctions from scratch every time. Although templates are a great timesaver, you still have to manually replace every element in your template.

To ease the pain, Template Filler (`www.templatefiller.com`) automatically processes your template, prompts you for the entries you'd like to make, and then presents the finished HTML. You'll wonder how you ever worked with templates without it. Best of all, you can use the site for free!

Before heading off to use Template Filler, you need to prepare your template. Don't worry; it takes only a few minutes. To help Template Filler know what parts you'd like to replace, you need to mark each replaceable section in the template with a set of double brackets. For example, your template likely has a place to include the title of your item inside the auction description. It may look something like this:

```
<p><strong>Item Title Goes Here</strong></p>
```

Although the preceding template doesn't take any time at all to modify by hand, it's a good example of the potential benefits of using Template Filler. When you begin working with long templates filled with HTML code and many entries, you'll realize what a pain manual template updates can be. Plus, you can avoid the frustration of posting an auction only to realize later that you forgot to change one of your entries. To modify your auction template for Template Filler, surround the section you'd like to replace with double brackets, like this:

```
<p><strong>[[Item Title Goes Here]]</strong></p>
```

Now follow these steps to give Template Filler a try:

1. **Go to** `www.templatefiller.com`.

   The Template Filler Web site appears at the Step One page. Figure 8-4 shows the Step One page with a template entered (it's the longer template introduced later in the chapter).

2. **Enter the preceding example template (the one with the double brackets) and then click Process Template.**

   The Step Two page appears.

3. **Type an example item title into the Item Title Goes Here entry and then click Replace Template Entries.**

   The template output appears on the Step Three page.

Step Three displays your completed template. Template Filler automatically replaces every placeholder (text surrounded with double brackets `[[like this]]`) found in your original template. The site also displays a preview of the template you created. If you want to change the entry title (Item Title Goes Here), just change your template so that the title you want to see is inside the double brackets, like `[[Item Title]]`. The code would look like this:

```
<p><strong>[[Item Title]]</strong></p>
```

Figure 8-4:
Template
Filler Step
One.

Although the standard text entries that Template Filler uses work fine for short entries, such as item names, shipping prices, or short tag lines, they don't work well for longer entries. For paragraphs, you want Template Filler to provide a text entry box, much like the one eBay uses for the item description. The clever folks at Template Filler already thought of this and have devised a way for you to get a text entry box. Inside your template, include a colon followed by the word `text` after the entry name. This tells Template Filler to display a larger text entry box instead of the short single line entry. Figure 8-5 shows the Step Two page where you'd fill in the placeholders found in the following sample template:

```
<table border="1">
<tr>
  <td><p><strong>Item Title</strong></td>
  <td><p>[[Item Title]]</p></td>
</tr>
<tr>
  <td><p><strong>Item Condition</strong></td>
  <td><p>[[Item Condition:text]]</p></td>
</tr>
</table>
```

Figure 8-5:
Template
Filler Step
Two.

Notice that the line `<td><p>[[Item Condition:text]]</p></td>` includes the name of a new template entry: `Item Condition`. You probably need a few sentences to adequately describe the condition of an auction item. To get a text entry long enough to handle several sentences, the template includes the necessary `:text` after the template entry name, inside the double brackets. Template Filler replaces each placeholder with the values you enter in Step Two. Figure 8-6 shows the completed template HTML code from the previous sample template.

Template Filler also makes it easy for you to change your images each time you use your template. You can set up an entry in your template to always display an image from your Web site. The template prompts Template Filler to ask you for the image name each time. Or, if you don't always use images from the same place, set up your template to allow an entire URL.

Here's a template entry that prompts for the image name:

```
<img src="http://www.yourWebsite.com/images/[[Image
          name]].jpg">
```

Figure 8-6:
Template
Filler Step
Three.

Notice that the preceding template entry includes the Web site address, image folder name, and image file extension (.jpg). All you have to enter is the name of the image file. However, you must be certain that you upload your images into the same place on your Web site each time!

The following template entry allows you to use an image from any site:

```
<img src="[[Image URL]].jpg">
```

This example gives you the flexibility to include an image from any Web site. However, this method is more time consuming if you always include a photo from the same place.

Part III
Stepping into Some Programming

The 5th Wave   By Rich Tennant

"I think I've found a way to increase mug sales on the auction site, but which do you like better? The folding menu of hellfire we get if we use JavaScript? Or the cross-fading multiple images of burning torment that CSS provides?"

In this part . . .

Given enough time, energy, tools, and motivation, anybody can build a dugout canoe. True, you need a tree, an axe, the aforementioned amount of time, and plenty of water (it's probably hot there in canoe country), but you can probably finish the job without any special instructions. Why? Because most everybody knows that a dugout canoe looks like half of a large, hollowed-out log. If you can find a big enough log and go after it long enough with your axe, then a cool dugout canoe eventually emerges into the world.

On the other side of the boat-development universe, you discover the folks who make boats for use in races like the America's Cup. Given enough money, effort, money, energy, computer time, and money, they can bring forth plans to build the most amazing boat that ever sailed into any race on any body of water. Luckily for my budget, very few people actually *need* something as mysterious and wonderful as an America's Cup yacht, but it's still nice to know that the serious engineers can whip together something awesome with a little advance notice.

In the earlier chapters of this book, you dive into the basic realm of HTML. Now you get to move onward into more "serious" programming that takes you beyond stuff you can accomplish with mere HTML. Whether it's developing some simple eBay tools of your own or adding new features to your auctions with some well-placed JavaScript, this part opens the door to the intermediate level of your high-tech adventure. It even gets into some techniques for automating e-mail responses far beyond that capacity of your normal e-mail application. It also outlines ways to plan and organize your work for maximum efficiency.

There's still a time and place for the basic techniques, but now you're ready for something more. Although you might still cruise a few online rivers in your HTML dugout canoe, your business needs the speed and performance of those sleek machines in the big races, and with the information in this part, you can make it happen. Go get 'em, captain!

Chapter 9

Elementary Geeking for Advanced Profits

. . . .

. . . .

Top-notch auction descriptions and Web sites use more than just simple HTML. By using JavaScript, DHTML, and more sophisticated HTML, you can take your auctions to the next level. These gizmos, often called *scripts,* are plentiful on the Web and offer an unlimited palette of engaging and handy tools. Although many are useful only for showing off a particular geeky technology, many are perfect for the world of eBay. Scripts perform many useful functions; they power interactive navigation menus, perform calculations (useful for shipping calculators), and add animated effects.

Creating impressive auction descriptions takes time and effort. However, the work is worth it because they can earn you higher profits. Enhancing your auctions with nifty Web gizmos doesn't have to require a ton of work. You don't need to be a certified pocket-protector-wearing geek to spice up your auctions with high-tech add-ins. Many don't require any technical knowledge; just copy the code into your auction, and you're done!

You can also use scripts to liven up your personal or company Web site because most scripts aren't limited to eBay. Many scripts are already available for free on the Internet; browse through www.javascript.com or www.dynamicdrive.com for a glimpse of what's available. This chapter focuses on resources you can tap for easy additions to your auctions; no programming experience necessary!

Putting Gizmos in Your Web Pages and Auctions

Gizmos, or nifty add-ons inside a Web page, provide an easy way to spice up a simple Web site or auction description. Gizmos give visitors a new way to communicate with you or interact with your Web page. Fitting right inside a Web site, gizmos are easy to add and don't require technical expertise.

Web page gizmos consist of two parts, the stuff you see and the stuff you don't see. The part you see is the actual gizmo, whether it's a shipping calculator, advertising banner, or page view counter. Web code, called a *script,* works in the background to make the gizmo work. Scripts fit into the HTML that makes up the Web page. Web pages and auctions can include many gizmos. Figure 9-1 shows examples of a page counter, simple banners, and a dynamic PayPal banner. Don't worry if you don't know how these work; this chapter gives you the lowdown!

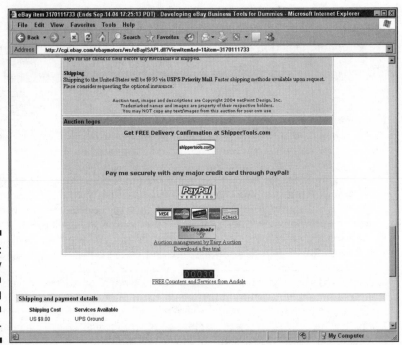

Figure 9-1: An eBay auction including auction scripts.

Gizmos, like kitchen appliances, come in a variety of shapes and kinds. Some, like a toaster, are easy to use; just plug them in and go! Others require more expertise and some setup (think of an oven). Best of all, you have lots of options to choose from. When you find a gizmo that displays a photo slide show, chances are that several other scripts out there can do the same thing (and maybe add some neat features).

Web sites offering free gizmos are plentiful. A quick search for JavaScript or DHTML turns up countless entries. Most sites include categorized lists of scripts and a search tool. Take a look through the listings to get an idea of what's available.

Although most scripts are free to use, many include a copyright notice that you must not remove from the HTML code. (Scripts include clear warnings inside the code's comments when the author requires a copyright notice.) Using a script author's code without including the copyright notice is stealing; don't do it. Many authors spend countless hours on their scripts, so give them the credit they deserve.

Tech-savvy individuals aren't the only ones posting nifty Web components. Many businesses that you already partner with make their code collections available. For example, PayPal publishes an extensive array of Web code for you to use.

You may run across sites that offer *paid* gizmos. Although you must pay a one-time or subscription fee, typically these scripts offer technical support and better quality. Most site operators test the scripts carefully before putting them up for sale. Paid scripts often utilize a special program running on the company's servers. This gives the script more flexibility and power, providing you with more options for your auctions.

As with many things, you can get carried away with scripts. Many of the options available are cool but can be downright annoying to users. Remember to take a moment to think about your customers. Always ask the question, "Will this help my customers learn about and buy my products quickly and easily?" If the answer is no, think twice about adding the latest nifty script to your auction.

Although popular, the dreaded Snow Flake script is a great example of what *not* to do. The script displays falling snow across the entire page, as shown in Figure 9-2. It appears to be a cute effect, but it distracts your customers from what's most important: your item! Stay away from scripts that don't help your bidders.

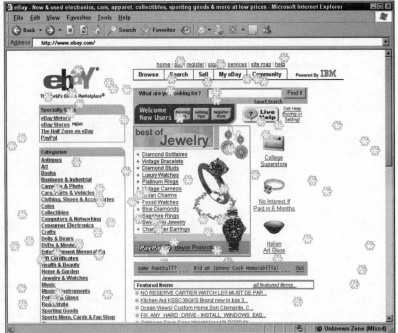

Figure 9-2:
The dreaded
Snow Flake
script at
work.

Getting started with scripts

How do you harness all this free code? Many times, you can simply copy a
script from an online directory, then drop it right into your auction or Web
site. Each gizmo includes a script (often computer code and HTML) that,
when added to your auction or Web site, activates the gizmo. Add the code
into your auction description where you want the gizmo to show up.

Scripts come in many flavors, from pure HTML code to hybrid scripts that mix
programming code with HTML. However, understanding how a script works
is not a prerequisite for using it. Someone else took the time to develop and
test the gizmo, and you get to reap the benefits. In the chapters to come, this
book shows you how various scripts tick, giving you the foundation for creating your own (or modifying one to meet your specific needs).

Scripts fall into two main categories:

- **No changes necessary:** With these scripts, you can just copy the code
  exactly as you see it into your Web site or auction description.

- **Some assembly required:** Although the author has done all the work, a
  few pieces require some customization. For example, if you're adding a
  shipping calculator to your Web site, you may have to add your zip code
  to the script.

The *no changes necessary* gizmos are the easiest to use, requiring no modifications before putting them to work. Just add the code to your Web site or auction where you want the gizmo to appear, and you're done.

When using a *some assembly required* script, don't forget to perform the necessary customization; otherwise, the script won't work as expected. Although some of the most useful scripts require some simple changes, they usually aren't difficult to perform. The changes are usually clearly spelled out in the script instructions. Some Web sites (PayPal is a great example) even provide a Web-based tool to automatically create the script with all the customizing done for you. When you're ready to dig into more powerful scripts that require more complicated customization, take a look at Chapter 10.

Dealing with eBay's JavaScript limitations

Unfortunately, not every script works within eBay auctions. Scripts have two issues to contend with in an eBay auction: technical code limitations and eBay's JavaScript policy. Each limit the use of JavaScript, a programming language used in many gizmos.

Because eBay allows sellers to put HTML only in the body of the Web page, the `<HEAD>` area of the HTML isn't available. Although many scripts instruct you to put code into the `<HEAD>` section of the HTML page, you can often include the code in the body without experiencing any problems. Most times, the script must appear before the HTML that calls it. If a script instructs you to put some code in the `<HEAD>` section, just add it to the top of your auction description. That way, all your description HTML code follows, making the script happy.

eBay's HTML and JavaScript policy offers another hurdle to overcome when adding JavaScript to your auctions. eBay designed its JavaScript policy (go to `pages.ebay.com/help/policies/listing-javascript.html` or search for JavaScript inside eBay's help area) to protect eBay members from malicious JavaScript scripts (yep, they're out there). If you attempt to use a banned JavaScript code in your auction description, eBay returns an error. For more details, check out the section "Rules for Playing in eBay's Coffeehouse" in Chapter 10.

Driving Faster Payments with Better PayPal Links

In a perfect world, every winning bidder would submit payment within minutes of an auction's close, and cash flow and time savings would be incredible. Of course, this isn't a perfect world, and nothing eats up precious time like trying to encourage a bidder to complete the transaction. Although some bidders simply like to take their time, many are either intimidated by or lazy about wading through numerous screens to finish the auction process. They've won the auction, often the most exhilarating part of eBay, and paying is seen as an annoyance better left for another day.

To make life easier, the folks at PayPal created a service where buyers and sellers could exchange funds quickly and securely. Offering an easy way for smaller sellers to accept credit card payments, PayPal became one of the Web's most popular payment services.

Thankfully, PayPal understands the buyer mentality. Sellers often add simple PayPal logos to their auction to encourage bids from PayPal members. While a simple PayPal banner isn't a bad addition to your auctions, the PayPal Smart Logo, shown in Figure 9-3, takes simplicity one step further. The Smart Logo gizmo sits politely in your auction page, proudly advertising your acceptance of PayPal payments. Plus, visitors curious about PayPal can click the logo, taking them to the PayPal Web site (you even earn a commission if visitors sign up for a PayPal account after using your link). However, the magic happens after the auction closes: The script that creates the logo link automatically changes to a big yellow Pay Now button.

Now when your auction closes and the winning bidder is looking over it, he or she can just click the Pay Now button to submit payment. The buyer doesn't have to worry about sending a check or money order. PayPal makes the payment process quick and easy.

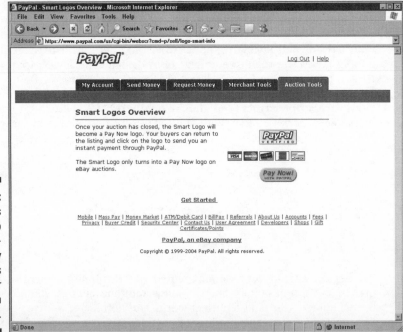

Figure 9-3:
PayPal's Smart Logo automatically changes when your auction closes.

To make it as simple as possible to add PayPal banners to your auctions, each banner comes customized with your account information encoded into the script. There's no cost; PayPal wants to help you add logos, promoting their service. PayPal's Manual Logos page described in the steps below lists several logos for use in eBay auctions or your Web site. The logos don't require any manual changes. However, you must have an active PayPal account to retrieve the banner code.

Perform the following steps to add a Smart Logo PayPal banner to your auction:

1. **Open the PayPal home page at** www.paypal.com.
2. **Enter your Email Address and Password, then click Log In.**
3. **Click the large Auction Tools tab.**
4. **Under the Add PayPal to Your Listings heading, click the Manual Logos link.**
5. **Scroll down to the Smart Logo section.**
6. **Highlight and copy the HTML inside the text box.**
7. **Paste the code into your auction description where you'd like to include the logo. Most sellers add the PayPal logo to the bottom of each auction description.**

Although PayPal offers automatic logos, you have more control over the placement of the logos if you manually insert them. When activated, PayPal's automatic logo system looks to see if you've posted any new auctions, adding a PayPal banner to any auctions it finds. The automatic logos display at the bottom of the auction description, prefaced with an unsightly message, shown in Figure 9-4, On Jul-21-04 at 22:25:34 PDT, seller added the following information:. Ugh. After putting a lot of time and energy into making your auction descriptions look their best, don't let PayPal botch it up. Pass up the automatic logos and insert a Smart Logo into your auctions yourself; they look better when integrated into your custom auction template.

Figure 9-4:
Skip the ugly automatic PayPal logos and add the logo manually to your template.

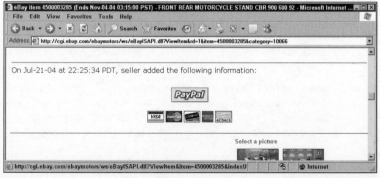

Dressing Up Your Auctions with DHTML

Dynamic HTML (DHTML) gives you more control over the look of your Web pages than plain HTML. DHTML isn't really a language of its own; instead, it combines HTML, JavaScript, and Cascading Style Sheets (CSS) to create impressive Web pages. (For more on what you can do with JavaScript and CSS, turn to Chapters 10 and 11, respectively.) DHTML scripts can animate text, create stunning image effects, and display appealing menus.

DHTML scripts are an easy way to improve your auction's visual appeal. Because of DHTML's modular nature, you typically can drop a script into your auction without disrupting the rest of the auction description.

The biggest drawback to DHTML is its client-side nature. In the Web world, some things take place on the Web server, and others happen on the user's computer, inside the Web browser. Servers manage lists of products, respond with the Web page and images the user has requested, and accept information entered into a Web site. Those actions all happen on the *server side*.

Actions that happen on the user's computer are called *client side*. They include displaying JavaScript animations, figuring out what size of text to display, and translating an HTML file into the Web page you see on-screen. Client-side actions save the server a ton of processing time, making the Web faster. The downside is that client-side scripts (such as JavaScript and DHTML) must rely on the *client*, or visitor's Web browser, to display the page correctly. If visitors have all the latest software, that's not a problem. However, if visitors are using older browsers, they may not see all your nifty effects. When you add a script to your Web page, look for any compatibility information. Typically, online script libraries include listings of what browsers the scripts work with.

DHTML scripts that work effectively with many different browsers take time to develop and test. Thankfully, other individuals have undertaken this task for you. DHTML makes a great addition to your auctions as they're easy to add. You don't need to understand DHTML code to use it in your auction descriptions or Web site. The Web offers a wealth of free scripts. Take a look through these extensive script libraries, and you're sure to find something useful for your auction:

- ✔ **Dynamic Drive** (`www.dynamicdrive.com`): From simple text animations to complicated menus, Dynamic Drive has scripts that create almost every effect imaginable. Its large script archive will keep you satiated.

- ✔ **Dynamic HTML Central** (`www.dhtmlcentral.com`): Although this site doesn't showcase as many scripts as other sites, the selection offers more detailed installation instructions as well as more polished scripts. The site also offers tutorials to help feed your customization craving.

✔ **CodeToad** (`www.codetoad.com/dhtml/`): Sporting a large script archive (over 200 scripts), CodeToad makes it easy to find something to fit your site. It also includes tutorials and articles as well as information about other programming languages, should you feel adventurous.

✔ **HotScripts.com** (`www.hotscripts.com`): This is yet another site offering a broad range of scripts for a variety of languages. The DHTML scripts found their way into the site's JavaScript category. With over 1,000 scripts, you may have to dig around a bit to find what scripts suit you.

✔ **Need Scripts** (`www.needscripts.com`): Again, you need to dig down into the JavaScript section to find what you're looking for. However, you can branch out and find help with other programming languages as you develop your skills.

✔ **SiteScripts** (`www.sitescripts.com`): SiteScripts goes with the quantity over quality theory. It offers a broad range of scripts (over 500), but you may have to try more than one script before finding the one that fits the bill.

When you're looking for an easy way to create a customized animation for your auction or Web site, you'll find that freebie scripts just don't offer the options you need and may take time to customize. DHTML scripts and programs available for purchase come in handy. Several developers offer programs that build DHTML scripts on the fly. That means you can change the script to match your needs and the program will output the DHTML script for you to use. No programming experience necessary. The programs frequently offer an interface that feels a bit like a WYSIWYG editor for DHTML scripts. The following list includes several examples, and a quick search online turns up a broad range of other options:

✔ **OpenCube** (`www.opencube.com`): A software developer with scripts in use on many large sites, OpenCube offers a tremendous suite of applications to solve your DHTML troubles. In particular, its Visual QuickMenu Pro application gives you the tools necessary to create stunning menus for your Web site. Plus, the Web Effects DHTML program fills out your repertoire, offering a variety of animations and effects.

✔ **Apycom Software** (`www.dhtml-menu.com`): Offering a polished menu script, Apycom Software gives sellers an inexpensive way to add animated page navigation.

✔ **Softcomplex** (`www.softcomplex.com`): Softcomplex's inexpensive scripts offer a variety of different functions, from animated menus to custom calendars. The site also includes a custom menu builder.

✔ **Xtreeme** (`www.xtreeme.com/dhtml/`): Although more expensive than other options, the DHTML Menu Studio from Xtreeme gives you real flexibility. The program creates menus that don't require any DHTML or JavaScript knowledge. See Figure 9-5.

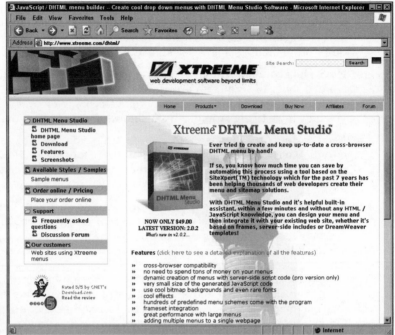

Figure 9-5:
Xtreeme's
DHTML
Menu Studio
home page.

Be careful to test any script you find (or contact the author) *before* buying. Wherever possible, take advantage of trial versions to try out the code the program creates. Some scripts may not pass eBay's JavaScript restrictions. Thankfully, eBay's auction listing form alerts you if it finds anything unacceptable. To learn more about eBay's rules, see "Rules for Playing in eBay's Coffeehouse" in Chapter 10.

Encouraging Customer Interaction with a Form

My favorite type of e-mail from eBay users has no subject and simply says, "Is it in good condition?" That's it!

I'm sure you received e-mails like that — every seller gets a few. You have many auctions running, and a potential buyer e-mails you to ask about an item but forgets to provide the important details you need to answer. Thankfully, you can help your prospective bidders help themselves by adding a contact form to your eBay auctions. This is a great way to prequalify customer communications coming your way.

Imagine having your customers fill out a brief form that asks them the nature of their question and automatically includes the auction number and a link to the auction. Wouldn't that be great? You could get creative and add more questions. But be careful not to make your form too complicated or involved, or your potential bidders may give up and buy elsewhere!

Contact forms aren't the only use for forms in your eBay auction. You can include a feedback box that encourages visitors to rate your auction design as well as enables them to send requests for a particular item.

You can add a form to your auction in two ways:

- ✔ **Simple e-mail:** Adding a simple two-part form to your auction is easy. Your bidders can select a topic and then fill in the e-mail body. You can control what the subject line contains, making it easy to filter incoming mail. The only downside is that you have limited options for expanding your form.

- ✔ **Form processor:** By adding a separate script (outside of eBay) that processes your auction forms, you have almost limitless options. Every form field type works, and you have no limit on the number of entries you can request. Unfortunately, setting up a custom processing script on your own Web site requires some work. Thankfully, other Web developers have done the work and offer form processing as a service (Check out `www.responders.com`, `www.formbreeze.com`, and `www.email-form.com`.)

Each option has benefits and challenges. The simple e-mail form, shown in Figure 9-6, is quick to add and easy to work with, but it's limited. The form processor approach offers a wide array of options but requires you to have your own Web space (or another service) and more technical expertise.

The example below draws upon JavaScript commands to include a link to your auction and the item number. The following steps show you how to add a simple e-mail form to your auctions:

1. **Decide where to place the form in your auction template.**

   You probably include a section toward the end of your auction description that lists purchase terms, shipping details, and contact options. This makes a great spot to include your e-mail form.

2. **Add the form header HTML code and insert your e-mail address.**

   Insert the following code, which uses a standard HTML `<form>`, remembering to drop in your e-mail address in place of *YourEmailAddress*.

```
<form action="mailto:YourEmailAddress" method="POST" enc-
    type="text/plain">
```

3. **Insert special JavaScript code.**

   The JavaScript code adds two hidden fields to your form, giving you the URL of the auction the e-mail came from and ensuring that you'll know what auction number the sender is inquiring about.

```
<script language="JavaScript">
<!-- // Start
  function returnItemNumber() {
    var itemURL = location.href;
    var tempURL = itemURL.substring( itemURL.indexOf(
        "item=" ) );
    if ( tempURL.indexOf( "&" ) != -1 ) {
      itemNumber  = tempURL.substring( 5,
        tempURL.indexOf( "&" ) );
    } else {
      itemNumber  = tempURL.substring( 5 );
    }
    return itemNumber
  }
  var itemNumber  = returnItemNumber();
  htmlCode =  '<input type="hidden" name="itemURL"
        value="' + location.href + '">'+
          '<input type="hidden" name="itemNumber"
        value="' + returnItemNumber() + '">';
        document.write( htmlCode );
// End -->
</script>
```

4. **Include HTML form fields.**

   After the special JavaScript code, add any form fields you'd like potential bidders to fill in. For the example, the code includes a drop-down list with possible question categories and a text box for the bidder's question. Feel free to get creative, adding more fields (although you don't want to get too carried away; bidders won't take time to fill out your form if it's long). Your HTML editor (Chapter 3 introduces several) can help create the HTML for additional form fields.

```
<select name="formReason">
  <option value="--None Selected--" SELECTED>---</option>
  <option value="Shipping Questions" SELECTED>Shipping
        Questions</option>
  <option value="International Bidding">International
        Bidding</option>
  <option value="Item Questions">Item Questions</option>
  <option value="Feedback Questions">Feedback
        Questions</option>
</select>
<br>
How may we help you?<br>
<textarea cols="30" rows="5" name="body">
</textarea>
```

5. Throw in the "submit" button and close the HTML `<form>` tag.

Finally, include the submit button and the closing form tag `</form>`.

```
<input type="submit" value="Send">
</form>
```

That's it — you successfully created your e-mail reply form. To use it, just drop the finished code into your auction at the point where you want the reply form to appear. Figure 9-6 shows the form in action.

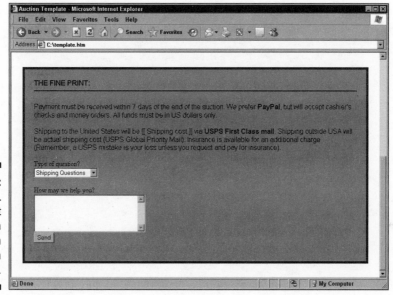

Figure 9-6: HTML contact form shown inside an auction template.

Chapter 10

Caffeinating Your Auctions with JavaScript

In This Chapter

▶ Finding a place for JavaScript

▶ Playing by eBay's rules

▶ Putting JavaScript to work in your auctions

*T*he Web has made incredible strides in transforming itself from a small academic exchange into the new millennium's digital playground. Like encyclopedias, early Web pages didn't think; they merely existed to provide information. However, as the Web has developed, so too have the technologies that power the Internet.

JavaScript fills a void in the Web programmer's toolbox, adding *logic* to a Web page. Originally developed by Netscape, JavaScript is a simple scripting language created to enhance Web pages. JavaScript powers many of the Web's interactive features, from forms to images that respond to mouse movements. This chapter introduces the most useful JavaScript features for eBay sellers, including images that change, forms that send e-mail, and search tools. By using the scripts in this chapter, you can add new interactive and moving elements to your auctions.

Where JavaScript Fits into the Programming Pantheon

Strictly speaking, HTML isn't a programming language; it's a markup language. Its many features exist to describe what visitors see on the screen. Font sizes, image placement, colors, and links exist in the world of HTML.

JavaScript takes HTML, a visual layout language, and drops in honest-to-goodness programming. JavaScript adds *conditional execution* (a fancy way of saying that it can decide which of several options to choose), loops (repeating the same commands), and interactivity. It can do math, validate form entries, generate animated menus, and perform visual effects.

JavaScript hides on Web sites everywhere. Although you may not know it, chances are you encountered a site utilizing JavaScript today. If you listed a new auction item, JavaScript powered the category selection box, filtering eBay's category list to make it easier to find the category you need.

You fit JavaScript inside a page's HTML, right alongside regular HTML elements. A section of JavaScript starts with a beginning `<SCRIPT>` tag and ends with a closing `</SCRIPT>` tag. The script tag tells your browser to expect JavaScript code. Inside the script tags, you include JavaScript code.

While not mandatory, you should include HTML comment tags (`<!--` and `-->`) around the body of your JavaScript. Otherwise, a browser that doesn't understand JavaScript (some old browsers are out there) will display the raw code on your Web page. Not very pretty!

The following example begins with the standard HTML tags you'd use for every page (`<html>`, `<head>`, and `<title>`). Then inside the `<body>` of the page, the example uses JavaScript's `document.write` command to output `Hello World!` to the Web browser. Following the preceding suggestion, the code uses HTML comment tags to enclose the JavaScript.

```
<html>
<head>
  <title>JavaScript Test</title>
</head>

<body>
  <script language="JavaScript">
  <!--
    document.write("Hello World!");
  //-->
  </script>
</body>
</html>
```

Because JavaScript is a client-side language, the user's computer — the client — must support JavaScript in order for the special features to work. The good news is that most browsers include JavaScript support. JavaScript has been around since the mid-'90s, so chances are good that your visitors can enjoy your latest JavaScript creations. eBay has enough confidence in JavaScript to use it.

Rules for Playing in eBay's Coffeehouse

To keep members safe from malicious JavaScript code, eBay places limitations on the JavaScript that you can use in your listings. (You can read the full policy at `pages.ebay.com/help/policies/listing-javascript.html` or by searching for `JavaScript` inside eBay's Help section.) In general, eBay forbids JavaScript or HTML that performs any of the following activities:

✔ Writing files to the visitor's hard drive (for example, loading a program, reading or writing cookies, or modifying the Windows Registry)

✔ Displaying automatic pop-up windows

✔ Linking to scripts stored outside eBay

✔ Automatically forwarding visitors to a different page

✔ Using code that attempts to fool eBay's JavaScript validation

Rather than cancel auctions that use forbidden JavaScript, eBay catches scripts that violate eBay policy during the auction listing process. Although eBay's documentation says that the error begins with `Disallowed JavaScript/HTML Syntax`, it doesn't. The error that eBay displays, as shown in Figure 10-1, doesn't offer much assistance in understanding what part of your code violates eBay policy. Table 10-1 lists some of the most common JavaScript codes that violate eBay's JavaScript/HTML policy.

Figure 10-1: The dreaded JavaScript error appears at the bottom of this page.

Table 10-1	JavaScript That's Forbidden by eBay
Code	*Reason*
`<script src="">`	Links to code stored outside of eBay
`<IFRAME>`	Links to code or HTML stored outside of eBay
`.cookie`	Reads/writes cookies to visitors' PCs
`eval()`	Bypasses eBay's JavaScript validation
`window.open`	Opens another Web page
`window.location`	Redirects visitors to another page

eBay's JavaScript restrictions shouldn't cramp your efforts to spice up your auctions. Scripts that use forbidden JavaScript commands typically aren't the kind of scripts you want in your auctions to begin with because they often produce auctions that annoy potential buyers.

Harvesting fresh JavaScript from online fields

If you can find the time to write JavaScript from scratch for your auctions, that's great. But if you're like most people, you'll want to save time by using some of the many free scripts available online. Developers submit their scripts to online directories, and more often than not, you'll find a script that fits your needs. Plus, online directories offer a great opportunity to find out about the many tasks that JavaScript can help with.

Using free JavaScript gizmos saves time, enabling you to focus on your business. Scripts typically include complete instructions, making for a painless integration. A quick search for JavaScript on your favorite search engine will turn up countless possibilities, so I've put together a list of sites for you to start with:

✔ **JavaScript City** (www.javascriptcity. com): Not content to just list numerous free scripts and tutorials, JavaScript City hosts a massive JavaScript forum. With over 50,000 posts, you're likely to find an answer to your JavaScript questions.

✔ **JavaScript Kit** (www.javascriptkit. com): In addition to free scripts, JavaScript Kit includes a number of tutorials, helping you develop your JavaScript skills. If you're considering learning to write your own JavaScript, you'll definitely want to take a look at this site.

✔ **JavaScript Search** (www.javascript search.com): This is another excellent resource when you need a script that performs a specific function. Its extensive script collection contains some unique entries (check out the "Ask Mustafa" game).

✔ **The JavaScript Source** (javascript. internet.com): Internet.com, a long-time source of helpful Internet geekery, offers an extensive JavaScript code collection. You'll find over 2,000 free scripts.

Ready-to-Serve Scripts, Freshly Brewed!

Spicing up your auctions doesn't have to take all weekend — or even all of your lunch hour. The following scripts offer an easy way to harness the power of JavaScript. They make it easier for potential bidders to return to your item listings, recommend your auctions to friends, or see more pictures of your item. The last script helps you research items on eBay, creating a quick search line in your browser.

Because most of these scripts are designed to go into your auction text, I designed them with eBay's JavaScript rules in mind.

Protecting your e-mail address from unwanted exposure

You want good communication with your customers — heck, every seller wants that. Because eBay transactions take place in the online world, communicating through e-mail makes a lot of sense. To facilitate precisely that kind of thing, eBay includes that nifty little Ask Seller a Question link on each of your auction pages. That link gives your customers an easy way to find you and ask you questions. Because of the way eBay designed it, your customers get to pose their queries *without* discovering your e-mail address in the process. eBay created that tool to let your customers freely contact you and, at the same time, to protect your e-mail address from the ever-present problem of junk e-mail.

Adding the same sort of communication link on your Web site involves using a mailto: link. When customers click the mailto: link on your Web site, their browser automatically starts their e-mail program and creates a new message.

Unfortunately, it didn't take long for the world's spammers to realize that behind every mailto: link sits a valid, monitored e-mail address just waiting for messages. To make the most of this "opportunity" (as they see it), spammers designed robotic software that visits Web pages (including eBay auctions and About Me pages) and scans them for mailto: links. Whenever the robot program finds a mailto: link, it adds the e-mail address — in this case, *your* e-mail address — to its evil database of new spam recipients.

Thanks to the clever JavaScript that follows, you can foil those address-collecting spambots while still giving your customers easy, one-click access to your e-mail address through a regular mailto: link.

The script in Listing 10-1 tricks the spambots because those robots only read and scan raw HTML code without processing any scripts or other programming the code contains. When a spambot comes across this bit of JavaScript, it doesn't recognize anything in it. It can't find an e-mail address or a mailto: link, so it just shrugs and continues to some other site. Score one for the good guys!

But if the spambot can't find the `mailto:` link, why does it appear for your customers? It works because your customers look at the HTML code *after* their Web browser finishes processing everything. When the browser receives the JavaScript in Listing 10-1, it runs the code, which then builds a valid HTML `mailto:` link. The customer's Web browser recognizes the HTML code and displays the finished link, ready for clicking.

Listing 10-1:   Creating a mailto Link for Your E-Mail Address

```
<p>If you have questions about our auctions or products, just

<script type="text/javascript">
<!-- // Start

  // The email address goes in the line below
  emailAd=('ebay' + '@' + 'linguaplay.com');

  // This statement builds the HTML mailto link directly
  // in your customer's web browser
  document.write('<a href="mailto:' + emailAd + '">' + 'email
        us.</a>');
// End -->
</script>

We'll reply within one business day.</p>
```

In this example, the script creates a `mailto:` link for the e-mail address `ebay@linguaplay.com`. To put a different e-mail address into the script, follow these steps:

1. **Find the line that starts with** `emailAd=`.

   This line of code puts together the three parts of the address: the account name, the at sign (@), and the domain name.

2. **Replace the word** `ebay` **with your e-mail account name.**

   Only put in the portion of your address that sits to the left of the at sign.

3. **Replace the domain** `linguaplay.com` **with your e-mail domain name.**

   Put the whole domain name in there, including the `.com`, `.net`, or dot-whatever suffix at the end of the domain.

That's it — you just put your e-mail address in there and made the script your own. Feel free to play around with the wording that displays on the customer's screen by customizing it according to your needs. As written, the script displays If you have questions about our auctions or products, just email us. We'll reply within one business day. The `mailto:` link itself sits behind the words `email us`.

Making it easy for visitors to bookmark your site

Retailers spend inordinate amounts of money on advertising, encouraging potential buyers to come back and visit again. There's a reason, too: From a business perspective, it costs a lot less money to *retain* a current customer than it does to *find* a new one.

The same thing holds true in the online world. Unless you sell a one-time-use product or service, you need to keep your eBay business in front of your happy customers, with the goal of turning them into *returning* customers.

JavaScript makes it easy to add a link inside your auction that adds a bookmark to your eBay Store (or any other Web site for that matter). While some technical limitations make it tough to help potential bidders come back later, make it easy for them to add a bookmark to your eBay Store.

The following example code adds a link to your eBay auctions that lets customers create a bookmark to your eBay Store. You can include the code anywhere in your auction text. Wherever you put it, make it somewhere prominent and visible so your customers see the link (and hopefully click it).

```
<a HREF="javascript:window.external.AddFavorite
        ('http://www.ebay.com/stores/STORENAME/',
        'eBay Store - My Store Name');">Add my
        eBay Store to your Favorites</a>
```

Although it looks a little dense, you can make your own version of it with just a few steps. Here's how to do it:

1. **Start by opening your favorite HTML editor and creating a new file.**

   By building your code in a new, blank HTML file, you can easily test and tweak the code without worrying that you might break something in your auction text.

2. **In the Body section of the HTML file, type the first part of the code,**
   `<a href="javascript:window.external.AddFavorite('`.

   This section of code opens the link (the `<a href` part of the code) and begins putting together the JavaScript itself.

3. **Next, type the Web address that you want to add to your customer's Favorites list.**

   Make sure you include the `http://` part at the beginning of the address; otherwise, the link won't work in your customer's Favorites list.

4. **After the Web address, type an apostrophe, a comma, a space (just hit the spacebar), and then another apostrophe.**

   This odd mixture of punctuation and a space prepares the code for the next thing you want to add: a name for your link in the customer's Favorites list.

5. **Type the text that identifies your link in the customer's Favorites list.**

   Although creativity counts, keep your text relatively simple. Include your store name and maybe the word *eBay* somewhere so the person remembers why he knows you. After that, get ready for more punctuation.

6. **After the link name, type this odd-looking collection of symbols:**

   ```
   ');">
   ```

7. **Finally, type the text that appears in the link itself when the customer looks at your auction. At the end of the text, add** `</a>`**, which closes the HTML link and puts the finishing touch on the script.**

   As with the name of the Favorites entry back in Step 5, keep this text simple and obvious. Something like the example text *(Add my eBay Store to your Favorites)* works very well.

When you finish, your code should look much like the example, except that it features the Web address of your eBay Store as well as whatever other customizations you put in. At this point, test your script by opening the file in your favorite Web browser and clicking the link. If the link doesn't appear correctly or you don't get a new entry in your Favorites by clicking it, double-check your work — particularly the peculiar little punctuation marks in Steps 4 and 6.

Adding an e-mail a friend link

Although eBay automatically includes an Email a Friend About This auction link, it appears at the bottom of the page, making it easy for buyers to overlook. A better way to encourage potential buyers to share your auction with friends is to add your own link in a prominent place inside your auction.

Listing 10-2 adds a small e-mail entry form. Auction visitors can enter a friend's e-mail address and then click the Send a Link button. The JavaScript kicks in to send an e-mail to the address entered along with a link to your auction.

Listing 10-2:   Adding an E-Mail Entry Form

```
<SCRIPT LANGUAGE="JavaScript">
<!-- // Start
  function emailAuctionLink() {
    var singleReturn = "\n";
    var doubleReturn = "\n\n";
    var emailSubject = "eBay Auction - Thought you'd be
            interested";
    var emailBody = "Check out this auction!" + doubleReturn
            + document.title + singleReturn + location.href;
    var emailURI     = "mailto:" +
            document.mailForm.email.value + "?subject=" +
            escape( emailSubject ) + "&body=" + escape(
            emailBody );
    window.navigate(emailURI);
  }
//  End -->
</script>

<form name="mailForm">
Tell a friend about this auction!<br>
<input type="text" name="email" size="40" value="Enter their
            email address" onFocus="this.value=''"><br>
<input type="button" value="Send a link"
            onClick="emailAuctionLink();">
</form>
```

To add the Send a Link form to your auction, add the code in Listing 10-2 (also found on the CD) into your auction description where you want the form to show up. You don't need to change a thing; the script works right out of the box.

Creating an image slide show

You don't add a bunch of photos to an online auction just so the display looks nice. Nope, those photos serve a serious business purpose. Product photographs sometimes make or break online sales. Your customers naturally want to see the item they're considering, but if you shove too many photos into your listing, it makes navigation tough for the poor, photo-overloaded customers.

eBay offers its own solution to the multiphoto problem, but (of course) it wants some money for its efforts. Granted, at $0.15 per photo and $0.75 for a slide show, the fees seem reasonable. But if you sell the same products week after week, month after month, and you include several photos and a slide show in each auction, those little fees start adding up to big dollars coming straight out of your pockets.

Why not save all that money by creating your *own* slide show and adding it to your auctions *for free?* With a little effort and the JavaScript gizmo that follows, you can create your own custom slide shows. Because the slide show appears inside your regular auction text, eBay doesn't charge anything for it.

This slide show lets you include several images into a nice, small space on-screen. That prevents the kind of on-screen clutter that distracts and dismays some online buyers. After your customers look at a picture, they can click the Next and Prev buttons (as shown in Figure 10-2) to see the next image in your show. It's easy for the customers and free for you. Life just doesn't get better than this.

The script in Listing 10-3 creates your image slide show. Don't let the size of the script throw you — yes, it's big, but you only need to work with a few select parts. The complex-looking part of the script handles the on-screen controls and stores the list of available images. You just change the entries in bold when using the script for your auctions.

To use the script in Listing 10-3, you must host each slide show photo on your Web site or at a photo hosting service. See Chapter 4 for more details.

Listing 10-3: Creating Your Own Slide Show

```
<script language="JavaScript">
<!-- // Start
  currentPhoto = 1;

  if (document.images) {
    // Change these variables to match your images and image
         count
    // Put the number of images in your slideshow into the
         photoCount line below
    photoCount   = 3;
    photo = new Array(photoCount+1);
    // Each photo in your slideshow needs the following two
         entries.
    // Be sure that each photo has its own number inside
    // the brackets. Enter a full URL for IMAGE URL (like
    // http://www.yourwebsite.com/image.jpg.)
    photo[1] = new Image();
    photo[1].src = "IMAGE URL";
    // Code for second image
    photo[2] = new Image();
    photo[2].src = "IMAGE URL";

    // Code for third image
    photo[3] = new Image();
    photo[3].src = "IMAGE URL";
```

```
   // To add another image, copy the code for image three
   // above, increase the photo index (change 3 to 4)
   // and replace the photo URL.

;

   // The rest of the script (from here to the /script
   //       marker below) needs no changes, regardless of what
   //       you did above.
   }
 function prevPhoto() {
   currentPhoto--;
   if ( currentPhoto < 1 )
     currentPhoto = photoCount;
   document.images['Photos'].src = photo[currentPhoto].src;
 }

 function nextPhoto() {
   currentPhoto++
   if ( currentPhoto > photoCount )
     currentPhoto = 1
   document.images['Photos'].src = photo[currentPhoto].src
 }
// End -->
</script>
```

To put Listing 10-3 to work, you need to perform several changes:

1. **Add an entry for each image in your slide show.**

   The script includes two lines for every photo in the slide show. The example slide show has three photos. Each photo entry uses the following form:

   ```
   photo[X] = new Image();
   photo[X].src = "IMAGE URL";
   ```

   Insert the two preceding lines (or change the values in the script) for each of your photos. Be sure that each photo has a unique number, called the photo index (replace the X entry). Your first photo must use 1, the next photo must use 2, and so on.

2. **Update the** photoCount **variable.**

   Find the line inside the script that starts with the following:

   ```
   photoCount =
   ```

   Change the value at the end of the line to match the number of photos you included in the script. The value you enter for the photoCount variable should match the highest photo index used in the code.

3. Add the script code to your auction.

The script code must come before the HTML that follows. So add the script section of the slide show at the top of your auction description.

With the script portion of the slide show complete, use the following HTML code to insert the slide show into your auction. Include the HTML code at the point in your auction text where you want the slide show to appear. This code tells the browser to process and show the JavaScript elements that you just created. Treat this just like any normal text in your auction because that's how the Web browser sees it.

```
<p align="center">
  <a href="javascript:prevPhoto()">Prev</a> -- <a
         href="javascript:nextPhoto()">Next</a><br>
  <!-- Change the URL of the photo in the SRC attribute below
         so it matches the first image listed above, then
         sit back and let the JavaScript do the rest -->
  <img name="Photos" border=0 src="FIRST IMAGE URL">
</p>
```

Before you drop this code into your auction, you must make one change. The HTML code jump-starts the slide show by displaying the first image. You must change the HTML so that it matches the first image of *your* slide show. In the HTML code, find the following line:

```
<img name="Photos" border=0 src="FIRST IMAGE URL">
```

Enter the URL of your first image (photo index 1) in place of the entry `FIRST IMAGE URL`. Take a look at the finished slide show in Figure 10-2.

Figure 10-2:
Image
slide show
preview.

Adding an eBay search tool to your browser's context menu

Internet Explorer offers a great timesaving shortcut for searching on eBay (or search engines). This gizmo creates a new menu item on the *context menu* (which pops up when you right-click on something) that, when you highlight a word or phrase, automatically pops up an eBay search.

It's always important to research the market price for items you're looking to sell. Unfortunately, taking time to do a thorough search isn't always practical. With this timesaving script, it's much easier to track down competitive items. Give the script a try, and you'll wonder how you ever lived without it. Take a look at the Search eBay context menu option in Figure 10-3.

Adding the Search eBay context menu option to your browser requires modifications in your Windows Registry. Remember, changes to the Registry can render your computer inoperable if performed incorrectly. To make life easier, the CD includes a file that automatically performs the necessary changes.

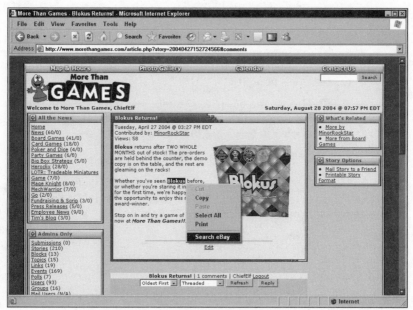

Figure 10-3:
An incredibly useful context search.

Follow these steps to add an eBay search option to your browser's context menu:

1. **Create an HTML file with the following code:**

```html
<html>
<head>
  <title>eBay Search</title>
</head>

<body>
  <script language="JavaScript">
  <!-- // Start
    var searchURL = new
        String("http://search.ebay.com/");

    var myWindow   = window.external.menuArguments;
    var myDoc      = myWindow.document;
    var mySelection = myDoc.selection;
    var myRange    = mySelection.createRange(  );
    var mySearch   = new String(myRange.text);

    window.open( searchURL + mySearch );
  //  End -->
  </script>
</body>
</html>
```

2. **Save the file to your main** `C:` **drive (making it easier to perform the upcoming Registry update) with the name** `eBaySearch.html` (`c:\eBaySearch.html`).

3. **Finally, locate the** `eBaySearchReg.reg` **Windows Registry update file on the CD. Right-click on the file and choose Merge from the pop-up menu. Click Yes to accept the changes.**

4. **Exit Internet Explorer to activate the changes.**

To try out your new eBay search shortcut, open a Web page, highlight some text, and then right-click on it to see your new menu. Choose Search eBay to automatically open eBay with your search term.

Chapter 11

Formatting with Cascading Style Sheets

*I*n the ancient days of the Web, when Internet maps showed vast uncharted realms labeled *"Here there be dragons, Macintoshes, and AOL Users,"* things like page formatting didn't get much attention. Sharing documents and information with people across the country (and around the globe) was so exciting that people didn't bother making their pages pretty.

Fast forward to today, where beautifully designed sites fill the Web. Keeping a visitor's attention practically requires that your pages look clean and professional. Taking the time to develop your auction design pays off with higher sale prices and more frequent bids. In a very real way, visitors gauge your legitimacy by evaluating your auction page. Like a store that looks run down and in disrepair, a poor auction design warns customers to proceed with caution.

At first, online sellers tried to solve their layout problems with HTML tables. Although it worked in the beginning, developers quickly ran into unsolvable paradoxes as they nested tables within tables within tables in their quest for the perfect page layout. It was into this crisis of design and development that *Cascading Style Sheets* (known as *CSS* for short) came onto the scene, charging in like a heroic knight battling the forces of darkness (or something like that).

Thanks to its myriad options, CSS puts a lot of power in your hands. But options bring complexity, which is why CSS remains a challenging technology. This chapter helps you through some of those early challenges by introducing CSS, a Web coding language that expands HTML's creative options.

Is CSS really worth the time?

eBay users sold millions of items without using a bit of CSS code in their auctions. So you might wonder, "Should I invest the time to use CSS in my auctions?" The decision to use Cascading Style Sheets comes down to control. How much control do you want over your auction text? Making an auction look its very best requires absolute control. It involves telling the browser exactly how large to make every heading and paragraph and ensuring that the text has the right feel. HTML alone can't do that — but HTML augmented with CSS can. By using CSS, you also get:

✔ **Many neat formatting options:** If you want to change the spacing between letters to spice up a heading, CSS, not HTML, makes it work. Text shadows, word spacing, and line heights are just a few options that CSS adds.

✔ **Simpler updating for your Web site or auction:** Using a CSS container to create classes of CSS rules makes it easy to change your Web site's look. Every part of the page that uses the shared rules immediately updates when the shared rules change. Planning to change the font for your entire auction? Make one change in the shared CSS rules, and the entire page changes. If you were to make that same change with plain HTML, you'd have to manually change every instance of the old font.

Although CSS shines best when applied to a whole Web site (eBay itself relies on CSS to organize pages), this technology offers a lot for simple auction text, too. Once you see the power of CSS in action, plain old HTML loses a lot of its luster, believe me.

The chapter takes a hands-on approach to CSS, explaining how to use CSS to change font sizes and color, modify an entire page with one edit, and create advanced borders and text boxes. Use the concepts and code to liven up your text, jazz up your page design, and quickly update your auction layout. As you put these examples to work, you also see how the rudiments of CSS work, which makes further study a lot easier.

When (and if) you really want to dive into the depths of CSS, pick up a copy of *Cascading Style Sheets For Dummies,* by Damon Dean. If we tried to cover even *half* of the stuff that he does, this chapter would turn out *way* too long. (And nobody wants to see *that* happen.)

Giving Auctions a Lesson in Style

Cascading Style Sheets offer lots of options for formatting and laying out a Web page or eBay auction. They go far beyond what you can accomplish with plain HTML alone. But rather than replacing HTML, CSS *extends* HTML to provide a number of specific benefits:

- ✔ Flexible text formatting
- ✔ Exact text placement
- ✔ Simpler upkeep of your home page or auction template

Although CSS accomplishes this by adding new ways to format almost every HTML tag, CSS isn't HTML — it's a completely separate technology that simply *coexists* with HTML. CSS code fits into HTML tags, and gets processed along with the HTML itself.

CSS code consists of two parts, called *containers* and *rules:*

- ✔ **Containers** are little HTML code crates that hold CSS rules. To make life interesting, CSS containers come in several types. When your Web browser finds a container in your HTML code, it shifts gears and gets ready to process whatever it finds inside the container as a *rule.*
- ✔ **Rules** are specific CSS instructions that change what the browser does with your page's content. CSS rules always follow the same pattern: They begin with a characteristic, and end with the value you want to assign to the characteristic. CSS rules govern text sizes, colors, and fonts, as well as the location of text and images on the screen. Frankly, CSS rules do so many things that it's easy to get lost among all of the options.

You can't have rules without containers, and you can't use containers without rules. Without the container, your Web browser would overlook and ignore the CSS rules on your page. If you leave out the rules, then the browser has nothing to do when it cracks open a container. Each part relies on the other; neither one stands by itself.

Here's an example of some simple CSS code in action:

```
<p style="color: red;">This text's font shows up red.</p>
```

In this example, the `style=` tag forms the CSS container around a simple rule: the `color: red;` part of the code. The `style=` informs the Web browser that some CSS code waits ahead, so that when the browser reaches the `color: red;` part it knows what to do with the instructions.

Together, the code above tells the browser to change the text color of the current paragraph — and only the current paragraph — to red. Why did it know to limit the change to the current paragraph? Because the container (the `style=` tag) sits inside a normal, boring HTML paragraph tag (`<p>`).

TIP

Memorizing countless CSS codes isn't practical unless you're planning to take up Web design professionally. Thankfully, software developers have created tools that build CSS rules for you. These tools give you menus and prompts that guide you through assembling the perfect CSS for your auctions. TopStyle (www.bradsoft.com/topstyle/), shown in Figure 11-1, and Style Master (www.westciv.com/style_master/) offer easy ways to develop CSS without typing a bit of CSS code.

Because CSS expands HTML instead of replacing it, sometimes you can accomplish the same task by using either HTML or CSS. For example, to change the text color for a paragraph, you can use standard HTML codes or special CSS attributes inside HTML:

```
In HTML - <font color="Red">This text is red.</font>
In CSS - <font style="color:Red;">This text is also
         red.</font>
```

Notice that the CSS code is almost identical to the HTML version. The primary difference is the style attribute (the CSS container).

Figure 11-1:
Put software to work creating your CSS rules.

Taming your text formatting

The power of CSS really shines when you're working with text formatting, especially font sizes, because you can alter the appearance of an entire page (or Web site) by editing one line of code. Auction headings, for example, are frequently larger than the rest of the auction text. The following two examples display larger text sizes:

```
HTML - <font size="+1">This text is "bigger."</font>
CSS - <font style="font-size:16pt;">This text is exactly
          16pt.</font>
```

The HTML example displays the text one step larger than normal. What does *one step* mean? That depends, because each Web browser interprets `size` `"+1"` a little differently. With this HTML example, you know that the text will show up larger on the page, but you don't know exactly how large.

CSS solves font size confusion. Unlike HTML, CSS rules can specify exactly how big to make the text. CSS removes any doubt about how the browser should display Web content. The size value, often specified in points, is just like the sizes found in a word processor.

Updating your pages with class

One of CSS' best features is that it enables you to quickly and easily assign the same formatting to multiple parts of a page (or even an entire Web site). With HTML, changing the font size of every heading within a page can be a real headache. But with CSS, you can make the change a snap.

You can apply CSS rules to every element on a page or to only the elements specified with the CSS `class` container. CSS rules have the power to change how text is displayed on an entire page, without requiring numerous changes throughout the HTML. With CSS, changing the text size, color, and font for an entire page is easy.

Classes, a special kind of CSS rule, provide conditional formatting. With conditional formatting, you apply your CSS rules only when necessary. For example, CSS rules can specify a class called `SectionHeading`. Then whenever `SectionHeading` shows up, the HTML includes a CSS `class` container to activate the CSS rule. You can change every instance of the `SectionHeading` by simply updating the CSS rule once. As a conditional format, only the headings you specifically apply the class to receive the formatting.

Cracking the CSS Code

Using CSS inside HTML requires two parts: CSS rules and CSS containers. The CSS rules specify how the HTML should change, and the container fits the rules into the HTML. One cannot exist without the other.

Understanding CSS rules

Though you don't need to know CSS inside out to take advantage of it, it's a good idea to familiarize yourself with the concept of CSS rules. The following code shows a simple CSS rule:

```
color: red
```

This CSS rule consists of two parts: a property and a value. The property, `color`, is what the rule changes. The value, `red`, specifies what the property becomes. Properties and values are separated by a colon.

Putting rules to work in your auction descriptions is easy. The simplest method is to add a `style` CSS container to an existing HTML tag:

```
<p style="color: red;">This text is red.</p>
```

The `style` attribute applies the included CSS rules to everything inside the paragraph tags (`<p> </p>`). Style attributes can include more than one CSS rule, although each must be separated by a semicolon, as shown in the following example:

```
<p style="color: red;font-size:14pt;">This text is red and
          14pt.</p>
```

The preceding `style` attribute includes two CSS rules; one sets the text color as red, and the other sets the font size to 14 point.

Font sizes in CSS use one of two different scales:

- ✔ **Points,** which are similar to the sizes used by popular word processors (approximately ½ of an inch for those who are counting).
- ✔ **Pixels,** which relate to the dots on a computer screen. A typical computer screen displays just over 1,000 pixels across and just under 800 high.

If all this talk of points and pixels sounds complicated, that's okay; trial and error is often the best way to find just the right size. Most often, it's easiest to use points in your CSS. Try several different sizes to find what works for you.

Getting to know CSS containers

When marking up your text with HTML and embedded CSS containers, you use two different groups of HTML tags: block-level and inline tags. Each type of tag displays on-screen slightly differently, making it important to know which type makes the most sense for your CSS containers.

Block-level tags include a line break before and after the tag. Paragraph tags <p> and headings <h1> fall into the block-level group. <div> is also a common tag used to apply CSS rules to HTML. Two paragraph tags side by side, as shown in the following example, show up with line breaks in between:

```
<p>Paragraph 1</p><p>Paragraph 2</p>
```

Putting tags into the middle of a paragraph (or other block-level tag) requires an *inline tag*. Inline tags don't automatically include line breaks when displayed on the screen. <span>, <b>, and <i> are all inline tags. Use inline tags when you want to modify a portion of a paragraph with CSS, as shown in the following example:

```
<p>This paragraph would look silly if my <b>bold</b>,
        <i>italic</i>, and <span style="font-size:
        18pt;">super-size text</span> were on separate
        lines. Since I used the inline SPAN tag, they show
        up within the paragraph.</p>
```

Making changes a snap

Applying CSS rules to an entire page employs a different container: the <style> tag. This tag is a type of CSS container that applies CSS rules to the entire Web page. By using the <style> tag, you can update an entire page quickly and easily. Note that the <style> tag includes a set of HTML comments — <!-- and --> — at the beginning and end so that old browsers that can't display CSS rules won't display them on your page.

Here's an example of the <style> tag:

```
<style>
  <!--
  p {
    color: red;
    font-size: 14pt;
  }
  .heading {
    font-size: 18pt;
    font-weight : bold;
  }
  -->
</style>
```

This example adds a new twist to CSS rules with the selectors p and .heading. *Selectors* specify which HTML tags the rules inside apply to. A CSS selector starts by defining what HTML tag (or tags) it applies to and then uses braces to surround the CSS rules.

The .heading selector is a special type of selector that creates a CSS class. This type of selector applies only to HTML tags that include the class attribute. The following example shows how the class attribute fits into an HTML tag:

```
<p class="heading">This text will have the CSS rules from the
              .heading selector applied.</p>
```

The beauty of the CSS class is that many items in an HTML page can use the same class. With the class applied, you can update the entire page simply by changing the CSS rules inside the style container.

CSS makes maintaining your Web site and auction templates significantly easier than plain HTML. Rather than putting all the formatting into each section of the page, CSS makes it easy to apply one set of rules to the entire page. HTML forces you to include the same formatting everywhere it's needed.

The HTML way:

```
<font size="+1">Item Description</font><br>
A functional but stylish stapler, used gently.<br>
<font size="+1">Shipping Details</font><br>
Shipping available via USPS Priority Mail for $3.95.
```

The CSS way:

```
<style>
  <!--
  .heading {
    font-size: 16pt;
  }
  -->
</style>
<font class="heading">Item Description</font><br>
A functional but stylish stapler, used gently.<br>
<font class="heading">Shipping Details</font><br>
Shipping available via USPS Priority Mail for $3.95.
```

In the CSS example, you can change the font size simply by modifying the line font-size: 16pt;. But to change the font size in the HTML example, you need to make two edits — each size="+1" entry. Although this HTML example has only two occurrences of the larger font, imagine a Web site that includes tens or even hundreds of headings.

Putting rules to work throughout your auctions

CSS takes the `style` container one step further. Using the `@import` entry in a `style` container, CSS can apply the same set of CSS rules to more than one page or auction description. Each auction includes the `@import` entry that points to a shared file, located on your Web site. The file, a collection of CSS rules inside a CSS `style` container, tells each page what CSS rules to use. One update to the imported CSS rules updates every page or auction that links to it.

To use a shared set of CSS rules, use the following CSS container:

```
<style>
  @import url(http://www.mywebsite.com/common.css);
</style>
```

The `common.css` file, located at `www.mywebsite.com`, would look like the following example:

```
<STYLE>
<!--
  p, span {
    font-family: arial, helvetica, sans-serif;
    font-size: 10pt;
    color: Black;
  }
  .pageHeader {
    font-size: 16pt;
    font-weight : bold;
  }
-->
</STYLE>
```

Finding out more about available CSS options

The CSS rules available are too numerous to list. However, a number of excellent references and tools are available to help you develop your own CSS:

- *Cascading Style Sheets For Dummies* by Damon Dean
- *HTML 4 For Dummies* by Ed Tittel and Natanya Pitts
- HTML Help by the Web Design Group (`www.htmlhelp.com/reference/css/`)

- ✔ W3C (www.w3.org/Style/CSS/) — the W3C is a consortium that includes an exhaustive (and often complex) reference for Web languages, including CSS
- ✔ TopStyle software (www.bradsoft.com/topstyle/)
- ✔ Style Master software (www.westciv.com/style_master/)

Sprucing Up Your Auction Descriptions with Model Style Sheets

Now it's time to put CSS to work to draw your customers to your auction. Font sizes, letter spacing, and arranging your content within boxes are all important ways you can get the attention you want.

Getting specific with font sizes

The expanded font size options available with CSS make finding the size you want a breeze. Text can be almost any size, from incredibly tiny to ridiculously huge. Use a word processor to get a general idea of the text size that will fit your auction; make sure you're viewing the page at 100%.

The following style attribute includes a rule that makes the paragraph text 54 points in size:

```
<span style="font-size: 54 pt;">This text is MASSIVE</span>
```

Try using sizes from 7 point (very small) to over 80 (very large). See Figure 11-2 for examples of these sizes.

Grabbing attention with wider letter spacing

Increasing the spacing between letters in headings makes them jump off the page. Plain HTML can't easily accomplish different letter spacing, so the effect is not very common.

The following style attribute includes a CSS rule that makes the letter spacing in the paragraph 3 pixels wide:

```
<span style="letter-spacing: 3px;">This heading is WIDE</span>
```

Experiment with different letter spacing sizes to see what you like.

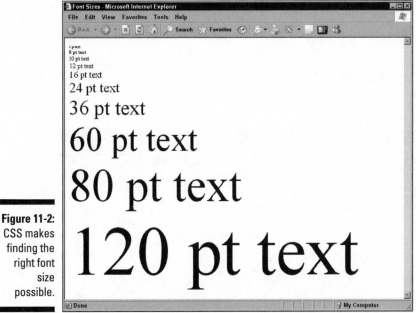

Figure 11-2:
CSS makes
finding the
right font
size
possible.

Separating sections with borders

CSS makes adding nifty borders and headings a breeze. Listing 11-1's style sheet transforms mundane level 1 headings into an interesting block header:

Listing 11-1:   Changing a Basic Heading into a Block Header

```
<style>
<!--
  H1 {
    background-color : Teal;
    color : White;
    font-family : Arial, Helvetica, sans-serif;
    font-weight : bold;
    letter-spacing : 3px;
    border : medium dashed Black;
    padding-top : 10px;
    padding-left : 10px;
    padding-right : 10px;
    padding-bottom : 10px;
  }
-->
</style>

<h1>Shipping Options</h1>
```

Include the preceding style sheet in the auction and then surround your headings with the H1 tag (`<h1>Heading text</h1>`). Compare the plain `<h1>` headings in Figure 11-3 to the fancier look in Figure 11-4 achieved using the preceding style sheet.

Experiment with different colors, padding sizes, and fonts. Several different border styles are available to use as well.

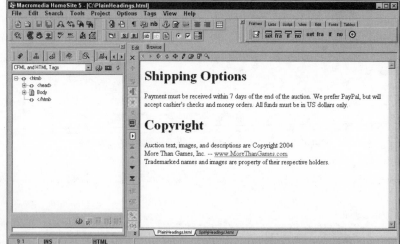

Figure 11-3:
Plain <H1>
headings.

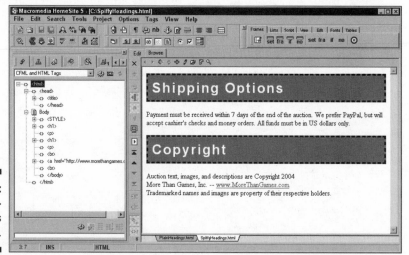

Figure 11-4:
Fancy <H1>
headings
with CSS.

Grouping text with boxes

Text boxes are a great way to set apart your auction description from the other items on eBay's standard-issue auction page. The entire auction description can go inside the box, or you can use a box for each heading. The style sheet in Listing 11-2 uses two different classes, one for the text box and the other for the box or section heading:

Listing 11-2: Text Box and Box Heading Style Sheet

```
<STYLE>
<!--
.box {
          background-color : Silver;
          font-family : Arial, Helvetica, sans-serif;
          border : medium double Black;
          padding-top : 10px;
          padding-left : 10px;
          padding-right : 10px;
          padding-bottom : 10px;
}

.boxHeading {
          font-weight : bold;
          letter-spacing : 3px;
          border-bottom-color : Gray;
          border-bottom-style : dashed;
          border-bottom-width : thin;
}
-->
</STYLE>

<div class="box">
  <div class="boxHeading">Shipping Options</div>
    <p>Payment must be received within 7 days of the end of
        the auction. We prefer PayPal, but will accept
        cashier's checks and money orders. All funds must
        be in US dollars only.</p>
    <p>Please include $4.90 for Shipping within the United
        States via USPS Priority Mail (including delivery
        confirmation and insurance).</p>
  <div class="boxHeading">Copyright</div>
    <p align="center">Auction text, images, and descriptions
        are Copyright 2004<br><b>More Than Games, Inc. --
        <a
        href="http://www.morethangames.com/">www.MoreThanG
        ames.com</a></b><br>Trademarked names and images
        are property of their respective holders.</p>
</div>
```

In the preceding example, the entire text box is surrounded by a `DIV` tag, and the `class="box"` CSS container that references the `.box` class is inside the CSS rules. Then each section inside the text box includes a `DIV` tag with a section heading. See Figure 11-5 for the results.

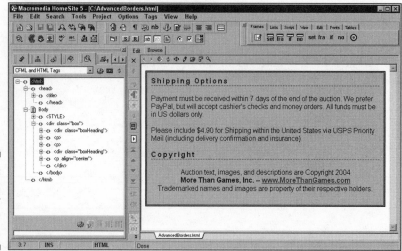

Figure 11-5: Preview the CSS in your favorite editor.

Chapter 12

E-Mail Automation Makes Message Handling a Breeze

. . . .

In This Chapter

▶ Taking a look at how e-mail works

▶ Finding the tools you need to create an e-mail application

▶ Building an e-mail processing application

▶ Setting up your computer to run the application automatically

. . . .

Managing communication with eBay and your customers is one of the most challenging tasks you'll face as an eBay seller. eBay sends a deluge of e-mails with information about every auction, and your customers send e-mails with questions about shipping, payments, and package status. Few chores sap so much time and seem to contribute so little to the bottom line.

Thankfully, computers offer timesaving tools that reduce the communication burden. Programming languages offer tools that integrate with your e-mail, helping you manage the flood of e-mail. Whereas Chapter 7 introduces features already in your e-mail application, this chapter focuses on what you can do with custom programs. You find out how to write a program that can open your e-mail mailbox and process the messages it finds.

Understanding the Technology Behind E-Mail

Before you receive your e-mail, a computer on the Internet (called an *e-mail server*) receives your e-mail and holds it for you, acting as an electronic mailbox. E-mail servers typically house hundreds of mailboxes. The keys to e-mail technology are the computer languages that send and receive e-mail from your e-mail server.

Most of the time, people never see or think about their e-mail server; it's a nebulous thing that floats out in the ether of the Internet happily doing its job. However, your *e-mail client* (the program on your computer that you use to send and read e-mail) maintains a close relationship with the e-mail server. E-mail clients usually use two languages (protocols) to send and receive e-mail: SMTP (Simple Mail Transfer Protocol) and POP (Post Office Protocol).

The computer *sends* e-mails from your computer to the e-mail server by using SMTP. The e-mail server takes care of forwarding the message on your behalf to another e-mail server until it reaches the destination. Many programming languages can also speak SMTP, giving you the power to send e-mail messages inside your custom programming code.

To *receive* e-mail, your e-mail client probably uses POP. Unfortunately, POP has a major drawback: Default mail-client configurations remove e-mail messages from your mailbox on the e-mail server and store them on your computer. Although that may not sound like a bad thing, it means you can't read e-mail from another computer if your e-mail client has already downloaded it. More importantly, your custom computer programs can't access e-mail that you've already retrieved via POP.

Thankfully, an alternative is available. IMAP (Internet Message Access Protocol) enables you to read e-mail with your e-mail client (because many support IMAP) and still access your e-mail from another computer or by using a computer program you write. IMAP leaves mail on the e-mail server so it's always available. Most Web e-mail (Web sites through which you can access your e-mail) programs use IMAP to read and store your messages. Unfortunately, because your e-mail stays on the server, your e-mail is only as safe as your e-mail server. If the server crashes, you lose your e-mail.

Most e-mail servers offer support for both IMAP and POP. To get the best of both worlds, you can configure your e-mail program to download e-mail via POP but leave messages on the server for seven days. Then your custom computer programs can access the e-mails by using IMAP (as long as you don't miss the seven-day window).

Gathering the Tools You Need to Make an E-Mail Processing Application Work

Getting your computer program talking to an e-mail server requires some specialized tools. You need help from your programming language, the computer you'll run your program on, and the e-mail server. Thankfully, if your program runs on the same computer as the e-mail server (which is typical when you're using a Web-based programming language), you have one less thing to worry about. To read e-mail programmatically, you need the following tools:

- **A programming language that supports IMAP or POP:** To connect to a POP or IMAP server, your programming language must include functions that connect to e-mail servers. If the language itself doesn't support e-mail access functions, a third-party developer may have tools that you can use to add IMAP or POP functionality.

- **Access to the e-mail server:** To read your e-mail, the program you write must have access to the e-mail server that you use. For Web-based programming languages, you shouldn't have to worry about server access. Your Web site (where the Web-based program resides) is typically located on the same server as your mailbox. Desktop programs offer a different challenge. You need to make sure that you're connected to the Internet when you run your program; otherwise, it won't connect to the e-mail server.

- **IMAP support on your e-mail server:** With almost no exceptions, e-mail servers support POP. However, IMAP support can be harder to come by. Check with your e-mail host to see if it supports IMAP.

This chapter includes examples written in PHP, a Web-based programming language. Although PHP includes functions that connect to IMAP and POP, some servers don't have PHP support activated; consult your server administrator about your options. Other Web-based programming languages that support IMAP and POP include Perl, CGI, and ASP. You can also access IMAP and POP from a desktop programming language, such as C++, Visual Basic, or Java. If your programming language doesn't include built-in functions, you may find that another developer has created a library that adds the necessary support.

If your Web host doesn't currently offer the support for POP or IMAP that you need, you're not out of luck — yet. You may be able to contact your host and request that it set you up with a special account that has the necessary programming support. If your host doesn't have programming language support, you may want to consider setting up a Web-based programming language on your desktop PC. PHP and ASP both run on Windows PCs. Take a look at *Active Server Pages For Dummies* by Bill Hatfield or *PHP For Dummies* by Janet Valade (both published by Wiley) for details.

Scripting Your Way to Automated E-Mail

This chapter uses PHP, an excellent Web-based programming language, to retrieve e-mail via an IMAP server. Although you can use POP, IMAP is a step above POP.

Avoiding common e-mail processing pitfalls

When working with your e-mail server, keep a couple of key concepts in mind:

✔ **When testing an application that opens your e-mail, make sure that you have e-mails to read!** Your program may not appear to work correctly if it doesn't have any e-mails to process. If possible, send yourself a few e-mails for testing purposes. However, make sure that your e-mail program doesn't download them immediately after they're sent; otherwise your application won't have any e-mail to read. One way around the e-mail client is to use a Web-based e-mail program provided by your e-mail hosting company. Ask your server administrator about Web-based e-mail availability.

✔ **Decide whether you need to enter your e-mail username and password each time you use your application.** Although you can store your e-mail username and password in your application, you may decide not to. If you're running a program on an intermittent basis, it's probably a good idea to use a login prompt that accepts your e-mail username and password. However, if you run a program daily to process your eBay mail, you'll likely need the login details coded into the application. For simplicity, the examples in this book use hard-coded login details.

✔ **Thoroughly test the application to ensure that you don't flood customers with automated e-mail.** When you develop a program that responds to e-mail, be sure that you test it thoroughly. Otherwise, your program

may end up sending a deluge of e-mail to unsuspecting recipients.

✔ **If your program gathers information from e-mails, verify the format often.** One of the most powerful functions of an e-mail application is reading your mail. However, if you teach your program to look for certain pieces of information (such as an auction number and description), you need to frequently check the e-mail format to make sure it hasn't changed. If eBay rearranges its e-mail format, your program may become confused. By looking at the format periodically and checking your program's output, you can catch changes quickly.

✔ **Consider using your application to process a secondary mailbox.** If your program goes haywire, you don't want it to churn through your mailbox, deleting every entry. To avoid this problem, you can set up your eBay and PayPal accounts to send e-mail to a secondary address that you use only for automated e-mails. Set up your e-mail processing application to access this secondary mailbox. That way, you limit the damage your program can do if something goes wrong.

Although programmatic access to your e-mail offers some challenges, the benefits for large-scale sellers outweigh any potential troubles. Managing the deluge of messages lightens the load and gives you more time to focus on the moneymaking aspects of your business.

Your programming language likely employs a different syntax for connecting to an IMAP or POP server, but the general process is similar to PHP. The Web abounds with helpful guides for getting IMAP and POP working with your preferred programming language. Visit www.google.com and enter *language*

IMAP guide or *language* **POP guide** where you replace *language* with the name of your programming language. Chances are, you'll find several helpful sites to guide you through the syntax you need.

Before you get rolling on your e-mail application, you want to test the connection between your program and the e-mail server. This chapter demonstrates how to access a generic e-mail server, but you can apply this method to your server setup. However, your mileage may vary.

If the examples don't work for you on your first attempt, you may need to make some modifications to suit your e-mail server. When appropriate, this chapter highlights settings you may need to verify with your server administrator.

Testing your connection with a simple e-mail listing

Before embarking on your journey towards programmatic e-mail peace and happiness, you need to test your IMAP connection. To do so, you can use the script in Listing 12-1, which accesses a mailbox and displays a list of e-mail messages within it.

The program first opens a connection to the IMAP server, requiring the server address, server options, and account login details. After it has connected to the IMAP server, the program uses several built-in functions to retrieve a list of folders and e-mail messages. After determining which details about each message to output, the program lists the folders and mail messages in the inbox.

To use Listing 12-1, you need to replace *mail.yourmailserver.com* with the address of your e-mail server, and *username* and *password* with your mailbox username and password, respectively.

Listing 12-1:   Testing Your IMAP Connection

```php
<?php

// Store connection details -- replace these!!
// Check with your server administrator for the address
// of your email server (usually mail.domainname.com)
$mailServerAddress  = 'mail.yourmailserver.com';
// Replace the username and password below with your
// mailbox's login values
$mailServerUsername = 'username';
$mailServerPassword = 'password';
```

(continued)

Listing 12-1 *(continued)*

```
// Server Connection String - Applies the protocol and
// encryption settings for the server
$mailServerDetails = '{' . $mailServerAddress .
        '/imap/notls/norsh}INBOX';
// Connect to IMAP server using details above
if ( $connectionIMAP = imap_open( $mailServerDetails,
        $mailServerUsername, $mailServerPassword) )
{
  // Start the page
  echo '<html><body>';

  // Output the folders in the mailbox
  echo '<h1>Mailboxes</h1>';

  // Retrieve an array of folders
  if ( $mailboxFolders = imap_listmailbox($connectionIMAP,
        '{' . $mailServerAddress . ':143}', "*") )
  {
    echo '<ul>';
    while ( list( $key, $val ) = each( $mailboxFolders ) )
    {
      echo "<li><p>$val";
    }
    echo '</ul>';
  } else {
    echo '<p>Failed to retrieve list of folders';
  }

  // Output a list of messages
  echo '<h1>Messages in the Inbox</h1>';
  echo '
<table border="1">
<tr>
  <td><p><strong>Date</strong></p></td>
  <td><p><strong>Subject</strong></p></td>
  <td><p><strong>From</strong></p></td>
</tr>';
  for ( $i = 1; $i <= imap_num_msg( $connectionIMAP ); $i++ )
  {
    $singleMessage = imap_headerinfo( $connectionIMAP, $i );
    echo '
  <tr>
    <td><p>' . $singleMessage->Date . '</p></td>
    <td><p>' . $singleMessage->subject . '</p></td>
    <td><p>' . $singleMessage->fromaddress . '</p></td>
  </tr>';
  }
  echo '</table>';
```

```
    // Close the IMAP server connection
    imap_close( $connectionIMAP );

    echo '</body></html>';
} else {
    echo '<h1>Sorry, the IMAP connection failed...check your
            settings again...</h1>';
}

?>
```

If your application successfully connects to the IMAP server and displays the messages in your mailbox, you're ready to begin making something useful out of it. See the next section for details on how to use your application to generate e-mail summaries.

If you didn't have success with the preceding test script, here are a few troubleshooting ideas:

✔ **Did you remember to change the connection details?** You need to include the mail server address (mail.yourdomain.com, for example) and change the variables that contain the username and password. Without the correct details, the connection fails.

✔ **Do you have the requirements covered?** Look over the server requirements in "Gathering the Tools You Need to Make an E-Mail Processing Application Work," earlier in the chapter, to ensure that your server and application pass.

✔ **Does your server use an encrypted connection?** Most servers don't use TLS, RSH, or SSH encrypted connections. However, if your server uses secure connections, you need to change the server connection string. If your server utilizes TLS, remove the /notls portion of the connection string. If your connection uses RSH or SSH, remove the /norsh portion of the connection string.

If you're still having trouble, contact your server administrator to verify all your settings. If possible, try another mail server to see if your mail server is causing the problem. Take a look at Chapter 21 for more troubleshooting tips.

Sending yourself summary e-mails

If you post a large volume of auctions, you know that keeping track of which auctions you (or your employees) have listed and which have closed is a formidable task. Fortunately, managing the flood of e-mail from eBay doesn't have to be a challenge. Your e-mail processing application can go through your e-mail, gather a list of the day's new listings and closed auctions, and e-mail you a summary.

Your application may optionally delete the messages after gathering them for your summary. But make sure the application doesn't delete the e-mails until after it successfully e-mails you the summary. Otherwise, the application might crash in the middle of the process with your eBay e-mails deleted, and then you'd be out of luck.

Before using Listing 12-2, you must change several settings to match your e-mail server and e-mail account settings. Replace *youremail@youremailserver.com* and *mail.youremailserver.com* with your e-mail address and the address of your e-mail server. Also, enter your e-mail username and password in place of *username* and *password*.

Listing 12-2: Generating Summary E-Mails

```php
<?php

// Store connection details -- replace these!!
// Check with your server administrator for the address
// of your email server (usually mail.domainname.com)
$yourEmailAddress   = 'youremail@youremailserver.com';
$mailServerAddress  = 'mail.youremailserver.com';
// Replace the username and password below with your
// mailbox's login values
$mailServerUsername = 'username';
$mailServerPassword = 'password';

// Server Connection String - Applies the protocol and
// encryption settings for the server
$mailServerDetails  = '{' . $mailServerAddress .
          '/imap/notls/norsh}INBOX';
// Connect to IMAP server using details above
if ( $connectionIMAP = imap_open( $mailServerDetails,
          $mailServerUsername, $mailServerPassword) )
{
  $listingConfirmationHTML = '';
  $listingEndedHTML        = '';
  $emailProcessedCount     = 0;
  for ( $i = 1; $i <= imap_num_msg( $connectionIMAP ); $i++ )
  {
    $singleMessage = imap_headerinfo( $connectionIMAP, $i );


    // Check for the subject string that denotes a listing
        confirmation
```

```
// Use somewhat odd syntax to get around PHP's strpos
      return value issues
if ( !( strpos( $singleMessage->fromaddress,
      'listingconfirm@ebay.com' ) === FALSE ) )
{
  $messageType                = 'Listing Confirmation';
} elseif ( !( strpos( $singleMessage->fromaddress,
      'endofauction@ebay.com' ) === FALSE ) ) {
  $messageType                = 'Auction Ended';
} else {
  // Message subject doesn't match one of the specifics
      we're looking for
  // So exit the loop
  continue;
}
// Flag the message for deletion (although the software
// doesn't complete the delete until the end of the
// process with the imap_expunge() function
imap_delete( $connectionIMAP, $i );

// The following lines return an array, use the 1 index
// to output the first entry found
ereg( "\(Item #(.+)\)", $singleMessage->subject,
      $itemNumber );
ereg( ": (.+) \(Item #", $singleMessage->subject,
      $itemTitle );

// Use array index 1 for the Number and Title. The PHP
      ereg
// search function puts the entire input string into
      index 0,
// then the first entry found in index 1
$emailHTML = '
<tr>
  <td><p>' . $messageType . '</p></td>
  <td><p>' . $singleMessage->Date . '</p></td>
  <td><p>' . $itemNumber[1] . '</p></td>
  <td><p>' . $itemTitle[1] . '</p></td>
</tr>';

switch ( $messageType )
{
  case 'Listing Confirmation':
    $listingConfirmationHTML .= $emailHTML;
    break;
  case 'Auction Ended':
    $listingEndedHTML .= $emailHTML;
    break;
}
$emailProcessedCount += 1;
```

(continued)

Listing 12-2 *(continued)*

```
    }

    if ( $emailProcessedCount > 0 )
    {
      // Prepare the email
      $headers  = "MIME-Version: 1.0\r\n";
      $headers .= "Content-type: text/html; charset=iso-
            8859-1\r\n";
      $headers .= "From: $yourEmailAddress\r\n";
      $emailSubject = 'Auction Summary';

      $titleHTML = '
      <tr>
        <td><p><strong>Type</strong></p></td>
        <td><p><strong>Date</strong></p></td>
        <td><p><strong>Item Number</strong></p></td>
        <td><p><strong>Item Title</strong></p></td>
      </tr>';
      $message = '
      <html>
      <head>
        <title>' . $emailSubject . '</title>
      </head>
      <body>
      <p><h1>Auctions Ended</h1>
      <table border="1">' . $titleHTML . $listingEndedHTML .
            '</table>
      <p><h1>Auctions Created</h1>
      <table border="1">' . $titleHTML .
            $listingConfirmationHTML . '</table>
      </body>
      </html>';

      mail( $yourEmailAddress, $subject, $message, $headers );
    }
    // Confirm deletion of the mail messages processed?
    // If so, remove the comment marks from this line:
    // imap_expunge( $connectionIMAP );

    // Close the IMAP server connection
    imap_close( $connectionIMAP );
  } else {
    echo '<h1>Sorry, the IMAP connection failed...check your
            settings again...</h1>';
  }

?>
```

This program works as a launching pad for your e-mail processing endeavors. It reads through every e-mail, looking for certain phrases or combinations of characters. The program locates any text between the specified start and end characters. For example, to retrieve the item number from the e-mail subject, the program retrieves everything between the characters (Item # and the closing parenthesis). PHP's powerful regular expression (a search method) function ereg handles the details.

For more information on creating regular expressions in PHP, check out *Apache, MySQL, and PHP Web Development All-in-One Desk Reference For Dummies* by Jeff Cogswell (Wiley). You'll find a wealth of knowledge on using regular expressions to retrieve the information you need from subject lines or e-mail bodies.

You might be wondering, "What else can I have my e-mail application do?" Here are some ideas you may want to try:

- ✔ **Store information in a database.** PHP applications often integrate with a MySQL database. Consider changing the preceding example so that it stores the auction details in a database instead of creating a summary e-mail.

- ✔ **Automatically e-mail your customers upon auction close.** Any time one of your auctions closes, eBay automatically sends you an auction close e-mail that provides details about the auction including closing date, final price, and winning bidder. Your application can read in the auction details contained in this auction close e-mail and then send out an e-mail requesting payment from your customer.

Your options are almost limitless. Think about what would make your life easier and get coding. By incorporating the powerful search functions, you can pull the details you need out of any e-mail. After you have the data, consider how to respond or store the e-mail details. By processing and removing e-mails, you'll clean up your inbox and save time!

Scheduling Your Operations

After you've created an e-mail processing program, think about running it at a set interval. Although you can fire it up only occasionally, you maximize the benefits of your e-mail application when it runs automatically. It's a good idea to run the eBay activity summary e-mail each evening or early in the morning. That way, you have a daily look at what's going on with your account, and the application clears out your mailbox before you begin the day (if you activate the delete portion of the program).

Depending on what kind of computer you use, you have a couple options for scheduling your programs to run automatically. Microsoft began including a scheduling application starting with Windows 98 called the Task Scheduler, shown in Figure 12-1. So if you use Windows, you probably have what you need already.

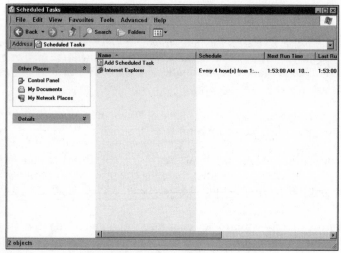

Figure 12-1:
The
Windows
Scheduled
Tasks
window.

Linux and UNIX users have the *cron* tool available for scheduling operations. Depending on the features your Web server provides, you may be able to schedule the server to activate your application. Some non-Windows hosting companies allow you to use cron. Talk to your system administrator for help setting up a cron job for your application.

Scheduling a custom desktop application doesn't pose any trouble at all. Visit the Windows Control Panel to find the Task Scheduler (depending on your version of Windows, it may be called Scheduled Tasks). Create a new task, point it to your application, and then specify how often the task should run.

Scheduling Web-based programs is a little more difficult and requires an additional step. You need to choose your Web browser as the task to run and then add the URL of your program in double quotes after the program. The Run line should look like this:

```
C:\PROGRA~1\INTERN~1\iexplore.exe "http://www.yourdomainname.
        com/yourprogram.php"
```

Part IV
Going API with eBay and More

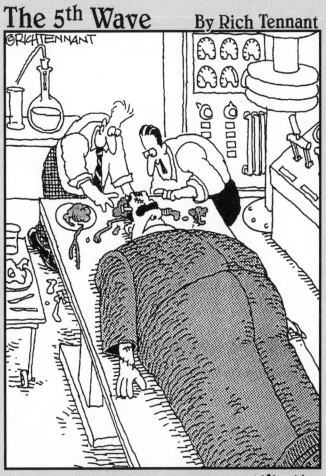

The 5th Wave   By Rich Tennant

@RICHTENNANT

"There's the PayPal payment notification!
I knew I'd printed it before the computer
crashed."

In this part . . .

Commanding an application program interface (API) sits at the pinnacle of your online programming world. You need all your technical wits about you to scale this peak. Armed with your understanding of HTML, your knowledge of a programming language like PHP, and lots of patience and dedication and a trimmed-back social calendar, you stand on the cusp of great and wonderful technical things.

Forget what the menus say. Ignore the limited tools that the *other* people use. If you control the API, you can make your own magic, develop your own tools, and seriously increase your potential for making money through eBay.

One word of caution: If you don't feel *completely comfortable* with things like HTML code and Web server controls, please flip back to one of the earlier chapters before tangling with the stuff in here. You need a solid foundation under you before getting into the truly high-tech, high-powered, and high-profit stuff described here. Really, you do. Your brain and your hairline will both thank me in the morning.

If you don't pick up something in this part the first time through, try it again a bit slower. Use the sample code included on the book's CD to help you past slow spots or across frustrating chasms of programming. With this book and its sample coding on the CD, you *can* do this. After all, you got this far, and you still have hair, right?

Chapter 13

A Brief Introduction to API Programming

*F*rom the dawn of personal computing, programs generally kept to themselves. Sure, they lived together on hard drives, but they rarely acknowledged each other's presence — and almost *never* actually chatted or shared any information. The programs behaved like neighbors in a subdivision, safe and content in the knowledge that they all lived alone together and that they liked things that way.

On the other hand, the people *using* the software didn't like all of this rugged individuality. They wished that the programs could get their collective acts together and start communicating with each other. Thanks to the advent of the Macintosh and Windows operating systems, that wish suddenly turned into reality. Although we take copying and pasting for granted today, not so many years ago the simple act of shifting raw text from a word processing document into a presentation slide without printing and retyping the whole thing practically brought tears to people's eyes. It was a religious experience.

Curiously, the first few waves of Internet-based applications suffered from the same problems as those rugged, individualistic applications of yore — namely the fact that they wouldn't talk to each other. Sure, Web sites do a pretty decent job of moving news, information, entertainment, and a host of other things back and forth between computers and people, but the Web sites never uttered a word among themselves. And, as before, the people using the technology gradually got tired of all that uppity digital snubbing. This time, they solved the communication problem with a technology called an *application programming interface* (or *API* for short).

APIs provide a language to let programs share data with each other. Over the last few years, the API concept has exploded in popularity because of its flexibility and its power. (Of course, the fact that lots of clever people figured out new ways to make money by using the power of API programming didn't hurt the whole enterprise either, but I digress.)

This chapter walks you through the broad concepts behind how APIs work. It explains each step in the API communication process and gives you a working knowledge of how programs talk to each other as well as what they say and how to decipher it.

 After you grasp the "big picture" of how APIs work, you can apply the knowledge almost anywhere. The same basics that make eBay's API work so well also drive the APIs for PayPal, the United States Postal Service, FedEx, UPS, and myriad other companies out there. Sure, the details differ for each of those systems, but every one of them abides by the same general API rules and concepts introduced in this chapter.

Grasping the Data Sharing Revolution

Advances in Internet technology, combined with spectacular innovations in what Web sites can really do, spurred the development of programs and systems that share data with each other. But why should anyone (apart from the conspiracy theorists out there) care about Web sites trading notes back and forth? It doesn't sound particularly important at first blush, but it represents a huge shift in how we, the people, interact with online programs and information.

When computer programs share data, the act of sharing separates the data from the program that carries it. That separation lets *you* — the person using the information — choose the program that best suits your needs for viewing, collating, and interpreting the data. You don't really care how that *other* program organized things because *your* program can handle it on its own. This simple change — separating the data from its program — puts power and flexibility into your hands instead of leaving it with the developers.

The fact-filled front page of Google News, shown in Figure 13-1, is a perfect example of a program in one place presenting data gleaned from somewhere else (or, in Google's case, from *many* other places). Not only does Google News offer an alternative interface, but it also combines data from many news sites and sources. Would you rather slog through ten individual news sites (each with its own unique interface and organization), or get all the information those sites offer spun together in a single glance at Google? There you have it — that's the power of programs sharing data.

Figure 13-1:
Google
News
displays
data from
many
sources.

To look at this another way, think about how you determine what movies are playing at your local cinema. You can look through the newspaper, check the Internet, call the theater, or read the signs posted outside the theater. Theaters provide movie schedules via numerous channels, letting you, the moviegoer, decide how you want to gather the information. In the same way, a computer program that shares its data with other programs enables users to decide which tool makes the most sense for them.

Most likely, you've visited a Web site recently that offered content from another computer program. For example, personal Web sites include national news headlines, online retailers display package-tracking details, and banks include stock quotes. In all these examples, the Web sites include information gathered from other computer programs.

Programs running on Internet-connected computers (called *servers*) contain valuable information *(databases)*. By teaching your Web site and computer programs to speak with these servers and access their databases, you open up a vast array of information for yourself and your customers.

Companies you may already conduct business with offer access to their extensive databases. For example, PayPal, eBay, UPS, and the United States Postal Service (USPS) all provide up-to-the-minute information for you to use on your Web site. Rather than send your customers to those Web sites for information, why not offer the information they need on your site?

In addition to asking other servers for information, your Web site can send information *to* other servers. For example, eBay allows members to post auctions and feedback by connecting directly to its servers (without visiting the eBay Web site). Chapter 15 describes how you can take advantage of these new features.

Harnessing this program-sharing harmony requires you to take a brief trip into the mildly geeky realm of computer programming. Companies that offer access to their servers write *application programming interfaces* (APIs) that detail how the communication takes place.

How APIs Work: The View from Way Up High

Until recently, only highly paid computer gurus had the know-how to convince one computer to share information with another. Because each computer system spoke a different language, developing an effective translation proved difficult. APIs solve the computer program translation challenge and make the process accessible for beginning programmers. Here is a brief rundown of what APIs do:

- ✔ Define a common language for each computer to use, simplifying the communication process.

- ✔ Offer a complete process that each computer follows, making data transfer a snap.

- ✔ Specify how the computers connect, what kind of information to share, and what language to speak. APIs perform a function similar to a language's spelling and grammar rules.

Although an API can describe how two programs on one computer talk back and forth, this book focuses on programs that communicate via the Internet. An API includes two components, the API documentation, or *specification,* and the API server:

- ✔ **The API documentation** offers programmers detailed instructions for talking to the API server. It gives exact details about what information to send, how to send it, and how the API server will respond.

- ✔ **API servers,** for the purposes of this book, run on computers connected to the Internet. They wait for an API program running on another computer to begin a computer conversation specified by the API documentation.

Companies offering API connections to their databases frequently require developers to pass a program certification and may require membership in their developer community. To use the eBay API, for example, you must join the eBay Developers Program (introduced in Chapter 14) and go through the application certification process. Certifying your API program ensures that it accurately communicates with the API server and doesn't include any glaring problems (bugs). The API documentation provides program requirements and steps to complete the program certification if required.

To help with the development process, companies typically offer a special API server, called a *development server* or *sandbox,* to test your API program against. (See Chapter 14 for the lowdown on eBay's Sandbox.) That way, you don't have to worry about accidentally posting a real auction or incurring fees while testing your program. The API documentation lays out what testing options the company makes available.

Talking to an API server

To make use of an *Internet API* (an API that connects to a program across the Internet), your computer or Web site needs a programming language. In general, Internet APIs require a language that can open Internet connections and understand the eXtensible Markup Language (XML). Thankfully, many programming languages pass the Internet API requirements test.

Programming languages capable of performing Internet API communication fall into two basic categories:

- **Languages that run on your computer:** Programming languages that operate on your computer can create programs just like the ones you're familiar with, from word processors to e-mail programs. These languages include C++, Java, and Visual Basic. These sophisticated programming languages can do more than just API communication; they can create complicated programs that do almost anything imaginable.

- **Languages that run on your Web site:** Programming languages for Web sites include PHP, ASP, and Perl. Web sites use programming languages to display *dynamic content* (content that changes each time you visit). Web sites that display news, stock quotes, and movie showtimes typically use a programming language to send Web browsers the pages users are looking for. A Web programming language also allows Web sites to use an API to contact the U.S. Postal Service to gather tracking information for customers' packages.

Selecting a programming language is akin in some ways to selecting a new TV: Many options exist, and they all perform the same basic task. However, each option has strengths and weaknesses. Certain features work more easily with one language than another. The final decision usually comes down to what you're most comfortable with and what fits in with the other products you already have. Most likely, you'll want to stick with the programming language your Web site already supports. However, feel free to try out several before making your final decision.

This book uses the Web programming language PHP to demonstrate how APIs work. Web programming languages offer a simpler interface design than traditional desktop programming languages and make your program available on any Internet-connected PC. The PHP principles demonstrated here work in any language, although the language syntax and functions may look and operate differently.

Understanding the API documentation

An API conversation between your API program and the API server consists of *requests* and *responses*. Typically, your API program creates an API request (based on the API documentation) and receives a response from the API server.

API documentation details how the API works. Typical API documentation describes what requests the API responds to. Requests vary in length; some simpler requests are short, and more complicated requests can be quite long. A more complicated request often requires more information and receives a more detailed response than a simple request.

APIs require an API program to format every request according to the API documentation. The request must first specify the request type (choosing from one of the options in the API documentation). An API may also require the API program to include additional data, such as a name, an e-mail address, a city, an auction title, and so on.

Take a look at the following sample USPS address validation API request:

```
<AddressValidateRequest USERID="xxxx" PASSWORD="xxxx">
  <Address ID="0">
    <FirmName>The White House</FirmName>
    <Address1></Address1>
    <Address2>1600 Pennsylvania Avenue NW</Address2>
    <City>Washington</City>
    <State>DC</State>
    <Zip5>20500</Zip5>
    <Zip4></Zip4>
  </Address>
</AddressValidateRequest>
```

The request starts with an XML `<AddressValidateRequest>` tag that tells the USPS API to check the addresses enclosed. The API's response, shown later in this section, provides corrections for any errors in the addresses given in the request and fills in any missing information. The `<AddressValidateRequest>` tag also includes `USERID` and `PASSWORD` attributes, reassuring the API server that the request comes from a valid user. Next, the request includes an address for the API to validate.

The address, enclosed inside the `<Address>` tag, includes address information enclosed by HTML-looking tags. The API documentation tells which fields to include. Each tag includes a single piece of information. The request includes the city name inside the `<City>` tag, for example.

Many APIs allow you to bundle multiple requests together. To simplify life, the USPS API address validation requests can include several addresses. The API documentation typically offers a way to differentiate each portion of the request. The address validation request includes an ID number for each address submitted (the preceding example includes a single address, `ID="0"`). eBay's API also allows you to retrieve information about several items in one request, helping your programs run faster and more efficiently.

The API spells out exactly what each piece of data — called a *field* in programmer speak — looks like. It describes

- ✔ What kind of information the field holds
- ✔ How many characters or numbers the field allows

A field type, also called a *data type,* tells whether the field holds letters, numbers, or a mixture of both. Numeric data types frequently restrict the highest and lowest numbers allowed, how many decimal places are acceptable, and whether negative numbers are allowed.

For example, the preceding `AddressValidateRequest` includes a Zip5 field. The API documentation requires you to include a five-digit number inside the `Zip5` tag. No letters are allowed, and the field must not include more than five characters.

Be careful to follow the API documentation's rules for field data types. If the request violates the documentation's rules, the API returns an error rather than the information you need.

Read through the data types in Table 13-1 to familiarize yourself with the most common data types.

Table 13-1	Some Common Data Types	
Data Type	*Description*	*Examples*
Integer	Whole numbers, positive or negative, with no decimal point	1, 5, 258, –45
Float	Really large numbers, or numbers with lots of decimal places (also called *reals* or *doubles*)	3.14159; 4,555,323,656
String	Text and numbers	The 56th page
Boolean	True or false value (usually 1 for true, 0 for false)	True, 1, 0
Time	Time of day	3:45 p.m., 1:35 a.m.
Date	Specific day	June 3, 2005

When creating an API request, you may not have to include every field. The API lists which fields you may omit (typically labeled as optional) as well as gives field lengths. The API documentation typically gives the maximum number of characters the field will accept and may also specify the minimum length.

After the API server receives your request, it sends an API response. Not wanting to leave anything vague, the API documentation details what the API response will include. The response definition often includes as much detail as the request definition. It may even include a list of every possible field value (the information stored in a field). After sending the preceding sample request to the USPS API, the API server returned the following response:

```
<AddressValidateResponse>
  <Address ID="0">
    <FirmName>THE WHITE HOUSE</FirmName>
    <Address2>1600 PENNSYLVANIA AVE NW</Address2>
    <City>WASHINGTON</City>
    <State>DC</State>
    <Zip5>20500</Zip5>
    <Zip4>0004</Zip4>
  </Address>
</AddressValidateResponse>
```

The response begins with a tag identifying the type of information to follow. The API documentation explains exactly what tags you'll find inside an AddressValidateResponse tag. The response includes a validated address for the address I submitted in the request shown earlier. You'll notice that the original request didn't include any information in the Zip4 field. The USPS API has helpfully given the correct values in it's `AddressValidateResponse`.

The API documentation also details the format to which the request and response must adhere. The APIs covered in this book utilize XML because it offers broad programming language support and enjoys strong Internet compatibility. (See the "A brief word about XML" sidebar for a brief explanation of how XML works.) As such, this book limits the discussion of response and request transmission to XML. Other information communication formats exist, but they're beyond the scope of this book. To find out more about XML, take a look at Ed Tittel's *XML For Dummies* (Wiley).

Organizing the conversation

With the API documentation in hand, your API program must embark on a multistep journey to complete the API communication process. Each step varies in complexity depending on which API your program utilizes and what programming language you select.

A brief word about XML

XML is a markup language (which uses tags, similar to HTML) that defines different types of information. XML tags help define what role each piece of content plays in the document. A computer program reading a word processing document stored as XML uses the XML tags to determine which parts make up the headings and which fit in as the body text.

You structure the tags so that content that belongs together (such as the various components of addresses used in the XML examples in this book) fits (or *nests*) inside grouping tags. The following example shows the `<Name>` and `<Email>` tags grouped together inside a `<Friend>` tag. You can include many `<Friend>` tags inside the `<MyXMLAddress Book>` tag, each with its own `<Name>` and `<Email>` tags.

```
<MyXMLAddressBook>
  <Friend>
    <Name>Bob Jones</Name>
    <Email>bob@bob.com</Email>
  </Friend>
</MyXMLAddressBook>
```

Although HTML, another markup language, has a fixed set of tags (`<b>` always means bold, for example), XML allows almost anything to be a tag. You can make up your own! In the preceding address book XML example, the `<Friend>` tag tells someone reading the document that the information they find inside relates to a friend.

APIs extensively use XML because it offers a structured, simple, and flexible method for package data. The receiving program can easily extract the necessary data and know exactly what that data relates to.

Connecting to another computer via an Internet API takes place in six steps:

1. **Gather inputs.**

   Before the API conversation starts, the program collects data from the user, databases, or other sources (system date, time, e-mails, and so on).

2. **Process the inputs and create an API request.**

   The program validates the inputs against the API documentation (data types, field length, and within range) and then encodes it into the API specified format (typically XML).

3. **Send the request to the API server.**

   With the request in hand, the program encodes the data, opens a connection through the Internet to the API server, and sends the request.

4. **Receive the API server response.**

   Depending on the API, an API response may simply report transmission success or failure, or it may return a detailed answer to the API request.

5. **Decode and process the response.**

   With the API response in hand, the program converts the response into a familiar format.

6. **Display or store the output.**

   Finally, the program displays and/or stores the data returned. In the case of simple success/failure responses, your program won't have much processing to do. When the response includes more detail, you'll need to equip your program to handle longer, more complex responses.

The section "Diving into More Detail on the API Process," later in this chapter, describes the preceding steps in more detail and gives examples of the specialized code needed to manage the communication process.

Talking back

Your API program can act like an API server, too. By creating an API program that accepts API connections from other computers, your program can accept API requests and respond to them.

For example, PayPal uses an API to contact your Web site when a PayPal payment comes through for you. That way, your Web program can listen 24 hours a day and know the instant a transaction takes place. API programs that act like a server are especially useful for recording your history of PayPal transactions. Chapter 17 introduces the PayPal API and provides a starting point for a transaction history.

Diving into More Detail on the API Process

Each step in the API communication process (described in "Organizing the conversation," earlier in this chapter) performs several specialized tasks. Because of the flexible nature of computer programming, each task often allows several different methods. How you choose to accomplish each task depends on the strengths and weaknesses of your chosen programming language.

Although the following examples utilize the open source programming language PHP, they illustrate the general methods employed to perform each API communication step. Your programming language may have different function names and punctuation (called *syntax*), but the logic works the same.

Step 1: Gather inputs

This first step creates a foundation for the communication process to follow. The program must gather answers to every question (you answer these questions by finding an input for every field) that the API requires in its request.

The program must first select one of the available request types allowed by the API. The program typically asks users what operation they'd like to perform. This important selection flags which part of the API documentation the API request must adhere to.

After your API program knows what field it must complete, it starts gathering the required data. Table 13-2 lists several places your program may find the data for each field. (Sometimes more than one location contains the same data.)

Table 13-2	Sources for API Data
Source	**Examples**
System info	Current date and time; API program network address and domain name
Hardcoding	Frequently used information (such as a list of APIs) that doesn't change often
User input	Web form fields completed by the user just before the API process
Database	Information entered by the user in form fields before the API process
Another API	An order ID from one API that is used in looking up package tracking

User input is the simplest method for gathering data. Storing frequently used information (an eBay user ID, API access ID, and so on) inside a database makes life easier. However, gathering the data via form fields makes troubleshooting easier because you can quickly change the values and limit the number of possible problems in your code.

Take a look at the following examples to see what the code behind each input looks like.

System info

Your programming language offers a wealth of information from its built-in functions. Use functions to fill variables with basic details, such as the date and time. The following code puts the current date and time into program variables:

```
$theCurrentTime = time();
$theCurrentDate = date();
```

Hardcoding

Passwords, server names, and file locations typically work best as hardcoded variables. Although your program could store the information in your database, you'd have to create a portion of your program to update the values. To keep your program simple, keep users away from dangerous settings. And for early testing, forcing a specific value into your program makes perfect sense. Plus, your program has the same value available every time it runs. Instead of pulling the values from a database, the following code assigns a specific value into each variable:

```
$myAPIUsername = 'username';
$myAPIPassword = 'password';
```

User input via Web form

Hardcoding just won't work for auction details that change. Any time you need new information from your user, you must offer a prompt. Search terms, auction titles, and item prices typically find their way into your application through a prompt. Unfortunately, unless you later store the information entered, it's lost when the user closes the application. Listing 13-1 illustrates a simple Web-based form that accepts a search string:

Listing 13-1:   A Web Form That Accepts a Search String

```php
<?php

// Check to see if user entered a search
if ( $_GET['action'] <> 'formProcess' ) {
  // Nope, no search performed. Since the user didn't search
  // offer the search form
  echo '
```

```
   <html>
   <head>
   <title>API Data Entry</title>
   </head>

   <body>
     <form action="' . $_SERVER['PHP_SELF'] . '">
       Enter Search: <input type="text" name="searchString"
         size="30">
       <input type="hidden" name="action"
         value="formProcess">
       <input type="submit">
     </form>
   </body>
   </html>
  ';
} else{
  // The user entered a search into the form. Store the
  // search terms into a variable.
  $mySearchString = $_GET['searchString'];
}

?>
```

PHP and MySQL database input

Databases are a wonderful place to store information. They're particularly useful for saving details about similar things. eBay item information fits into a database nicely; each eBay item includes the same information, a title, description, price, and so on. Using databases offers greater challenges than other input methods, but the potential value is worth the effort. Your database can store information about your auction. Listing 13-2 shows a program that retrieves a list of auctions from a database:

Listing 13-2:   Retrieving Auction Lists from a Database

```
<?php

// Hardcoded values for server address, username, password,
// and database name
$server = 'localhost';
$user   = 'myUsername';
$pass   = 'myPassword';
$db     = 'myDBName';
// Using the values above, connect to the database
$link   = mysql_connect($server, $user, $pass);
mysql_select_db( $db, $link );


// Locate auction that matches a previous search
```

(continued)

Listing 13-2 *(continued)*

```
$query = "SELECT * FROM AuctionList WHERE itemNumber =
          $itemNumberSearch";
// Retrieve the database results
$result = mysql_query( $query, $link );
$row = mysql_fetch_object( $result );
// Store the database entries into variables
$itemNumber      = $itemNumberSearch;
$itemTitle       = $row->itemTitle;
$itemStartingBid = $row->itemStartingBid;

?>
```

At this point in the API process, the API program stores all the field values in memory (by using programming variables). The next step in the API process converts these field entries into the format required by the API documentation.

Step 2: Process the inputs and create an API request

Before creating the API request, your API program must validate each input. Unfortunately, users often enter data that isn't valid for a given field. The API program must check each field entry against the API documentation to ensure that it meets the API's criteria. For example, a numeric field called `Price` needs a value like `5.00`, not `five dollars`.

Almost every API field will have a maximum length, specified in the API documentation. Listing 13-3 illustrates a simple way to check that a field fits. The `CheckLength` function uses a programming function to verify that the `fieldValue` falls within the `maxLength`.

Listing 13-3:   Ensuring a Field Fits with the CheckLength Function

```
<?php

function CheckLength ( $fieldValue, $maxLength )
{
  if ( strlen( $fieldValue ) >= $maxLength ) {
    return 0;
  } else {
    return 1;
  }
}

if ( CheckLength( 'My Field entry text', 10 ) ) {
  echo 'The field entry passes the length test';
} else {
```

```
    echo 'The field entry fails the length test';
}

?>
```

The if statement uses the CheckLength function to see if My Field entry text is less than or equal to the maximum field length, hardcoded as 10. The code outputs a message letting the user know whether the text passed the length test.

Many methods to test entry validity exist. A quick search online reveals numerous Web sites with validation code for almost any problem. E-mail address validation currently ranks as one of the most challenging problems. However, you can likely find a Web site within a few minutes that offers code validating for the type of entry you're working with. Try searching on the terms email validation, date validation, and string validation. To help narrow down the results, include the name of your programming language in the search (for example, PHP email validation).

When your program encounters an invalid entry, it must alert the program's user and get a replacement. The API process returns to Step 1 (described in the preceding section) to correct the faulty data. Simple programs alert users to an error and then make them start over, forcing them to fill in *all* the fields again even if only one was incorrect. More sophisticated programs store the valid entries for the user, requiring the user to fix only the problem entry. During testing, feel free to require a complete restart when you encounter an error. However, consider making your program more user friendly, or you (and your other users) may become frustrated using it.

To find out more about validating field entries, read the *For Dummies* book for your programming language. Take a look at Table 13-3 at the end of this chapter for a list of books to check out.

After your program validates each field, it embarks on the conversion process. Each field must fit into the data format required by the API documentation. The program takes the field entries out of memory and puts them into the API specified format.

Although many data formats exist, the APIs covered in this book all utilize XML. The API documentation details exactly what the XML request must look like. Your program fills in the blanks by using the data gathered in Step 1. The following example shows how your program takes input — in this case hardcoded values — and inserts the input into the appropriate fields inside the XML request. The City value goes inside the <City> tag, the State value goes inside the <State> tag, and so on.

```
<?php

// Store values for use in the XML request
```

```
// (these are hardcoded)
$firm     = 'The White House';
$address1 = '';
$address2 = '1600 Pennsylvania Avenue NW';
$city     = 'Washington';
$state    = 'DC';
$zip5     = '20500';
$zip4     = '';
// Create a variable that contains the XML request
// with each value filled in
$xml = '
<AddressValidateRequest USERID="' . $myAPIUsername . '"
         PASSWORD="' . $myAPIPassword . '">
  <Address ID="0">
    <FirmName>' . $firm . '</FirmName>
    <Address1>' . $address1 . '</Address1>
    <Address2>' . $address2 . '</Address2>
    <City>'    . $city . '</City>
    <State>'   . $state . '</State>
    <Zip5>'    . $zip5 . '</Zip5>
    <Zip4>'    . $zip4 . '</Zip4>
  </Address>
</AddressValidateRequest>
';

?>
```

APIs may allow more than one request *nested* together. Notice that in the preceding example the AddressValidateRequest includes a single address, prefaced with the entry <Address ID="*x*">. This information tells the API server which address the data inside relates to. The API documentation for the USPS Address Validation API allows up to five addresses. The API response uses the address IDs to match up the response for each address with the request. Check your API documentation to see when you can include nested requests. Nested requests save your program time because they don't have to connect to the API server as often.

Step 3: Send the request to the API server

Connecting to the API server and sending the request requires very little code. Web programming languages often include functions that make the connection process quite painless.

Desktop programming languages, on the other hand, may cause some grief. They typically require helper programs or components to open connections to Internet servers. Consult the documentation for your programming language for help.

Sending the XML to the other server isn't necessarily a small task. The Web uses a special encoding scheme to send XML data from one system to another. Some characters have special meaning in the Web world (slashes, spaces, single and double quotes, and so on), depending on the programming language. Your program must replace or *flag* (a process called URL encoding) these characters before sending the XML.

Your program must not skip the encoding process. Thankfully, encoding the XML requires only a line or two of code. Without this encoding, the API server may not understand your request and will likely return an error, and troubleshooting an encoding problem makes for a long day. Unfortunately, only certain characters require encoding, so your program will work fine until you include a character that requires encoding. Your program will plod along without any trouble until one day it can't handle a special entry that requires special encoding. Figuring out encoding problems can make life difficult, so take the time to test thoroughly the first time through.

APIs that transfer sensitive data may require the API connection to take place across a secure (HTTPS) connection. The code to accomplish a secure connection isn't longer or more complicated, but it may require special software. Some programming languages include functions to create an HTTPS connection. For example, PHP requires a programming library called CURL to perform HTTPS connections. CURL allows both HTTP and HTTPS connections, enabling you to use one connection method for both encrypted HTTPS and nonencrypted HTTP connections. Consult your programming language's documentation and your Web host to find out what you have available.

HTTP (unencrypted connections)

PHP's `fputs` function (other programming languages offer a similar command) can, among other things, send information to another computer system. The code in Listing 13-4 packs up information that the USPS API requires and adds special connection settings, called *headers*. Then it opens a connection to the USPS API server by using the `fsockopen` function and finally sends the data.

Listing 13-4: Sending Data to the USPS API

```php
<?php

// Package the request
$request  = '';
$APITitle = 'Verify';
$request  = 'API=' . $APITitle . '&XML=' . $xml;

// Prepare the connection header information
// Transmit the API location and request length
$header  = '';
$header .= "POST /ShippingAPI.dll HTTP/1.0\r\n";
```

(continued)

Listing 13-4 *(continued)*

```
$header .= "Content-type: application/x-www-form-
            urlencoded\r\n";
$header .= "Content-length: " . strlen($request) . "\r\n\r\n";
// Open the connection to the API Server
$APIConnection = fsockopen('production.shippingapis.com', 80,
            &$err_num, &$err_msg, 30);
$postalproblem  = 0;
// Check for a valid API server connection
if ($APIConnection) {
  // Send everything
  fputs( $APIConnection, $header . $request );
}

?>
```

HTTP and HTTPS (encrypted connections)

Offering a simpler way to send API data, CURL (a special program used for transferring information between computers) performs several menial steps in the API process. Unfortunately, not every server has the luxury of using CURL.

You'll notice that the code in Listing 13-5 doesn't include complex header commands because CURL does that for you! Like Listing 13-4, the sample packs up the API data. Then the program uses `curl_` functions to open the connection and send the data. CURL offers an added benefit: The following code also takes care of receiving the response from the API server (covered in the next section).

Listing 13-5: **Using CURL to Send Data to an API**

```
<?php

// Requires the CURL package (http://curl.haxx.se/)
// Package the request
$request  = '';
$APITitle = 'Verify';
$request  = 'API=' . $APITitle . '&XML=' . $xml;

// Create a connection to the API server
$APIConnection = curl_init();
// Set some connection options
curl_setopt( $APIConnection, CURLOPT_URL, "http://production.
            shippingapis.com/ShippingAPI.dll" );
curl_setopt( $APIConnection, CURLOPT_POSTFIELDS, $request );
curl_setopt( $APIConnection, CURLOPT_RETURNTRANSFER, 1 );
// Send the request -- and receive the response
$response = curl_exec( $APIConnection );
curl_close( $APIConnection );

?>
```

Step 4: Receive the API Response

After sending the API request, your program should wait for the API server's response. Your program could simply send the request and exit, but you wouldn't know whether the API server received your request. Most API servers return an answer to the API requests, so ending the program without receiving the response is just as silly as calling a friend, asking a question, and then hanging up before hearing his answer.

Unless the API documentation specifies otherwise, the API response should come back in the same format as the request. The API documentation details what the response looks like and how to interpret the fields.

HTTP

An API application wouldn't be complete if it only sent data. Your program must accept the response from the API server. The following code waits for the API server to respond, storing information as it arrives. After the API server finishes sending the response, the program closes the connection.

The following code in Listing 13-6 replaces the last few lines of Listing 13-4 in Step 3. Listing 13-4 sent the response and then closed. Now in Listing 13-6, the program sends the data and waits for the response.

Listing 13-6:   Sending Data to and Waiting for a Response from the API

```php
<?php

// Continue if the program has a valid API server connection
if ($APIConnection) {
  socket_set_timeout( $APIConnection, 40 );

  // Send everything
  fputs( $APIConnection, $header . $request );

  // Get the response
  $socketstatus = socket_get_status( $APIConnection );
  $response     = '';
  // Keep going until the API server stops sending data
  while ( ( !feof( $APIConnection ) ) && (
          !$socketstatus['timed_out'] ) ) {
    // Check to make sure the connection hasn't closed
    $socketstatus = socket_get_status( $APIConnection );
    // Store another 256 characters of the reponse
    $response .= fgets( $APIConnection, 256 );
  }
}
// Close our connection to the API server
fclose( $APIConnection );

?>
```

HTTP and HTTPS

Because CURL automatically returns the response during the connection process, receiving the response doesn't require any additional code.

Just as your API program encoded the API request, the API server sends an encoded API response. Your programming language may automatically decode the response for you, or you may have to decode it by using a function.

Step 5: Process the response

After the program stores the decoded XML in memory, the API program works through the XML and stores the data. Each field has a value that the API program can discard, if not useful, or save. The API program can store useful values in a database or display them for the user.

Processing the response may pose a challenge if the request and response allow for more than one entry (address, auction item, package, and so on). A package-tracking search request may return a list of different package location entries. The previous address validation example allows the program to request validation of multiple addresses. The API program must handle responses containing one or more entries.

Due to XML's complicated nature, your response processing must strike a balance between extreme complexity and limited functionality. Simple XML parsing code handles the output from the current API, but it may have trouble if the XML changes. Although more complicated processing code can handle anything the API server throws at it, the code may take a long time to develop and test. It's best to stick with something simple that you understand rather than attempt to force a sophisticated XML processor you don't completely understand into your program.

Listing 13-7 uses a simple string function `split` to divide the XML response into manageable pieces. First, the program divides the reponse so that each address falls into its own variable. Then the program stores the address information inside.

Listing 13-7:   Using the split Function to Manage the XML Response

```php
<?php

// Get the XML inside the "AddressValidateResponse" tags
$myAddressList = array();
// Split the XML string into an array so that each array
          index has one address
$addressXMLArray = split("<Address ", getXMLInside(
          'AddressValidateResponse', $xml ) );
// Loop through the array of addresses
```

```
for ($i = 1; $i <= count( $addressXMLArray ) ; $i++) {
   // Store the address items from the XML into array variables
   $myAddressList[ $i ]['FirmName'] = getXMLInside(
            'FirmName', $addressXMLArray[ $i ] );
   $myAddressList[ $i ]['Address1'] = getXMLInside(
            'Address1', $addressXMLArray[ $i ] );
   $myAddressList[ $i ]['Address2'] = getXMLInside(
            'Address2', $addressXMLArray[ $i ] );
   $myAddressList[ $i ]['City']     = getXMLInside( 'City',
            $addressXMLArray[ $i ] );
   $myAddressList[ $i ]['State']    = getXMLInside( 'State',
            $addressXMLArray[ $i ] );
   $myAddressList[ $i ]['Zip5']     = getXMLInside( 'Zip5',
            $addressXMLArray[ $i ] );
   $myAddressList[ $i ]['Zip4']     = getXMLInside( 'Zip4',
            $addressXMLArray[ $i ] );
}

?>
```

Step 6: Display the output

Depending on the API request, your program may display the results of the API process. Simple API conversations require a simple success or failure message, whereas more complicated API requests may involve detailed output.

Output for a complex response may require an API program capable of handling variable size responses. Package-tracking details frequently include a list of package details, including the various stops along the way to delivery. The display for such a response must allow output of each line of delivery status.

Simple output to screen

The simplest method of outputting data from the API response is to display it on the screen. The code in Listing 13-8 works through the myAddressList variable created in Step 5, adding each entry to the Web page:

Listing 13-8:   Displaying the Output on the Screen

```
<?php

// Go through each Address entry in the array
for ( $i = 1; $i < count ( $myAddressList ); $i ++ ) {
   // Output the address number as a heading
   echo "<br><br><b>Address Number $I</b><br>";
```

(continued)

Listing 13-8: *(continued)*

```
  while ( list( $arrayIndex, $arrayValue ) = each(
          $myAddressList[ $i ] ) ) {
    // Output each part of the address
    echo "$arrayIndex: $arrayValue<br>";
  }
}

?>
```

Store results in MySQL Database

Often, it's a good idea to store the data received into your program's data-base so that it's available later. Otherwise, you'd have to perform another API request. The code in Listing 13-9 stores the addresses in a database table:

Listing 13-9: **Storing the Results in a Database Table**

```
<?php

// Hardcoded values for server address, username, password,
// and database name
$server = 'localhost';
$user   = 'myUsername';
$pass   = 'myPassword';
$db     = 'myDBName';
// Using the values above, connect to the database
$link   = mysql_connect($server, $user, $pass);
mysql_select_db( $db, $link );

// Go through the addresses stored in the myAddressList array
for ( $i = 1; $i < count ( $myAddressList ); $i ++ ) {
  // Start the SQL Query
  $query = "INSERT INTO myAddressTable SET ";
  // Get the first set of address components and add to query
  list( $arrayIndex, $arrayValue ) = each( $myAddressList[ $i
          ] );
  $query .= "$arrayIndex='$arrayValue'";
  // Loop through the rest of the address components
  while ( list( $arrayIndex, $arrayValue ) = each(
          $myAddressList[ $i ] ) ) {
    // Add each to the query, with a comma before each
    $query .= ", $arrayIndex='$arrayValue'";
  }
  // Run the SQL query to add the address to mySQL db
  $result = mysql_query( $query, $link );
}

?>
```

The Language Chat

Two broad categories of programming languages exist, those that power dynamic Web sites and those created to write stand-alone applications. Web-based programming languages include PHP, ASP, and Perl. Visual Basic, C++, and Java make up the most common stand-alone, or *desktop,* languages.

Using a programming language designed for desktop development gives you incredible control over the application. From advanced data processing to almost unlimited interface options, desktop languages give you complete flexibility. Desktop languages also appear to run faster (compared to Web languages). Desktop languages suffer from several drawbacks, though. The development software typically costs more than Web languages, and with the amazing flexibility comes a degree of frustration with the number of options and settings you have to contend with.

Web programming languages enjoy simplified interface creation, cross-platform program availability (meaning they can run on any computer with a Web browser), and inexpensive development tools. Unfortunately, they sacrifice flexibility and feel slower than desktop applications (because you must wait for your Internet connection to load each screen).

Your programming language selection will likely depend on what you already have available. Most of the popular programming languages just mentioned have similar capabilities. Differences among programming languages typically don't concern beginning and intermediate programmers.

To make your API development as easy as possible, you'll probably use the language that your Web site host offers. ASP, a Microsoft programming language, runs on Web servers using Microsoft Internet Information Server (IIS), and PHP, an open source language, runs on Linux or UNIX Web servers. Contact your Web host to find out what languages your Web site supports.

Table 13-3 lists programming language resources, all published by Wiley.

Table 13-3	Programming Resource Books
Language	*Book Title*
N/A	*Beginning Programming For Dummies*
PHP	*PHP & MySQL For Dummies*
ASP	*Active Server Pages For Dummies*

(continued)

Table 13-3 *(continued)*

Language	Book Title
.NET	*.NET Web Services For Dummies, ASP.NET For Dummies, Visual Basic .NET Database Programming For Dummies, Visual C++.NET For Dummies*
Perl	*Perl For Dummies*
Visual Basic	*Visual Basic 6 For Dummies* (for Windows)
C++	*C++ For Dummies*
Java	*Beginning Programming with Java For Dummies, Java & XML For Dummies, Java 2 For Dummies*

Chapter 14

Diving into the eBay Developers Program

Many folks claim that geeks are antisocial, but reality paints a very different picture. The Internet overflows with high-tech, geek-focused message boards, user groups, and developer communities. These gatherings of software developers and other technical enthusiasts fill an important need in the vast realm of application programming. Antisocial or not, even the most experienced programmers have difficulties when learning a new language. Online communities make a welcome source of help and support during those stressful times. (Besides, it gives the *really* technical people a safe place to be themselves away from everybody else.)

Online programmer communities give users an outlet for airing their frustrations, finding answers to their questions, and discovering new things they never imagined were possible. Almost every programming language enjoys numerous developer community Web sites and forums — take a look at the Web site listings in Chapter 18! Some developers even gather offline to exchange information and ideas during conferences and trade shows.

eBay values its development community, largely because they know that the company's success depends a great deal on the innovations that developers create for eBay members. That's why eBay launched the aptly named *eBay*

Developers Program. With its combination of resources and communications tools, the Developers Program makes life better for programmers at all skill and interest levels.

This chapter introduces the Developers Program, from the point where you first find the Web site, through registering as a developer and getting your login ID. It also gets into the somewhat complicated world of eBay API licenses (which you first run into during the Developers Program signup process). You also find out about some of the great resources available through the Developers Program, like the discussion areas and the Sandbox, where your applications go to play while you work on them (really, I'm not making this up).

What the eBay Developers Program Does for You

The eBay Developers Program offers many of the same benefits of other online developer communities, giving budding eBay developers a place to find out more information and network with other developers. Most importantly, the Developers Program is your ticket to using the API. You cannot access the eBay API without first joining the Developers Program.

While many online communities offer free membership, eBay does not. Developers seeking to test eBay applications or create programs for their own use slide in relatively cost-free. Individual memberships, geared towards smaller sellers and hobbyists, incur charges only when "certifying" an application for use with eBay's systems (more on that later). Commercial memberships, designed for heavy users of the eBay APIs or those selling eBay software, carry an annual membership fee and incur charges for each API call made after exhausting the monthly ration of free calls. The next section, "Do You Have a License for That API, Sir?" goes into detail about each membership option.

Offering more than just a community of eBay programming enthusiasts, membership in the Developers Program entitles you to begin developing eBay applications with the eBay API tools. (eBay doesn't allow nonmembers to access the API or documentation.) You also find sample code and helper programs, such as the Software Development Kit (SDK), which gives you a jumpstart on your application.

Your eBay Developers Program adventure begins at the program's home page (`developer.ebay.com`), shown in Figure 14-1. The main page offers links to the various program resources as well as the latest program news. You also find links to other helpful pages, including the Developer Education site.

The Developer Education Program offers courses for eBay bidders, sellers, and developers. The program also offers certification for consultants who assist other eBay users and developers seeking to utilize the eBay API. The courses are inexpensive, and most are available online. See the section "Getting with the Program: Discussion, Classes, and More," later in this chapter, for more on this program.

The Developers Program features the API documentation. As Chapter 13 explains, the API documentation details all the available request types and the responses your program should expect. The documentation goes into incredible detail, explaining data types, field sizes, and possible errors.

eBay's comprehensive guide includes an excellent getting started section as well as usage guidelines and several appendixes. The appendixes cover important issues including antispam rules, data types, and details for international API programming.

Program membership also may include paid technical support and the use of eBay marketing tools. Whether you have access to technical support and marketing tools depends on which license tier you choose when joining the program. The next section introduces each membership tier and details the differences.

Do You Have a License for That API, Sir?

eBay requires each Developers Program member to select a license tier during the signup process. Like many memberships, the license tier determines what you get, and how much you pay. Each license tier offers different membership fees, cost per API call performed, support options, and more. Review the options carefully, starting on the inexpensive side as you first get started. If you change your mind later, eBay offers a way to upgrade your license tier. However, you'll have to pay the applicable annual fee.

This section gives you an overview of the available license tier options. Because the Developers Program changes frequently, check the Developers Program Web site for the latest options, features, and pricing structure.

eBay distinguishes their four license tiers into two categories:

✔ The **Individual** license tier (it's the only license tier available in the Individual license category) offers the easiest (and least expensive) entry into the development program. It's designed for individuals and organizations that plan to use the API to support their personal eBay activities only. Individual tier members may not sell their application or allow other eBay members to use it. eBay also limits Individual tier members to 50 API calls on the production server and 5,000 calls to the Sandbox test server per day.

✔ **Commercial** licenses allow you to resell or license your API program to other eBay users. However, you pay a higher cost for that flexibility. Commercial license tier members enjoy unlimited production API calls per day, but eBay charges for each call beyond the monthly ration.

Diving into the eBay Solutions Directory

Designed to showcase the resources available from eBay and third-party eBay developers, the Solutions Directory (located at solutions. ebay.com) offers an alternative to creating an application on your own. If all this talk of APIs, license tiers, fees, and database programming seems a bit daunting, that's okay! The Solutions Directory may already include an application that meets your needs. If not, you'll find plenty of developers willing to help craft a solution, custom-fit to your business.

If you're already an experienced eBay developer (or dream of becoming one), consider listing your solution in the directory. However, you must join one of the Commercial license tiers before eBay allows you to list your application. eBay also limits the number of solutions you may list, based on the license tier you select. Members selecting the Basic, Professional, or Enterprise commercial license tiers receive one, three, or five directory listings, respectively.

eBay differentiates the license tiers by membership and API call fees and what support options are available. eBay affords members joining one of the Commercial license tiers one or more entries in the eBay Solutions Directory (see the "Diving into the eBay Solutions Directory" sidebar), eBay's listing of eBay friendly software and services, and marketing support logos. eBay also offers Platform Notifications (automated messages from eBay to your API program) for commercial licensees. The sections that follow go into detail about each license tier option.

Each license tier includes:

✔ Full access to Developers Program events, news, and training offerings.

✔ Full access to the free technical resources on the Developers Program Web site including the discussion forums and Developers Program newsletter.

✔ Access to eBay's test system, called the *Sandbox*. Individual licensees may send 5,000 API requests per day, whereas Commercial members have unlimited access. (For more on the Sandbox, see "Testing Your Application in the Sandbox," later in this chapter.)

When selecting a license tier, ask yourself the following questions:

✔ **Do you plan to let others use your application?**

If you answered yes, even if you don't plan to sell your program, you must go with one of the three Commercial license tier options. Members selecting the Individual license tier may not distribute their applications to others.

✔ **How many API calls will your application make?**

It's tough to predict how many calls your program will make to perform a given function. When in doubt, go with the Individual license tier. That way, you can test your program and gauge the number of calls you'll really need. Then, if necessary, upgrade your membership later.

The Individual license tier gives members 50 free API calls per day. After that, eBay stops responding to API calls (with two exceptions, covered later). Members selecting one of the three Commercial license tiers enjoy unlimited API calls per day. However, eBay charges a fee for call performs. Fortunately, the Basic Commercial license tier includes 30,000 free API calls each month. To help encourage you to keep selling, eBay allows every member to make unlimited AddItem and RelistItem (the calls used to list a new eBay auction or relist an item that closed) API calls.

If you're planning to write a simple application to support your small eBay business, selling fewer than 200 products a month, you'll probably get along fine with the Individual license tier membership. On the other hand, if you sell a lot of items on eBay and expect to create a powerful auction management system that automatically downloads transaction information, sends feedback, and performs searches, you'll probably need to choose one of the Commercial license tiers.

✔ **Will you need eBay's Paid Technical Support team?**

When you're really in a pinch and need official eBay technical support, eBay offers a dedicated support team. Members who select the Individual tier may not contact the Developer Technical Support team. Only Commercial license tiers may utilize Developer Technical Support.

However, each time you bring a technical issue to the Developer Technical Support team, you rack up a $195 fee (provided they solve your problem within two hours — otherwise, the fee goes up). To help out, eBay includes one or more free support cases with each Commercial license tier.

You can find an in-depth comparison of each license tier (shown in Figure 14-2) at the Developers Program Web site at `developer.ebay.com/DevProgram/membership/services.asp`.

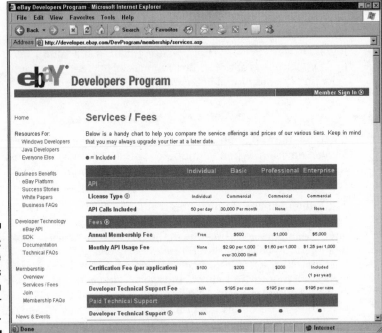

Figure 14-2: The Developers Program License Tier comparison.

Individual license tier

When developing API applications for yourself or your company, the Individual license tier likely fits the bill. With this license tier, eBay forbids you from sharing your application with other eBay members and restricts your application to 50 API calls per day. Unless you expect to use your application heavily, the Individual tier should meet your needs. eBay offers AddItem and RelistItem API calls (used to list a new eBay auction or relist an auction that closed recently) free of charge — a nice benefit! eBay would hate to slow down your auction postings!

With the exception of program certification (more on that later), the Individual tier offers a cost-free avenue for satisfying your API cravings. You don't pay an annual membership fee and you don't pay for API calls. However, you don't have access to Paid Technical Support options, you can make only 50 API calls a day (the rest are blocked — with the exception of AddItem and RelistItem), and you receive no marketing support.

The following list gives an overview of the Individual Tier license terms:

- ✔ No annual membership fee
- ✔ 5,000 free Sandbox API calls per day for testing
- ✔ Development and certification of one program
- ✔ Any applications you write must be self-certified ($100 fee) before you can use them with the live eBay system
- ✔ 50 free API calls per day (AddItem and RelistItem don't count against your daily limit)
- ✔ No paid technical support options

Although you must live within the API call limits, the price is right.

Commercial license tiers

If you want the ability to resell your application or need more than 50 API calls per day, select one of the Commercial license tiers. To cater to differing developer needs, eBay offers three different Commercial license tiers: Basic, Professional, and Enterprise.

All three Commercial tiers share the following features:

- ✔ Unlimited Sandbox API calls for testing
- ✔ Creation of multiple applications (the Individual tier allows only one)

✔ As with the Individual tier, free AddItem and RelistItem calls (which don't count toward included monthly API calls for the Basic Commercial license tier)

The key differences between the three tiers revolve around the fee structure, included API calls, paid technical support, and Solutions Directory listings. The Basic license tier is cheapest with a $500 annual membership fee. Annual fees for the Professional and Enterprise license tiers ring in at $1,000 and $5,000, respectively.

The following list gives an overview of the terms for each of the three Commercial license tiers:

✔ Annual membership fee: $500 for Basic, $1,000 for Professional, and $5,000 for Enterprise

✔ Unlimited Sandbox access free of charge

✔ Certification of multiple applications

✔ Certification fee of $200 per application

✔ API call pricing as follows:

  • **Basic license tier:** 30,000 API calls per month free of charge. API calls above 30,000 cost $2.90 per 1,000.

  • **Professional license tier:** No free API calls. Calls cost only $1.60 per 1,000.

  • **Enterprise license tier:** $1.25 per 1,000 API calls with no free calls included.

From a cost perspective, the Basic license tier offers the lowest fees until you hit around 100,000 API calls per month. The Professional license tier offers the lowest fees if you have between 500,000 and 1,000,000 API calls per month. After you hit 1,000,000 API calls a month, the Enterprise license tier delivers the best deal at a measly $20,000 for API calls and the annual membership fee. If you can afford $20,000 in annual eBay API fees, put this book down and give the authors a call, because we're always available for rent or long-term lease.

Joining the Developers Program

Your journey into the world of API programming starts when you join the eBay Developers Program. After you've signed up, you enjoy access to the API documentation, Sandbox API test server, and developer community. With your membership in hand, you can begin creating tools to make your life easier.

Before you start the membership application, you must have an eBay user ID and password. If you haven't registered with eBay yet, visit the eBay home page and then click the Register link at the top of the page. Registration takes only a few minutes. After you have an eBay user ID in hand, follow these steps to join the Developers Program:

1. **Click the Member Sign In link at** `developer.ebay.com`**. Then click the Join link next to the Not Yet a Member heading. Finally, click the Join Now button.**

   The five-page membership form walks you through entering relevant contact details, choosing your license tier, and indicating your acceptance of the eBay developer license. The process takes five to ten minutes.

2. **On the first page of the membership form, fill in the information for you or your company as well as contact information for the primary business contact, primary developer, and accounts payable contact.**

   If you're planning to develop API applications for yourself, the membership form goes pretty quickly. You can indicate that the Primary Developer and Accounts Payable contacts match the Primary Business contact. Otherwise, you need to enter the contact details for each individual in your organization.

3. **Enter the PayPal e-mail account address you will use to pay any API fees.**

   Don't panic! If you choose the Individual license tier, you don't pay for Sandbox use when testing your application. The only fee you pay is the certification fee, should you choose to go down that road.

4. **Complete the Intended API Use section, selecting the appropriate responses from the drop-down lists.**

5. **Complete the You, Your Company, and eBay sections. When you're done, click Next.**

   Page 2 of the membership form appears, which reviews the basic differences between the Individual and Commercial API licenses.

6. **Look over the license options, verify that you're at least 18 years old and are authorized to enter into legal contracts on behalf of your company, and then click Next to head to page 3.**

7. **On page 3, select one of the four API licenses.**

   Take one last moment to review the choices because this decision greatly impacts your interactions with eBay. Down the road, you can upgrade, but it will require a new API license.

8. **After selecting your license tier, select the Developer Technical Support Tier you need.**

   Members selecting the Individual license tier must choose the Individual Tier support option. Commercial license tiers enjoy the upgraded Per Case Tier support.

9. **Check the box next to each permitted API feature you plan to support in your program. Click Next.**

   The page automatically disables features not available within the selected license tier. Page 4 appears, with more terms to accept.

10. **Select the check boxes to signify that you agree to the terms and conditions for the API license. Click Next.**

    The next page includes any additional terms and conditions you must agree to based on the API uses you select.

11. **Enter your eBay user ID and password on page 5 to complete the API signup process.**

Getting with the Program: Discussion, Classes, and More

To encourage developers to use the eBay API, eBay offers several tools to help you get started with the Developers Program and keep up-to-date. The eBay Developer Education Program, Developer Newsletter, Weblog, and Developer Community Forums offer insight into the development process.

As a member of the eBay Developers Program, take advantage of every support tool available. You'll save yourself time and energy when you lean on the experience and understanding of others. Chances are, if you're dealing with a problem or question, someone else has already been there.

Figure 14-3 shows the Developers Program process diagram (available at developer.ebay.com/DevProgram/membership/overview.asp). This chapter and Chapter 15 walk you through everything you need to work through the process quickly.

Developer Education Program

The eBay Developer Education Program (developer.ebay.com/education/) offers official training from eBay. Available in instructor-led and online learning formats, the classes cover a broad range of topics. From basics like *Lifecycle of an eBay Listing* to *Building and Maintaining a Robust eBay Application,* the Developer Education Program covers the topics necessary to quickly bring you up to speed on eBay development.

Figure 14-3:
The eBay
API
develop-
ment
process.

You can take classes a la carte or as a series with an eye toward one of eBay's certifications. The eBay Certified Engineer and eBay Certified Consultant certifications offer interested individuals an opportunity to demonstrate their technical skills. The Consultant certification leans more towards the "nontechnical" side of eBay, whereas the Engineer certification focuses on programming expertise. If you're looking to offer your services to help other eBay members, the Consultant certification is for you. If you're more interested in developing API programs, go with the Engineer certification.

eBay charges relatively low fees for online courses. Courses typically cost between $25 and $70, and certification exams cost $150. Although the courses offer an excellent foundation for passing the certification exams, eBay doesn't guarantee that you'll pass after taking the suggested preparation courses.

Newsletters and Weblog

eBay gives you several tools for staying up-to-date with the growing developer community. eBay's Developer Newsletter offers a periodic update via e-mail for eBay developers (available online at `developer.ebay.com/DevZone/community/newsletter/`). The newsletter offers news about Developers

Program changes, upcoming events, and links to other helpful resources. Best of all, eBay maintains an extensive archive of previous newsletters, so you'll find over 30 past newsletters to pore over (in your copious free time).

Weblogs (*blogs* in online slang) have quickly become one of the Web's biggest trends. Weblogs center around posts, similar to journal entries, organized by date and topic. Members can even post comments about the posts. The Developers Program Weblog includes regular posts on many topics of interest to eBay developers.

Often less formal than other modes of communication, the blog gives you an inside look at what's new on eBay. Frequently, the most timely information shows up on the Developers Program Weblog. Like the Developer Newsletter, the blog (at `ebaydeveloper.typepad.com`) maintains an extensive archive going back to early 2004.

Community forums

Online forums ring in as one of the Internet's most important contributions to software development. By giving developers a place to discuss and collaborate on applications, forums speed up the programming process.

In the eBay community forums, you'll find help from other developers just like you as well as eBay's technical support staff. If you're struggling with a particular API call or concept, someone else probably has already figured out an answer or can help you find one. You'll be amazed at the level of expertise that forum members have. With few exceptions, other members offer solid advice and solutions, saving you precious time.

After you're familiar with the APIs, take time to read the message boards. You may have an opportunity to help someone else out.

Testing Your Application in the Sandbox

After joining the Developers Program, you probably want to get your program started. The Sandbox is a safe place to test your program without worrying about ringing up a significant eBay listing fee bill on the production servers.

The Sandbox, shown in Figure 14-4, acts like a mini-eBay, although every item and transaction are fictional. You can register an account, list auctions, place bids, and more. The Developers Program Web site includes a complete list of supported features at `developer.ebay.com/DevZone/get-started/sandbox.asp`.

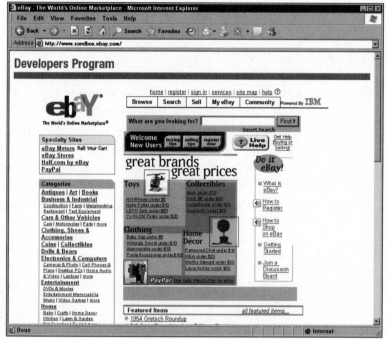

Figure 14-4:
The
developer
Sandbox
(which looks
a lot like
eBay).

To use the Sandbox, you need to register test users. To create (and validate) a Sandbox test user, follow these steps:

1. **Go to the Sandbox Web site at** `sandbox.ebay.com`. **Click Sign In at the top of the page and then click the Register button.**

2. **Complete the registration form, using a working e-mail address.**

   Because the Sandbox operates just like eBay, you must enter information that eBay can verify during the registration process. Be sure to remember the user IDs and passwords for your test users.

3. **Click I Accept This Agreement.**

   Even though you're not really registering on eBay (or actually accepting the terms of the agreement), you must still click the I Accept This Agreement button to continue the registration process.

   The Sandbox site e-mails you at the e-mail address provided.

4. **After you receive the confirmation e-mail from the Sandbox site, click the confirmation URL in the e-mail.**

   You must click the confirmation URL to complete the registration process.

5. **Get your API security keys (if you haven't already).**

   When you register with the Developers Program, you should receive an e-mail with your API security keys (an App ID, Cert ID, and Dev ID). If not, you can request another copy at `developer.ebay.com/DevZone/ContactUs.asp`.

6. **Point your browser to the API Test Tool, shown in Figure 14-5, at** `developer.ebay.com/DevZone/Build-Test/test-tool.asp`.

7. **Select Sandbox from the Host drop-down list and then paste in your Dev ID, App ID, and Cert ID. Enter your test user's user ID and password.**

8. **Select ValidateTestUserRegistration from the Select a Request Template drop-down list. Then click Submit.**

   The XML should automatically fill in your username and password in the appropriate XML tags.

   After you click Submit, the Sandbox returns a response.

9. **Take a look at the response that the Sandbox returns.**

   The message inside the Status should read `Success`. If not, eBay encountered a problem with the ValidateTestUserRegistration API call. Read the request XML for any error messages and then go back to Step 6 and try again.

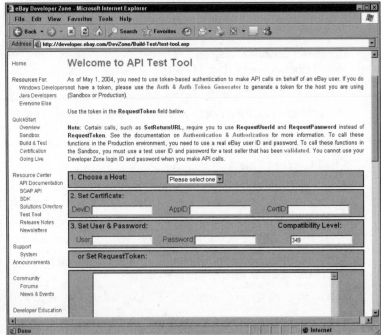

Figure 14-5:
eBay
Developers
Program
API Test
Tool.

After you've registered a test user on the Sandbox, you're ready to begin posting auctions and placing fictional bids.

Whether you chose the Individual or Commercial license, you'll have plenty of Sandbox API calls available to test your program. Although the Individual license limits you to 5,000 API calls to the Sandbox per day (Commercial licensees enjoy unlimited access), that should be more than enough for most development projects.

The Last Step: Certifying Your eBay Application

After you've thoroughly tested your program in the Sandbox, you can certify your application for use with the live eBay servers. Without certification, eBay doesn't allow access to the production servers that host real auctions. Certification ensures that applications pass eBay's usage guidelines and use the API efficiently.

Members who select the Individual license tier work through a different certification process than those who choose one of the Commercial license tiers:

- **Individual** license tier developers may complete the self-certification process with a reduced fee. However, programs passing the self-certification process receive limited access (only 50 API calls per day), and eBay actively monitors the program for compliance with certification guidelines.

- Members who choose one of the **Commercial** license tiers may complete the standard certification process, which utilizes an eBay support staff member for application review. After reviewing your application, the staff member provides a test plan that your program must successfully execute.

Applications may have to pass a recertification if eBay makes substantial changes to the API license or if your program changes "significantly." eBay defines significant changes as using new API calls, adding new features that use API calls (even if you've used the API call before), or changing the frequency of an API call. Your program may also require recertification if eBay revokes your certification (should your application fail to comply with your license).

The standard certification process typically takes between five and seven days, and the self-certification proceeds at your pace. You can complete the self-certification requirements as quickly as you like. Unfortunately, if you need your application certified in a hurry, eBay doesn't offer a priority certification option, so you'll definitely want to plan ahead. However, be careful to ensure that your application is ready because a failed certification effort requires recertification — and payment of another certification fee.

eBay offers an excellent overview of the development process that includes answers to frequently asked questions about the Sandbox and application certification at `developer.ebay.com/DevProgram/membership/overview.asp`. Click a specific process component for more details.

Chapter 15

Exploring the eBay API

In This Chapter

▶ Talking with eBay via the API

▶ Using eBay's new security scheme

▶ Moving forward with the eBay API

eBay's API gives you (and perhaps your customers) an opportunity to bypass the eBay Web site. The API provides almost all seller-related functionality that the Web site offers. However, instead of having to use the sometimes clunky Web interface, you can develop programs that quickly and efficiently perform transactions for you.

Posting even a handful of auctions manually through the Web interface can be time-consuming. Instead of having to enter each auction by hand, your API program can pull item information from a database and then begin the auctions automatically. Interested in speeding up the auction close process? No problem; the API can help automate feedback and gather bidder details. eBay's API offers almost limitless possibilities.

Preparing for a Conversation with the API

eBay's API supports two different *protocols* (computer communication languages) for sending your API transactions to eBay. Both XML over HTTPS (a secure Web communication language) and the SOAP API protocols offer access to eBay's databases. As a developer, you can choose whichever protocol you prefer or are most comfortable working with. Here's a brief rundown of the two protocols:

✔ **XML over HTTPS:** The XML API offers the broadest programming language support. Many languages offer XML support and can handle HTTPS communication. eBay began support for the XML API in November 2000. Unfortunately, the XML API requires the most complicated programmatic processing to communicate with eBay. The program must handle conversion of program data into XML and decode the response XML into program readable variables.

✔ **SOAP API protocol:** To make life easier, eBay released support for the SOAP API protocol in March 2004. Although SOAP requires a special SOAP client program to operate, it gives developers an opportunity to delegate the often tedious API communication process. SOAP takes care of the communication between your application and eBay, simplifying many troublesome issues including data conversion into XML, input validation, and response decoding. SOAP automatically translates program variables into API language and back again. Unfortunately, eBay's API calls available via SOAP and programming language support aren't as extensive as the XML API. You can find out more about eBay's SOAP progress at `developer.ebay.com/DevZone/soap.asp`.

As an alternative to XML over HTTPS and the SOAP API protocol, eBay offers a special *Software Development Kit* (SDK). The SDK simplifies the development process by alleviating the need to deal with XML and HTTPS communication, similar to SOAP. Unfortunately, shortcuts in the development world come at a price. Here are some downsides to using the SDK:

✔ Doesn't offer as much flexibility as the XML API for changing how your application communicates with eBay

✔ Supports only the Microsoft Windows platform, leaving UNIX, Linux, and Mac developers in the dark

✔ Provides very technical documentation, making it difficult for new programmers to effectively use the SDK

On the plus side, the SDK provides a foundation for developing eBay applications rapidly. Taking care of much of the communication grunt work, the SDK lets you focus on adding features, not digging through complex API communication protocols. However, despite its timesaving features, you may want to steer clear of the SDK unless you're an experienced programmer.

The following two examples show the difference between the XML API and the SDK. The XML API must handle the troublesome details of connecting to and communicating with eBay. The SDK handles the challenging details, making the code shorter and easier to read. Choose the method (XML API or SDK) that works best for you.

Getting the `GeteBayOfficialTime` via the XML API looks like this:

```php
<?php

// Build API Request
$eBayRequest = '<?xml version="1.0" encoding="iso-8859-1" ?>
<request>
  <RequestUserId>xxxxxx</RequestUserId>
  <RequestPassword>xxxxxx</RequestPassword>
  <ErrorLevel>0</ErrorLevel>
  <DetailLevel>0</DetailLevel>
  <Verb>GeteBayOfficialTime</Verb>
</request>';

$eBayHeaders = array (
            "X-EBAY-API-COMPATIBILITY-LEVEL: 349",
            "X-EBAY-API-DEV-NAME: xxxxxx",
            "X-EBAY-API-APP-NAME: xxxxxx",
            "X-EBAY-API-CERT-NAME: xxxxxx",
            "X-EBAY-API-CALL-NAME: GeteBayOfficialTime",
            "X-EBAY-API-SITEID: 0",
            "X-EBAY-API-DETAIL-LEVEL: 0"
);

// Requires the CURL package (http://curl.haxx.se/)
$APIConnection = curl_init();
curl_setopt ( $APIConnection, CURLOPT_SSL_VERIFYHOST, 0);
curl_setopt ( $APIConnection, CURLOPT_SSL_VERIFYPEER, 0);

curl_setopt( $APIConnection, CURLOPT_HTTPHEADER,
            $eBayHeaders); // Set the eBay Headers
curl_setopt( $APIConnection, CURLOPT_URL,
            'https://api.sandbox.ebay.com/ws/api.dll' );
curl_setopt( $APIConnection, CURLOPT_POST, 1 );
curl_setopt( $APIConnection, CURLOPT_POSTFIELDS, $eBayRequest
            );
curl_setopt( $APIConnection, CURLOPT_RETURNTRANSFER, 1 );

$response = curl_exec( $APIConnection );
curl_close( $APIConnection );

// Output only the contents of the EbayTime tag
ereg( "<EBayTime>.+</EBayTime>", $response, $responseArray );
echo $responseArray[0];

?>
```

Retrieving the `GeteBayOfficialTime` API call via the SDK is much shorter than the preceding XML API:

```php
<?php

// Set up an API session with the COM SDK component
// Replace the "xxxxxxx" values with your details
$apiSession = new COM("eBay.SDK.API.ApiSession");
$apiSession->Developer      = 'xxxxxx'; // DevName
$apiSession->Application     = 'xxxxxx'; // AppName
$apiSession->Certificate     = 'xxxxxx'; // CertName
// Be sure to use a Sandbox Username/password
$apiSession->RequestUserId   = 'xxxxxx'; // eBay Username
$apiSession->RequestPassword = 'xxxxxx'; // eBay Password
$apiSession->Url             =
          "https://api.sandbox.ebay.com/ws/api.dll";

// Create an eBay Time call
$apiTime = new COM("eBay.SDK.API.GeteBayOfficialTimeCall");
$apiTime->ApiCall->ErrorLevel = 1;
$apiTime->ApiCall->ApiCallSession = $apiSession;

// Execute (and output) the eBay official time
echo $apiTime->GeteBayOfficialTime();

?>
```

Before you get started with the eBay API, you need to register with the eBay Developers Program and create a Sandbox test user, as covered in Chapter 14. After you have your Developers Program membership and have validated your test user (using the eBay API Test Tool, which is explained in Chapter 14), you're ready to get moving on your API program.

Implementing eBay's Authentication and Authorization Process

Before getting started with the main eBay API calls, you need to set up your application to handle eBay's new Authentication and Authorization (called *Auth and Auth* for short) process. Working through the example in this section, you perform your first API calls and gather code samples to help you build your own API application. Throughout this section, you implement several different API calls, building a foundation for integrating eBay's other API calls into your application. The Auth and Auth process is one of the more challenging in API programming. When you finish adding Auth and Auth to your application, you're ready to dive into eBay's other API calls.

On May 1, 2004, eBay changed its user authentication process. Programs can no longer store eBay user IDs or passwords. Instead, eBay has created a new process that offers improved security by giving applications a method for accessing eBay on behalf of a user without having access to the user's eBay user ID and password. Instead of sending an eBay user ID and password with API requests, eBay requires something new: an *authentication token* (also called a request token). The authentication token acts like a passcode into the eBay API on behalf of the user. More importantly, authentication tokens expire after a certain period of time (as determined by eBay). This ensures that an application can't access eBay on the user's behalf indefinitely. eBay users can even revoke authentication tokens (causing them to expire) on the My eBay page.

eBay offers two methods for your program to create an authentication token:

✔ **Use a token generated on eBay's Developers Program Web site (with the authentication token generator):** This method is simple and makes getting your first eBay application started much easier. If you're developing an application under the Individual tier license, you probably want to go with this option. (See Chapter 14 for more on licenses and tiers.)

✔ **Send users through eBay's login system:** This option makes sense for Commercial tier applications that must support many eBay users.

After eBay generates a token, it maintains the token record until the expiration date. If the user logs in with your application, eBay sends the existing token to your application instead of generating a new token. To help your application, eBay includes a special token `Expiration` tag inside each API response when a token will expire within seven days. When the expiration notice begins appearing, your program can automatically prompt you to generate a new token.

Before diving into the token generation options, your application must have a unique identifier (required by the authentication system). Two applications using the same identifier by accident will experience problems accessing the API. The identifier tells eBay which application to forward token generation requests to. Simple applications likely need only a single unique identifier. More complicated applications may want to handle token requests differently depending on the location inside the program; in such cases, multiple unique identifiers may make sense.

eBay offers two methods for creating your unique identifier, called an `RuName` (see the "Authentication and Authorization" section of the API documentation for the latest information at `developer.ebay.com/DevZone/docs/API_Doc/Developing/AuthAndAuth.htm`):

✔ **Create your own identifier:** You can develop your own unique identifier. However, a chance exists that you'll choose the same identifier as another developer, causing problems for both of you. To reduce this risk, eBay recommends that you create an identifier with the form `company_identifier-application_name-use_case_identifier`:

- `company_identifier`: A value that relates to your company name

- `application_name`: Your application's name

- `use_case_identifier`: Which part of your application the `RuName` relates to

Each portion of the identifier should contain no spaces or special characters. For ease of use, choose only letters and numbers, using the underscore (_) character in place of spaces.

✔ **Get an eBay-assigned identifier:** To guarantee that your `RuName` doesn't conflict with another application, eBay offers a special administrative API call: `GetRuName`. The `GetRuName` call generates a unique identifier for you. Your program doesn't need to call the `GetRuName` on a regular basis; instead, you create an `RuName` (or several if you have the need) during development. The code that follows creates an `RuName` for your application.

The identifier method you choose depends on the kind of application you're trying to create. For applications you create for yourself under the Individual tier, you'll likely create your own identifier because a conflict with another application wouldn't create massive chaos. Commercial applications, on the other hand, can't afford any incompatibility issues, so having eBay assign an identifier makes more sense. After you have your `RuName` in hand, you're ready to develop your token generation process.

This chapter uses a block of shared code for every example. To make the examples work, you must include the section of shared code in Listing 15-2. The shared code includes programming comments that mark the beginning and end of the shared code. The CD includes the code shown in this chapter.

The following API call example (Listings 15-1 and 15-2) includes the shared code that you need for other examples in this chapter. The first section, Listing 15-1, goes at the top of your program. The code in Listing 15-2 goes after it.

Listing 15-1:   Code Specific to This API Call

```php
<?php

// Modify these values for your sandbox or production
// UserID and password. Used only for "administrative"
// API calls like GetRuName and SetReturnURL
```

```
$eBayUserID    = 'xxxxxxxxx';
$eBayPassword = 'xxxxxxxxx';

// Optional values
// You may optionally add a "UseCaseID" that allows
// your application to handle multiple RuNames
$appCaseID     = '';

// API Call Name
$eBayCallName = 'GetRuName';

// Build API Request
$eBayRequest = '<?xml version="1.0" encoding="iso-8859-1" ?>
<request>
  <RequestUserId>' . $eBayUserID . '</RequestUserId>
  <RequestPassword>' . $eBayPassword . '</RequestPassword>
  <Verb>' . $eBayCallName . '</Verb>';
// Determine whether to add optional UseCaseID
if ( $appCaseID <> '' )
  $eBayRequest .= '  <UseCaseId>' . $appCaseID .
        '</UseCaseId>';
$eBayRequest .= '
</request>';
```

Listing 15-2:   Shared Code Used by Other API Calls

```
//
// SHARED CODE
// Use the code below this point for other API
// calls later in this chapter
// Some values may require changes for API version
// or eBay country code (SiteID)
//

//
// REMEMBER: Modify these values to match your application
//
$eBayDevName  = 'xxxxxxxxx';
$eBayAppName  = 'xxxxxxxxx';
$eBayCertName = 'xxxxxxxxx';
// This code won't work unless you update the values above

$eBaySiteID         = '0';   // Change to match your country
                             // See API docs for details
$eBayDetail         = '0';
$eBayCompatibility = '349'; // This will change as eBay
                             // updates the API

$eBayHeaders = array (
        "X-EBAY-API-COMPATIBILITY-LEVEL: " .
        $eBayCompatibility,
```

(continued)

Listing 15-2 *(continued)*

```
            "X-EBAY-API-SESSION-CERTIFICATE: " . $eBayDevName
        . ';' . $eBayAppName . ';' . $eBayCertName,
            "X-EBAY-API-DEV-NAME: " . $eBayDevName,
            "X-EBAY-API-APP-NAME: " . $eBayAppName,
            "X-EBAY-API-CERT-NAME: " . $eBayCertName,
            "X-EBAY-API-CALL-NAME: " . $eBayCallName,
            "X-EBAY-API-SITEID: " . $eBaySiteID,
            "X-EBAY-API-DETAIL-LEVEL: " . $eBayDetail
);

// Requires the CURL package (http://curl.haxx.se/)
$APIConnection = curl_init();
curl_setopt ( $APIConnection, CURLOPT_SSL_VERIFYHOST, 0);
curl_setopt ( $APIConnection, CURLOPT_SSL_VERIFYPEER, 0);

curl_setopt( $APIConnection, CURLOPT_HTTPHEADER,
            $eBayHeaders); // Set the eBay Headers
curl_setopt( $APIConnection, CURLOPT_URL,
            'https://api.sandbox.ebay.com/ws/api.dll' );
curl_setopt( $APIConnection, CURLOPT_POST, 1 );
curl_setopt( $APIConnection, CURLOPT_POSTFIELDS, $eBayRequest
            );
curl_setopt( $APIConnection, CURLOPT_RETURNTRANSFER, 1 );

$response = curl_exec( $APIConnection );
curl_close( $APIConnection );

//
// End SHARED CODE
//


//
// Debug code -- include when calling administrative
// API calls (like GetRuName and SetReturnURL or when
// testing your API code)
//

echo '
<html>
<body>
  <textarea cols="60" rows="10">' . $eBayRequest .
            '</textarea>
  <br>
  <textarea cols="60" rows="10">' . $response . '</textarea>
</body>
</html>';

//
// End debug code
//

?>
```

Using an authentication token from the token generator

For your Individual tier application, the easiest solution for developing your program is to use an authentication token generated by the Developers Program token generator. Tokens typically last for 18 months (although eBay may change the length of time), so you don't have to worry about updating them very often. Keep in mind, however, that this method limits your program's flexibility because you need to manually generate a token and input it into your application for each eBay account. Figure 15-1 shows the eBay Developers Program token generator.

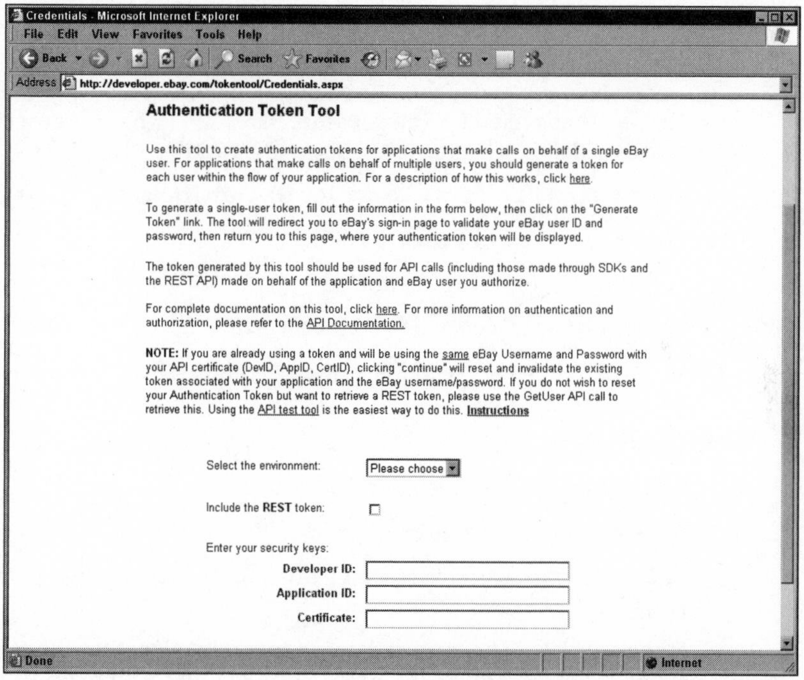

Figure 15-1: Developers Program token generator.

Your program can store the resulting authentication tokens from the token generator in a database or as a hardcoded variable entry in your program, or your program can request that users input (likely using Copy and Paste) the token each time they use the program.

Because the authentication token gives the program access to eBay on the user's behalf (with the user's user ID and password), you must treat it carefully. You should evaluate the location in which you store the token to ensure that others can't access it. If you suspect that someone else has a copy of your token, be sure to log into eBay and revoke the token. (To do so, log into My eBay and go to the eBay Preferences section. Under the Authorization Settings, you find a list of applications you've granted tokens to.)

Follow this process to create an authentication token with the token generator:

1. **Open eBay's Token Tool Web page at** `developer.ebay.com/ tokentool/Credentials.aspx`.

2. **Select the appropriate option from the Select the Environment drop-down list.**

   Choose the Sandbox option during testing and the Production option when you begin using your application. Ignore the Include REST Token option. That's used for the separate REST API (which is described in the nearby sidebar "Digging into eBay's REST API").

3. **Enter your API security keys (Dev ID, App ID, and Cert ID).**

4. **Click Continue to Generate Token.**

   The eBay Login page appears.

5. **Enter your user's user ID and password.**

   Use your test user credentials when creating a Sandbox authentication token.

6. **Click Sign In.**

   The Authorization page appears.

7. **Accept the authorization.**

   This is used to warn users that a third party will be using eBay on their behalf.

8. **Make a copy of the authentication token by selecting the token inside the text box and choosing Edit⇨Copy in your Web browser. You may want to paste the token into a document for use later.**

With an authentication token in hand, you can add it to your application's database, store it directly in the program code using a variable, or create a process in which users of your program enter the token in a form. Whichever method you choose, remember to safeguard your token so that no one can use eBay on your behalf without your permission.

Digging into eBay's REST API

eBay recently released an exciting new addition to the Developers Program, the Representational State Transfer (which gives it the clever acronym *REST*) API. The new API represents a significant departure from the existing XML and SDK APIs. First — and most impressively — REST doesn't require certification, allowing you to begin using the API on the production eBay system immediately. Better still, eBay doesn't charge for API calls through REST, making it a great choice if you're on a budget. Although the REST API offers only the `GetSearchResults` (used to search for eBay listings), it requires far fewer steps to set up and use than the full-fledged eBay API.

In its first incarnation, the REST API only helps you create a custom eBay search program inside your Web site or application. You control all the search parameters and features. Want to limit your users to only view your auctions? No problem! Best of all, you control how the search results look inside your Web site or application.

REST just recently joined the pool of tools in eBay's Developers Program, so nobody knows much about it yet. That should change soon, though, thanks to eBay's excellent REST API documentation and sample applications for ASP, ASP.NET, JavaScript, JSP, Perl, and PHP. As the REST API matures, you'll likely see it include many features beyond mere searching.

For the latest information about the eBay REST API, check out the following resources:

- ✔ **eBay's REST API site:** `developer.ebay.com/devprogram/resources/rest.asp`

- ✔ **REST API documentation:** `developer.ebay.com/devprogram/resources/eBayRESTAPIGuide.pdf`

Generating an authentication token dynamically

For commercial API applications, dynamic authentication token generation is the only viable solution. Your application must handle multiple users and token expirations (eBay currently validates a token for 18 months, after which it must be renewed). You need to evaluate how or if your program will store authentication tokens. Storing the tokens in a database or cookie makes it easier for users to pop in and use your application without having to enter their user IDs and passwords. If you decide to store your users' tokens, you must protect them carefully; tokens offer almost the same access to eBay as a username and password. If you decide not to store the tokens, instead holding them in memory until your program closes, your users will have to log in (either generating a new token or forwarding an existing token to your application). Of course if you don't store them, you don't have to worry about anyone stealing them!

Your program must perform several important functions to successfully implement automatic token generation:

✔ Employ a system for receiving authentication tokens from eBay after users log in. Applications perform this process differently depending on the type of application:

• **Web-based applications:** Due to the connected nature of Web-based applications, eBay's token generation process can send the token directly to the application. The application must first register URLs for successful and failed token generation attempts that eBay will send the authentication token to.

• **Desktop applications:** Because these programs typically cannot receive a token directly from eBay, the application must request the token (using the `FetchToken` API) after the user finishes entering the user ID and password.

✔ Send users to the eBay Web site to create a token and then process the result.

✔ Watch for token expiration (due to passing the expiration date, a user revoking the token, or eBay suspending the token due to suspicious activity).

To accept tokens from eBay, applications have several challenges to overcome. eBay's authentication token process isn't easy to implement, but the following sections help guide you through it.

No matter which type of application you're creating, Web-based or desktop, you must first send the user to eBay to sign in, creating or retrieving the authentication token.

Sending the user to eBay to create or retrieve a token

You need to send your users to eBay to create or retrieve a token when the application doesn't have a token on file or the token is about to expire (noted by the expiration tags in all API responses). When your program needs to fetch a token for the user, it must forward the user to eBay's Web site sign-in page. The production eBay site and Sandbox have different sign-in URLs:

✔ **Sandbox:** `https://signin.sandbox.ebay.com/ws/eBayISAPI.dll?SignIn`

✔ **Production:** `https://signin.ebay.com/ws/eBayISAPI.dll?SignIn`

Your application must include an `RuName` with the sign-in address and may include additional variables in the `RuParams` parameter. However, you must encode the variables in `RuParams` before including them; Listing 15-3 shows how. Your program receives the `RuParams` included in the response from eBay after the user signs in.

Listing 15-3: Sending the User to eBay to Create or Retrieve a Token

```php
<?php

$RuName  = 'xxxxxxxxxx';
$eBaySignInURL =
            'https://signin.sandbox.ebay.com/ws/eBayISAPI.dll?
            SignIn';

// Optional variables to include
$myVar1  = 'ProgramLocationA';
$myVar2  = 'CurrentActionC';
// Pack up the variables in a request string
$RuParams = 'myVar1=' . $myVar1 . '&myVar2=' . $myVar2;

// Send the user to eBay for signin (encoding the RuParams)
header( 'location: ' . $eBaySignInURL . '&runame=' . $RuName
        . '&ruparams=' . urlencode( $RuParams ) );
exit;

?>
```

Depending on what type of application you're creating, you need to communicate with eBay to retrieve the token resulting from the user's sign-in process. The following sections walk you through the steps necessary to retrieve the token after the user signs in. If your program can accept an HTTPS connection (most Web-based applications can), you probably want to use the Web-based application method, although you have the option of implementing the desktop application method. Desktop applications typically cannot accept an HTTPS connection from eBay and need to implement the desktop application method.

Web-based applications

Programmers creating Web-based applications have an easier time dealing with the authentication process. Rather than contacting eBay after the sign-in process to request the token (the way desktop applications must), your application registers a set of URLs that eBay contacts, automatically sending the token to your program.

To set up your application for accepting tokens from eBay, you need to follow two key steps:

1. **You must first register return URLs (one for successful logins and one for failed logins) with eBay.**

   The API sends the token to the registered URL after the user completes the sign-in process.

2. **You need to customize your application so that it can accept tokens that eBay sends to the URLs you registered.**

Return URLs may not use standard HTTP connections. Instead, due to the private nature of tokens, your accept and reject URLs must reside at an encrypted (HTTPS) URL. Be sure that you place your return URL processing scripts in your Web site's HTTPS area. (Check with your system administrator for help loading HTTPS pages.) The return URLs can't use query strings (myReturnURL.php?action=success), so you need to create two separate files: one for the successful token generation and one for failed attempts. To register your return URLs for the token generation process, your program uses the SetReturnURL API call. Be sure to create an RuName first because you need it to call SetReturnURL. Listing 15-4 demonstrates the SetReturnURL code.

If you've chosen an RuName already in use by another application, the API reports an error. Also, you can't use the add action more than once for the same RuName, or the API returns an error. If you need to make changes to the return URLs for a given RuName, use the update action.

Don't forget to include the shared code from Listing 15-2, earlier in this chapter. The following snippet won't work without it. To make life easier, you'll find the complete code (with shared sections already included) on the CD.

Listing 15-4:   Registering Your Return URLs for Token Generation

```php
<?php

// Modify these values for your sandbox or production
// UserID and password. Used only for "administrative"
// API calls like GetRuName and SetReturnURL
$eBayUserID      = 'xxxxxxxxx';
$eBayPassword    = 'xxxxxxxxx';

// Required Values
// Be sure to modify these values to match your
// application's URLs
$returnURLAction  = 'add'; // add, update, or delete
$returnURLRuName  = 'xxxxxxx';
$returnURLAccept  =
          'https://www.mywebsite.com/accept.php';
$returnURLReject  =
          'https://www.mywebsite.com/reject.php';

// Optional values
// Enter a URL for your privacy policy if desired
$returnURLPrivacyPolicy =
          'http://www.mywebsite.com/privacypolicy.php';
$returnURLReturnMethod  = '0'; // 1 or 0

// API Call Name
$eBayCallName        = 'SetReturnURL';
```

```
// Build API Request
$eBayRequest = '<?xml version="1.0" encoding="iso-8859-1" ?>
<request>
  <RequestUserId>' . $eBayUserID . '</RequestUserId>
  <RequestPassword>' . $eBayPassword . '</RequestPassword>
  <Action>' . $returnURLAction . '</Action>
  <RuName>' . $returnURLRuName . '</RuName>
  <Verb>' . $eBayCallName . '</Verb>';
// Add optional values
if ( $returnURLAccept <> '' )            $eBayRequest .= '
         <AcceptURL>' . $returnURLAccept . '</AcceptURL>';
if ( $returnURLReject <> '' )            $eBayRequest .= '
         <RejectURL>' . $returnURLReject . '</RejectURL>';
if ( $returnURLPrivacyPolicy <> '' )  $eBayRequest .= '
         <PrivacyPolicyURL>' . $returnURLPrivacyPolicy .
         '</PrivacyPolicyURL>';
if ( $returnURLReturnMethod <> '' )      $eBayRequest .= '
         <TokenReturnMethod>' . $returnURLReturnMethod .
         '</TokenReturnMethod>';
$eBayRequest .= '
</request>';
```

With the return URLs set, you need to update your program to accept the
response from eBay. eBay returns four values to the URL recorded with
`SetReturnURL`:

- ✔ `ebaytkn`: Authentication token.

- ✔ `tknexp`: Expiration date for the token.

- ✔ `username`: Username the user signed in with.

- ✔ **Custom values:** When you forward the user to eBay's sign-in page, you
  can include special values that eBay includes with the token response.
  Take a look at the `ruparams` explanation in the section "Sending the user
  to eBay to create or retrieve a token," earlier in this chapter.

The code in Listing 15-5 (included on the CD in this chapter's folder) accepts
the return values from the sign-in process, assigns those values to program
variables, and outputs them for debugging. The code works for both accept
and reject requests.

**Listing 15-5:   Accepting Return Values, Assigning Them to Program
              Variables, and Outputting Them for Debugging**

```php
<?php

// Go through all variables sent from eBay
//  - Store in local variables
//  - Include in debug details
```

(continued)

Listing 15-5 *(continued)*

```
while ( list( $key, $val ) = each( $HTTP_GET_VARS ) )
{
  // Remove special characters
  $val        = urldecode( stripslashes( $val ) );
  $$key       = $val;
  $debugMsg   .= "-- $key --\n$val\n\n\n";
}



//
// Debug code outputs the variables returned
//

echo '
<html>
<body>
  <textarea cols="60" rows="10">' . $debugMsg . '</textarea>
</body>
</html>';

//
// End debug code
//

?>
```

Desktop applications

Because a desktop application running on an end user's PC can't accept a connection from eBay, the program must contact eBay to retrieve the token. eBay created a special API call, FetchToken, to retrieve the token. Before you can use the FetchToken API call, your program must call the SetReturnURL API call and register empty values for the accept and reject URLs. Then you need to modify the address your application sends users to sign in, adding a new parameter: SecretID.

Your application has to call SetReturnURL only once for each RuName that you plan to use FetchToken for token retrieval. The code in Listing 15-6 alerts eBay that the application will use FetchToken for the given RuName.

Don't forget to include the shared code from Listing 15-2, earlier in this chapter. The following snippet won't work without it. If you're not comfortable putting the code together on your own, grab the complete, ready-to-edit code from this chapter's folder on the enclosed CD.

Listing 15-6:   Alerting eBay about Using FetchToken
for a Specific RuName

```php
<?php

// Modify these values for your sandbox or production
// UserID and password. Used only for "administrative"
// API calls like GetRuName and SetReturnURL
$eBayUserID       = 'xxxxxxxx';
$eBayPassword     = 'xxxxxxxx';

// Required Values
$returnURLAction  = 'add'; // add, update, or delete
$returnURLRuName  = 'xxxxxx';


// Optional values
$returnURLPrivacyPolicy = 'xxxxxx';
$returnURLReturnMethod  = '1'; // 1 or 0

// API Call Name
$eBayCallName           = 'SetReturnURL';

// Build API Request
$eBayRequest = '<?xml version="1.0" encoding="iso-8859-1" ?>
<request>
  <RequestUserId>' . $eBayUserID . '</RequestUserId>
  <RequestPassword>' . $eBayPassword . '</RequestPassword>
  <Action>' . $returnURLAction . '</Action>
  <RuName>' . $returnURLRuName . '</RuName>
  <Verb>' . $eBayCallName . '</Verb>';
// Add optional values
if ( $returnURLPrivacyPolicy <> '' ) $eBayRequest .= '
        <PrivacyPolicyURL>' . $returnURLPrivacyPolicy .
        '</PrivacyPolicyURL>';
if ( $returnURLReturnMethod <> '' )   $eBayRequest .= '
        <TokenReturnMethod>' . $returnURLReturnMethod .
        '</TokenReturnMethod>';
$eBayRequest .= '
</request>';
```

Next, you need to modify your code that directs users to eBay for signing in.
When using FetchToken, you must include a SecretID (sid) parameter. The
SecretID must be between 32 and 255 characters and should be unique to
your application. The SecretID identifies which instance of your application
sent a user to eBay's sign-in page. eBay recommends that you use the application's UUID (a unique identifier assigned by the operating system that

includes information about the user's PC and your application — see your programming language's documentation for details). You can create a dynamic SecretID, but you need to ensure that it can't ever match a SecretID created by another copy of your application running on a different computer.

Your program uses the SecretID when calling the FetchToken API call. The SecretID used in the FetchToken call must match the SecretID sent to eBay when the user signed in. Because you need the user's eBay user ID for the FetchToken API call, you can use it as a basis for creating a SecretID.

After the user signs in to eBay, your application calls the FetchToken API to retrieve the user's token, storing it for later use. The code in Listing 15-7 displays two links: one for signing in to eBay and the other for retrieving the token (after completing the sign-in process).

Don't forget to include the shared code from Listing 15-2, earlier in this chapter. The following snippet won't work without it. You need to put the shared code inside the following sample where the code comments indicate. To keep life simple, the included CD contains the following code with the necessary shared code already embedded inside. You can find the code in this chapter's folder.

Listing 15-7:   Displaying Two Links: For Signing in to eBay and Retrieving the Token

```php
<?php

// This value must match what the user enters upon
// sign-in. If not the FetchToken call will fail
$eBayUsername = 'xxxxxxxx';

// Change the RuName to match the application's RuName
// registered with the SetReturnURL API call
$RuName       = 'xxxxxxxx';

if ( $_GET['sid'] == '' )
{
    $eBaySignInURL =
            'https://signin.sandbox.ebay.com/ws/eBayISAPI.dll?
            SignIn';

    srand();
    $sid = str_replace( ' ', '', $eBayUsername . time() .
            time() * microtime() . mt_rand( 10000, 30000 ) );
```

```
   // Send the user to eBay for signin
   $eBaySignInLink = $eBaySignInURL . '&runame=' . $RuName .
         '&sid=' . urlencode( $sid );
   echo '<a href="' . $eBaySignInLink . '"
         target="_blank">Sign in to eBay</a><br>';
   echo '<a href="' . $_SERVER['PHP_SELF'] . '?sid=' .
         urlencode( $sid ) . '">Get Token from
         eBay</a><br>';
}
else
{
   // API Call Name
   $eBayCallName        = 'FetchToken';

   // Build API Request
   $eBayRequest = '<?xml version="1.0" encoding="iso-8859-1"
         ?>
<request>
   <RequestUserId>' . $eBayUsername . '</RequestUserId>
   <SecretId>' . urlencode( $_GET['sid'] ) . '</SecretId>
   <Verb>' . $eBayCallName . '</Verb>
</request>';

   //
   //
   // INSERT THE SHARED CODE FROM EARLIER CODE
   // EXAMPLES HERE
   //
   //

}
?>
```

It's a challenging road, but implementing eBay's new Authentication and Authorization scheme gives your users an additional layer of security. Best of all, it's one less thing for you to worry about. You no longer have to store usernames and passwords for your users.

After your application has the user's token in hand, it's ready to begin tapping the enormous resources eBay offers. You're ready to begin testing the many API calls eBay offers.

Taking Your Next Steps with the API

By implementing the eBay Authentication and Authorization scheme, you've already tried out several API calls. You're already well on your way to creating a fully functional eBay application.

Putting together all the components to send your first API request and receive a successful response represent most of the effort in adding an API to your applications. Now that you've performed several successful API communications, you're ready to branch out. eBay's API offers almost 100 calls, offering many different options.

Each API call operates similarly to the API calls you've already implemented. Other API calls have different inputs, but the process to send the request to eBay and retrieve the response works the same. Although the length of response may be different, extracting the information you need works similarly.

As you look at different API calls, you want to focus on three key pieces of information: the input fields, whether each field is optional or required, and the data type for each field. Armed with that information, you can format the request for the API call of your choice.

Your application must supply the API with every required field. The field data type tells you the type of information you can include in each field. Chapter 13 introduces data types and explains how to read the API documentation.

eBay's online API documentation — shown in Figure 15-2 and available at `developer.ebay.com/DevZone/docs/API_Doc/index.asp` — offers a detailed look at every API call, giving example XML, implementation notes, and detailed listings of inputs. You also find a complete listing of possible return values in the API response.

At this point, your biggest challenge is deciding what you want your application to accomplish. Take a look through the "Function Reference Guide" section of the API documentation to find an API call to power all your features.

Figure 15-2:
eBay's
Developers
Program
API
documen-
tation.

Chapter 16

Building Custom eBay Applications with Microsoft Office and the eBay API

*A*lthough posting auctions one at a time was fun when eBay first opened its doors, er, pages, to the public years ago, it's not the ideal use of your time these days. Applications that simplify the listing process through integration with your existing inventory systems save time and reduce the likelihood of errors. Tools that help with eBay searching and buying abound. Although the eBay interface works okay on a small scale, serious eBay business users can significantly benefit from using customized eBay tools.

If you're like many eBay business owners, you already own some or all of the Microsoft Office application suite — Word, Excel, Access, FrontPage, and the rest of them. Surprisingly, that means you *also* own a development tool suited for integration with eBay. Yup, you guessed it: those beloved Microsoft Office applications.

In March 2004, eBay and Microsoft joined forces to offer API support for the Microsoft Office System, taking the first tentative steps toward helping you develop custom eBay applications that work with and through Microsoft Office. With millions of experienced Office users lurking in businesses and homes around the world, Office certainly offers an attractive target user base.

As an added benefit, Microsoft Office brings a lot of valuable features to the development table. Your applications harness the database tools from Access or the analytical prowess of Excel. FrontPage speeds Web page development, doing many menial tasks for you. Rather than writing an entire application from scratch, Microsoft Office gives you a head start — or at least that's how it *should* work, in a perfect world.

This chapter offers an overview of the technical requirements, the development expertise, and the sheer degree of physical and emotional pain necessary to utilize the Microsoft Office System as an eBay application development tool. It also provides a list of resources you can refer to for further information because you'll need them. (Oh boy, will you *ever* need them.)

Mixing Oil, Water, eBay, and Microsoft Office

In an ideal world, you could create an Excel spreadsheet of your inventory and then instruct Excel to upload the items to eBay, creating a separate auction for each item. You'd drop in some simple code that would handle the listing process and communicate with eBay. eBay's sample application, shown in Figure 16-1, gives you an idea of what such an application might look like. The whole setup process would take a few hours to get up and running.

Unfortunately, this dream isn't a reality — yet. Integrating Microsoft Office with eBay offers some significant challenges. eBay's support for Microsoft Office hasn't reached a point where the average human can get started easily, so the development tools are better suited for experienced developers.

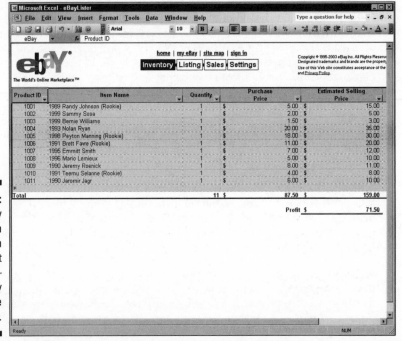

Figure 16-1:
eBay
integration
with
Microsoft
Excel —
an eBay
sample
application.

WARNING!

Is anybody there? Does anybody care? (Apparently not.)

In early 2004, eBay excitedly highlighted the possibilities of Microsoft Office integration on the Developers Program home page. It sounded like the Next Big Thing, with liberty, justice, profits, and easy development possibilities for all. But in the months since then, the much-vaunted integration vanished from the limelight and almost disappeared entirely.

Apart from the initial gush of delight, enthusiasm among developers for Office integration seems nonexistent. It's tough to find any mention of the integration efforts anywhere on the eBay Developers Program site at all. Granted, the site still provides a single, lonely sample application, but that hardly counts. Worse yet, discussion of Office integration on the Developers Program forums is almost nonexistent, which paints a picture of a completely disinterested development community.

Perhaps some new and exciting expansion of the program waits in the wings, but for now, it looks like the whole Microsoft Office integration program either got put on permanent hold or simply died at birth. It seemingly promised so much, but at this point, delivered very little. Stay tuned and see what, if anything, develops in the future.

Testing out the Microsoft Office integration with the sample application (found at `developer.ebay.com/DevZone/docs/Samplecode.asp` in the eBay Developers Program Web site) is not for the faint of heart. The sample doesn't explain how to install or use its code — you need to figure that out for yourself. In fact, the lone shred of documentation included in the sample details the programmatic interface used. The supposedly simple task of getting the sample program up and running requires familiarity with Microsoft's development tools and Web server. And the sample doesn't even support the Authorization and Authentication (*Auth and Auth,* as the developers usually describe it) system that went into place months ago.

To take advantage of the Microsoft Office System eBay integration, you need *serious* development experience with the following impressive list of technologies:

- **Object-oriented programming concepts and execution:** The eBay Software Development Kit (SDK) used to integrate with the Microsoft Office System leans heavily on the object-oriented programming model. You need to have a strong foundation in working with classes and objects.

- **Microsoft application development:** Whether you choose .NET or the simpler VBA, you need a solid understanding of Microsoft's programming options.

✔ **Microsoft Internet Information Server:** eBay's sample application requires special security and application setup in Microsoft's Internet Information Server. If you use an online host, you may be able to lean on your system administrator for help.

Although the experience necessary may seem steep, the payoff should be worth it, provided you ever get there. By integrating Office with eBay's API, you can develop applications that take advantage of Excel's information analysis and storage tools as well as FrontPage's Web layout and design capabilities. If you're feeling really enthusiastic, you can create an entire inventory system in Access and create an automated auction posting system.

What if you lack the stunning résumé that it takes to make Office carry on a profitable conversation with the eBay API? Unless you have some other driving reason to dive headlong into Microsoft Office development, turn your attention to Web-based application development with languages like PHP. They give you a *lot* more "bang for the buck" than Office integration in both the long-run and the short-term.

Gathering the Tools You Need to Put Office to Work

Although the experiential requirements for integrating eBay and the Microsoft Office System are steep, the technical requirements are not. To use the Microsoft Office System integration, you need the following tools:

✔ **Microsoft Office System applications:** The Microsoft Office System comprises an entire suite of applications, including the Office applications Word and Excel, as well as the lesser-known applications InfoPath, OneNote, and SharePoint. Thankfully, you don't need them all. You'll most likely use Excel 2003 and FrontPage 2003 for your eBay development. For more details about the Microsoft Office System, visit www. microsoft.com/office/system/.

✔ **eBay Developers Program Software Development Kit (SDK):** The SDK offers programmatic access to the eBay API, taking care of the gritty details necessary to communicate with eBay. It offers object-based access to the API through COM or .NET.

✔ **An Internet connection:** What good would the API be if your application couldn't talk to eBay?

After you have the necessary software, you're ready to get going with the eBay SDK inside Microsoft Office. The SDK gives you access to all the API's features including auction listings, item searches, and feedback management.

Finding Your Way with Online Resources

Getting the Microsoft Office System working with eBay can be a daunting task. However, other developers have gone down this road before and documented their experiences. To help you get going, I've included a list of helpful resources.

eBay SDK and API documentation

Your first resource is likely to be the official documentation on eBay's Developers Program Web site (available at `developer.ebay.com/DevZone/docs/SDK/` for the SDK and for the API). The API and SDK documentation detail all the functions included and the available parameters. The documentation offers guides that introduce each segment of the eBay/Office integration system, users, auctions, feedback, and more.

DevX.com

The DevX site has a pair of articles about application development with the Microsoft Office System to help you get started on your first application:

- ✔ "Monitor eBay Auctions with Visual Studio.NET" (`www.devx.com/webdev/Article/21341/`)
- ✔ "Integrate Your Inventory System with the eBay SDK" (`www.devx.com/dotnet/Article/19812/`)

Microsoft Office Developer Center

You can find out more about development for the Microsoft Office System at the official Microsoft Office Developer Center at `msdn.microsoft.com/office/` (shown in Figure 16-2). The site offers sample code, programming references, and access to the Office developer community. With details about development on each Office System application, this is a good place to find the help you need.

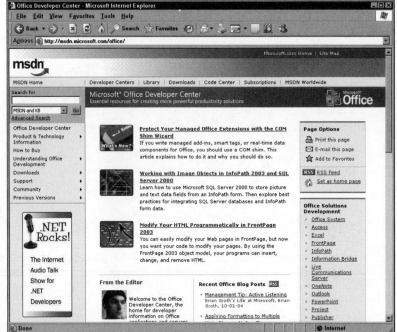

Figure 16-2:
The
Microsoft
Office
Developer
Center
home page.

Other For Dummies titles

The *For Dummies* series (Wiley) includes a number of titles that can help you with your development project:

- ✔ *Excel VBA Programming For Dummies* by John Walkenbach
- ✔ *Access VBA Programming For Dummies* by Alan Simpson
- ✔ *FrontPage 2003 For Dummies* by Asha Dornfest
- ✔ *ASP.NET For Dummies* by Bill Hatfield
- ✔ *Visual Basic .NET For Dummies* by Wallace Wang
- ✔ *Visual C++ .NET For Dummies* by Michael Hyman and Bob Arnson

Chapter 17

Visiting Other API Planets: PayPal, FedEx, UPS, and the U.S. Postal Service

In This Chapter

▶ Getting Instant Payment Notification (IPN) from PayPal

▶ Teaming up with the USPS

▶ Communicating with your friends at FedEx and UPS

Due to the open nature of programming APIs, numerous companies offer API access to their databases. They have an incentive to help make your life easier because you do more business with them and require less help than if you were doing things manually. Plus, you're a much happier customer if an API program makes your life easier.

As you evaluate companies to team up with, it's worth considering whether or not they offer an API. You can save yourself time and money by using your vendor's API tools. However, ask yourself whether the API really makes things easier. Often, that depends on how intuitive the Web interface feels. The easier and more configurable the Web site, the more time the API must save you before it makes sense for you to switch (from using the Web interface to an API program).

Enhancing Payment Processing with the PayPal API

PayPal has not released the bulk of its API tools for public use because they're still in testing. The API isn't ready for use in serious business applications. (PayPal welcomes developers to test and create programs but only for the Sandbox test server.) The good news is that PayPal will eventually support an API interface, but the bad news it that you may have to wait a while.

Thankfully, PayPal does offer one API tool that you can use now: Instant Payment Notification (IPN). This tool works like a reverse API. PayPal's server connects to your API program and sends you the details of every one of your PayPal transaction or status updates. Your program can record a complete transaction history for your account or react to the transactions. The transactions can trigger automated e-mail to you or your customers as well as open up Web site access to restricted areas.

Signing up for the PayPal API

Even though the PayPal API is still in development, you can begin developing an application. The process will hone your API programming skills, giving you an edge when working with other APIs. You just have to wait until the PayPal API goes live before putting your program to use.

To get started with PayPal's API program, you first need to sign up. To do so, follow these steps:

1. **Visit** `https://developer.paypal.com` **(shown in Figure 17-1).**

2. **Click the Sign Up Now link to start the quick and easy registration process.**

3. **Enter your basic contact information, answer a couple questions about your business and planned API use, and accept the User Agreement and Privacy Policy.**

4. **When you finish filling out the form, click the Sign Up button at the bottom of the page.**

   PayPal e-mails a confirmation notice to you.

5. **Click the link in the e-mail confirmation to validate your account.**

   You must validate your account in order to gain access to the Developer Central Web site.

After you've joined the PayPal Developer Program, you're ready to begin finding out about the API. PayPal's Developer Central offers documentation, frequently asked questions, and a users forum. To help get up and running quickly, take a look at the code samples.

Figure 17-1:
PayPal's
Developer
Central
welcome
page.

Although the API offers only limited functionality, the options available warrant some exploration. Transaction searches alone make the PayPal API worth looking into. The search options offer more flexibility than PayPal's Web interface, including searches by auction item number and amount. The API also powers automated refunds and mass payments.

Most importantly, the PayPal API offers transaction lookups. Your program can retrieve the payment details for your transactions. With the API, you can display transaction details on your own Web site or in an automated e-mail message.

What you can do with Instant Payment Notification

Even though the full PayPal API is in beta, the Instant Payment Notification (IPN) tool can power your business today. IPN sends you a notification every time your PayPal account processes or updates a transaction. With IPN, your program can

- ✔ Create your transaction history
- ✔ Trigger automatic e-mail responses
- ✔ Open restricted areas of your Web site

Best of all, the IPN sends a detailed record of the transaction to your API program. You can find the IPN documentation under the Merchant Tools section of the site or visit `https://www.paypal.com/us/cgi-bin/webscr?cmd=p/xcl/rec/ipn-intro`.

How the IPN process works

To send the transaction details, the IPN contacts your API program. In a sense, it's an API in reverse. Here's what happens when a transaction occurs:

1. **PayPal connects to your API program (acting as an API server) and sends the transaction information.**

   However, unlike a traditional API communication, your API program doesn't have to return a response. Plus, unlike eBay, PayPal doesn't require certification before sending your application into action.

2. **When your program receives the transaction details, it must contact PayPal via a standard API specially designed to validate the transaction. Validating the transaction involves sending the IPN API an exact copy of the transaction details and awaiting a response.**

   The validation step is important because it prevents hackers from sending your API program fake transactions.

   To verify the transaction, the IPN program sends the API a copy of the information received along with a command variable:

   ```
   cmd=_notify-validate
   ```

   Unlike most API programs that use XML, PayPal utilizes the simpler HTTP POST. Because PayPal sends the transaction details as an HTTP POST, it's easy to send it to the IPN API for validation. There's no conversion step to perform.

3. **If the transaction is valid, PayPal returns a VERIFIED response; otherwise, it responds with INVALID.**

A VERIFIED response tells you that the transaction actually happened through PayPal. INVALID should raise red flags in your program. Most likely, an error occurred in your program, or someone is attempting to hack your program.

It's important to note that a VERIFIED response doesn't mean you should begin processing an order. You still must go through PayPal's recommended validation steps (outlined in the IPN section of the PayPal Integration Manual). While it'd be nice to have a URL for the PayPal Integration Manual, PayPal's security features don't offer that luxury. To locate the Integration Manual, follow these steps:

1. **Go to the PayPal home page and log in.**

2. **Click the Merchant Tools tab, located at the top of the page.**

3. **Towards the bottom of the page under the heading Integrating with Backend Applications, click the Instant Payment Notification link.**

4. **In the Instant Payment Notification navigation bar on the left side of the screen, click the Manual link. Then click the Merchant User Manual & Integration Guide link.**

To further guard against fraudulent use of your API program, your program should also follow PayPal's other recommended checks, which include verifying payment status, item pricing, and the receiving account's e-mail address, and checking for duplicate transaction IDs.

To use IPN, you must have

✔ Web site space with API programming support. (See Chapter 13 for help choosing a language.)

✔ A Business or Premier PayPal account.

Creating an IPN program

Although IPN programs vary depending on what actions the programs take, the basic code to receive and validate the Instant Payment Notification works the same. The program must receive the information from PayPal and then use the IPN API to verify the data. (Glance through Chapter 13 for more information about the API process.)

Listing 17-1 handles the entire communication process with PayPal. It builds on the concepts from Chapter 13 and adds an e-mail debug process (because you don't see the output of the program). The program automatically e-mails you when an error occurs (or if you turn on e-mail debugging). Be sure to change the `paypalAccountAddress` entry — *youremail@yourisp.com* — to match your Business/Premier account e-mail address.

On your Web site, create a PHP file in which you store the code in Listing 17-1, which is your IPN program. Then use the address of your IPN program to set up IPN through your PayPal account, as described in the next section. Listing 17-1 is written in PHP, but you can apply the same general concepts to any programming language.

In several places in Listing 17-1, you'll notice large comment blocks (like the one that follows):

```
/****************************************************
 * Perform IPN notification history storage here *
 * using a database -- record a copy of every    *
 * IPN notification so that you have a record of *
 * possible hack attempts as well                *
 ****************************************************/
```

These comment blocks highlight places inside the example where you can insert your own code to perform processing that your business needs. Each comment gives a suggestion for what type of processing you might include.

Listing 17-1:   Receiving and Validating the Instant Payment Notification

```php
<?php

// Send Debugging email even if transaction passes
          Verification?
// (1 for yes, 0 for no)
// The mail() function requires Sendmail. If you use another
// email program, see
          http://us4.php.net/manual/en/ref.mail.php
// for details
$debug = 1;

// Enter account address for fraud protection and debug
// emails -- BE SURE TO CHANGE THIS TO YOUR EMAIL ADDRESS
$paypalAccountAddress = 'youremail@yourisp.com';

// Debug email setup
$subject = 'Debug output from IPN';
$debugMsg = "PayPal IPN Transaction\n\n";

// Begin the verification request with PayPal's special
          command
$request = 'cmd=_notify-validate';
```

```php
// Go through all variables POSTed from PayPal
//   - Store in local variables
//   - Add to verification request
//   - Include in debug details
while ( list( $key, $val ) = each( $HTTP_POST_VARS ) )
{
    // Remove special characters
    $val       = urlencode( stripslashes( $val ) );
    $$key      = $val;
    $request   .= "&$key=$val";
    $debugMsg  .= "$key - $val\n";
}

/***************************************************
 * Perform IPN notification history storage here   *
 * using a database -- record a copy of every      *
 * IPN notification so that you have a record of    *
 * possible hack attempts as well                  *
 ***************************************************/

// Send the verification request to PayPal
// Requires the CURL package (http://curl.haxx.se/)
$APIConnection = curl_init();
curl_setopt( $APIConnection, CURLOPT_URL,
        "https://www.paypal.com/cgi-bin/webscr" );
curl_setopt( $APIConnection, CURLOPT_POSTFIELDS, $request );
curl_setopt( $APIConnection, CURLOPT_RETURNTRANSFER, 1 );
$response = curl_exec( $APIConnection );
curl_close( $APIConnection );

// Prepare debug message if verification process found an
            error
$msg = "PayPal IPN Verification report:\r\n\r\n";
$msg .= "Response: $response\r\n\r\nIPN Verification
        Request:\r\n$request\r\n\r\n$debugMsg";

if ( $response == '' ) {
    // Didn't receive any response
        mail( $paypalAccountAddress, $subject . ' - Empty
        response received', $msg );
        exit;
} else {
        if ( $response <> 'VERIFIED' ) {
            // PayPal responded didn't respond with
        "VERIFIED"
    mail( $paypalAccountAddress, $subject . ' - Invalid
        response received', $msg );
            exit;
        } else {
```

(continued)

Listing 17-1: *(continued)*

```
              if ( $receiver_email <> $paypalAccountAddress
      ) {
                  // Invalid payment email address --
      possible spoof
    mail( $paypalAccountAddress, $subject . ' - Invalid
      Payment Email Address', $msg );
                  exit;
              }

      /************************************************
      * Perform the checks recommended by PayPal here *
      * (Account Email address check included above)  *
      * Add code to validate the following:           *
      *  - Duplicate transaction ID                   *
      *  - Payment status is COMPLETED                *
      *  - Price and item number/desc                 *
      ************************************************/

      /************************************************
      * Add code here to process the transaction if   *
      * it passes the checks above. Consider adding    *
      * db updates and automatic emails to you and     *
      * your customer                                  *
      ************************************************/

      // If $debug = 1 above, send debug email even though
          notification passed verification
      if ( $debug ) {
        mail( $paypalAccountAddress, $subject . ' - Payment
          notification VERIFIED', $msg );
      }
          }
}

?>
```

Activating IPN for your PayPal account

After you have the IPN program on your Web site, activating IPN for your PayPal account takes only a few moments. To set up IPNs, follow these steps:

1. **Log in to your PayPal account.**

2. **Click the Profile option.**

3. **Under the Selling Preferences heading, click Instant Payment Notification Preferences.**

4. **Click the Edit button.**

5. **Select the Instant Payment Notification check box.**

6. **Enter the URL of your IPN program and then click Save.**

PayPal offers a detailed testing process at `https://www.paypal.com/us/ cgi-bin/webscr?cmd=_ipn-test-about`. You can also find the testing procedure by clicking the Merchant Tools tab, then the Instant Payment Notification link under the Other PayPal tools heading, and finally, the Testing link in the menu on the left side of the screen.

The testing procedure details how to set up your accounts for testing. After you set up the accounts, the document walks you through performing a test transaction. Using Listing 17-1, you receive an e-mail with complete details about the IPN process. The e-mail contains the request, PayPal's response, and the value of every transaction variable.

After you've tested the IPN process and received the debugging messages, you're ready to customize the program to perform processing specific to your business. Although you can leave the code alone and receive notification of every payment change, the real power of the IPN comes when you put the notifications to use. Listing 17-1 includes placeholders (as described in the preceding section) for your own customized processing. Each placeholder sits inside a large PHP comment block, surrounded by asterisks. Think about adding automated e-mails sent to you or your customers and a database history of transactions. See Chapter 13 for sample database storage code.

Mailing Faster (And Cheaper) with the Postal Service API

The United States Postal Service (USPS) offers a wealth of API tools for you to use in your programs, including

- ✔ Package status information
- ✔ Shipping labels
- ✔ Rate calculators
- ✔ Address verification

The API gives you the tools necessary to build a sophisticated auction fulfillment system. Visit `www.usps.com/webtools/` (shown in Figure 17-2) to find out more about the program and download the API documentation.

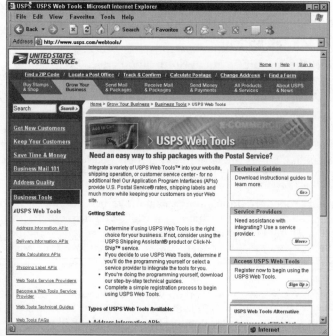

Figure 17-2:
The USPS
Web Tools
welcome
page.

The USPS API not only saves you time but saves you money as well. To
encourage you to use the electronic bar code labels, the USPS API gives you a
postage discount. For example, Delivery Confirmation for Priority Mail typically costs $0.45 in additional postage. When you use an Electronic Delivery
Confirmation label from the USPS API, Delivery Confirmation is free!

To showcase the API, the USPS developed the USPS Shipping Assistant (available at `www.usps.com/shippingassistant/`). The program runs on your
PC and showcases many of the API's capabilities.

Here's what you need to do to use the USPS API:

- **Registration:** To use the USPS API tools, you must complete the API registration process, which doesn't take long. You fill out a one-page form
  and then wait for your registration confirmation e-mail (it may take up to
  24 hours).

- **Testing:** With your username and password in hand, you can start testing your program with the USPS test server. When you're comfortable,
  you can begin running your program against the live service. However,
  several API services require certification. In general, any API that creates
  a bar code label or number must pass certification.

✔ **Certification:** To get certified, you have to create a set of sample labels by using the sample XML provided in the API documentation. You just print the labels and mail them to the USPS certification center; you don't have to pay a certification fee. If your labels pass inspection, you receive access to the live production servers. If your labels don't pass, you have to start over.

To maintain your certification, the labels must be readable by the USPS carriers' bar code scanners at least 95 percent of the time. If not, the USPS revokes your certification. If you're the only person using your API program, maintaining quality doesn't require much effort. Use a quality printer and throw away any labels that show smudges or streaks. If other people use your program, be sure to educate them about the importance of maintaining print quality.

Providing package tracking on your Web site

Offering a package status lookup on your Web site keeps your customers at your site and provides a helpful service. With the USPS API, providing this service is relatively painless. Listing 17-2 adds a form for customers to look up their package status on your Web site. Be sure to replace the USERID= and PASSWORD= entries with your USPS credentials.

Listing 17-2: **Adding a Form for Customers to Track Packages**

```php
<?php

if ( $confirmationno <> '' ) {
  //Get tracking info for given number

  $xmlTag = '';
  $xml   = '<TrackRequest USERID="userid"
            PASSWORD="password">';
  $xml  .= '<TrackID ID="' . $confirmationno . '"/>';
  $xml  .= '</TrackRequest>';

  // Requires the CURL package (http://curl.haxx.se/)
  // Package the request
  $APITitle = 'TrackV2';
  $request = 'API=' . $APITitle . '&XML=' . $xml;

  $APIConnection = curl_init();
```

(continued)

Listing 17-2: *(continued)*

```
curl_setopt( $APIConnection, CURLOPT_URL,
        "http://production.shippingapis.com/ShippingAPI.dl
        l" );
curl_setopt( $APIConnection, CURLOPT_POSTFIELDS, $request
        );
curl_setopt( $APIConnection, CURLOPT_RETURNTRANSFER, 1 );

$response = curl_exec( $APIConnection );
curl_close( $APIConnection );

// Check to see if the XML contains an "Error" tag
$error = GetXMLContents( 'Error' , $response );
if ( $error ) {
  // The response was empty, add an error message to the
        output -- include the USPS description
        $errorDesc = GetXMLContents( 'Description' ,
        $error );
        $tracksummary   = '<font color="#FF0000">The
    USPS server returned an error (listed below).
    Sometimes this happens because of Internet
    problems or heavy usage on the USPS computers.
    Click the refresh button in your browser to try
    again.<br><br>USPS Error: ' . $errorDesc .
    '</font>';
        } elseif ( $response == '' ) {
  // The response was empty, add an error message to the
        ouput
  $error = 1;
  $tracksummary   = '<font color="#FF0000">We encountered a
        problem communicating with the USPS tracking
        system. Sometimes this happens because of Internet
        problems or heavy usage on the USPS computers.
        Click the refresh button in your browser to try
        again.</font>';
        } else {
        // Get the package status summary from the
    XML tag TrackSummary
        $tracksummary        = GetXMLContents(
    'TrackSummary', $response );
  // Break up the list of TrackingDetails into an array
  $trackdetails        = split( '<TrackDetail>',
        $response );
  for ( $i = 0; $trackdetails[ $i ] <> '' ; $i++)
    // Go through the track details array and remove the
        XML tags
    // leaving a track detail description in each array
        value
```

```
      list ( $trackdetails[ $i ], $temp ) = split(
          '</TrackDetail>', $trackdetails[ $i ] );
      }

  echo '<p><b>Tracking Information - ' . $confirmationno .
          '</b><br>';
  echo $tracksummary . '</p>';
  echo '<p><b>Track Detail</b><br>';
  echo '<ul>';
  // Loop through the package tracking details
  for ( $i = 1; $trackdetails[$i] <> "" ; $i++ )
    echo '<li><p>' . $trackdetails[$i] . '</li>';
  // If no tracking detail found, dump out the generic
          message
  if ( $i == 1 )
    echo '<p>There are no tracking details at this
          time.</p>';
} else {
  // If no number entered, output our entry form
  echo '<p>Package Label Number<br>';
  echo '<form action="' . $SERVER[ 'PHP_SELF' ] . '">';
  echo '<input type="text" name="confirmationno" size="24"
          maxlength="20"> <input type="submit"
          value="Track"></p>';
  echo '</form>';
}

// This function pulls the contents out of simple XML tags
// Not suitable for tags that include attributes
function GetXMLContents ( $tag, $xml ) {
  list( $temp, $XMLContents ) = spliti("<$tag>", $xml );
  list( $XMLContents, $temp ) = spliti("</$tag>",
          $XMLContents );

  if ( $XMLContents == $xml ) {
    // Didn't find the XML tag
    return '';
  } else {
    // Found the tag, return the contents
  return $XMLContents;
  }
}
?>
```

Using bar-coded address labels

The USPS API also provides bar-coded address labels for your packages.
You supply the shipment type, shipping service, and addresses, and the API

provides the shipping label. This API operates similarly to the other APIs discussed. Take a look at Chapter 13 for general API programming help.

To use the API-supplied images, your program must decode the image data inside the XML response, and then the browser will recognize the image. Use Listing 17-3 to decode and display the image.

Listing 17-3: Deciphering and Displaying API Images

```php
<?php

// The code before this snippet must put the image
// data from the XML into the $labelXML variable

// Decode the XML image data (encoded with BASE 64)
$imageData = base64_decode( $labelXML );
// Change this, depending on what label type
// you request from the USPS in the API request
$imageType  = 'PDF';

if ( $imageType == 'PDF' ) {
    // Tell the browser what kind of image to display
    header("Content-type: application/pdf");
    header("Content-disposition: inline; filename=label.pdf");
    header("Content-length: " . strlen($imageData) );
} else {
    // Tell the browser what kind of image to display
    header("Content-type: image/jpeg");
    header("Content-length: " . strlen($imageData) );
}

// Output the image data
echo $imageData;

?>
```

Listing 17-3 stores the decoded image data in the $imageData variable. Then based on the type of image requested from the API server (PDF or JPG), it outputs the image and the required headers.

For Listing 17-3 to work, your program *cannot* output anything to the browser before or after this code. Otherwise, the browser will become confused and won't properly display the label.

As you explore the USPS API, be sure to take a look at the Rate Calculator tools. They can improve your shipping cost estimates and save you time. Your program can automatically enter the origin location and your common package sizes and weights.

Alternative solutions for low-volume shippers

The various API tools offer plenty of flexibility and power, but if you're a low-volume shipper, you may not be able to justify the expense of a custom solution. Creating your own API program can suck valuable resources away from your primary business, costing you money.

Many software developers have taken the time to utilize the API tools offered by FedEx, UPS, and the USPS for you. By leveraging hundreds or thousands of users, they spread the development cost across many customers. You can take advantage of their time investment and find tools that meet your needs without requiring your own development time.

Getting started with streamlined and reduced-cost USPS shipping starts with a trip to one of several online software vendors. Stamps. com (www.stamps.com) and Endicia Internet Postage (www.endicia.com) offer postage and shipping labels. The USPS Shipping Assistant (www.usps.com/shippingassistant/)

provides access to the API tools, although the challenging interface can be frustrating. ShipperTools (www.shippertools.com) offers reduced-cost electronic USPS labels with complete package history and omits the complexity and expense of online postage.

The major shippers also include links to help you find a software solution or custom developer:

✔ **FedEx:** www.fedex.com/us/
   solutions/integrator.html

✔ **USPS:** www.usps.com/webtools/
   providers.htm

✔ **UPS:** www.ec.ups.com/ecommerce/
   solutions/servprov.html

If you're short on time, consider contacting the service providers listed. They have the expertise necessary to help you develop a custom solution or find a suitable product already available.

Smoothing Your High-Volume Shipping with the FedEx and UPS APIs

After you've got the sale, your biggest goal is delivering the product as inexpensively as possible without creating any customer service problems. Order fulfillment efficiencies often separate successful from struggling online retailers and auction sellers. By streamlining your order fulfillment system, you reap the benefit of happier customers through lower costs, reduced shipping prices, faster delivery, and fewer lost packages.

Automated package labeling alone makes your business appear more professional and reduces your packing time drastically. Rather than handwriting your labels, you apply crisp, clean shipping labels. With a UPS or FedEx account, you don't have to waste time standing in line to get a package bar code label. Your program can also automatically pull address information from your customer database rather than force you to retype it each time.

In addition to electronic labels, integrated tracking tools give your customers a sense of security and save you time when looking up package status information. Imagine having your order database linked into your shipper's tracking database. By clicking a package, you receive the full package status. You no longer have to type tracking numbers into the shipper's Web site.

Your program can help estimate your shipping prices and delivery times by using the integrated rate and transit time API functions. You can get accurate estimates right from your order processing program without having to visit the shipper's Web site.

Exploring the FedEx API tools

FedEx offers the FedEx Web Integration Solutions (WIS) for developers looking to integrate their tracking and shipping functions into a Web site. The WIS home page resides at `www.fedex.com/us/solutions/wis/` (shown in Figure 17-3). WIS includes an API system for communicating with FedEx. The WIS offers an API component (called the Ship Manager) that you can integrate into your programs. There is also the Ship Manager Direct for advanced users interested in connecting directly to the API with XML.

You need a FedEx account number before registering to use the API. If you don't already have a FedEx account number, you can set up an account at `https://www.fedex.com/signup/`.

Follow these steps to sign up for the FedEx API:

1. **Click one of the Register links at the WIS home page (`www.fedex.com/us/solutions/wis/`) to begin.**

2. **Enter your contact details, FedEx account information, and type of business.**

3. **Under Communication Path to FedEx, select what development method you're planning to use. Here are your options:**

   • **FSM API:** This is really more of a Software Development Kit (SDK) than an API. SDKs seek to simplify your life by taking care of the nitty-gritty server communication details, letting you focus on the features your program needs. The FSM API connection method utilizes a specialized programming component from FedEx to simplify the communication process. The FSM API supports C, C++, Java, Visual Basic, VBScript, and JavaScript. If you're using a language that FedEx doesn't support (such as PHP), this method won't work for you.

- **FSM Direct:** This option has more in common with the APIs discussed throughout this book. Your program must create and send XML requests directly to the FedEx API server.

4. **Under Data Format, choose which data format you want to utilize: the older FedEx Tagged Transaction format or the newer industry standard XML format (called XML Tools in the form). To keep your programming job easier, go for the XML Tools option and then click the Submit button.**

If you choose the FSM API in Step 3, you can download the API as soon as you complete the form. If you choose FSM Direct, FedEx e-mails the links for the FSM Direct documentation. The requirements for test server access and program certification differ depending on the FSM option you choose. The documentation for each details the process.

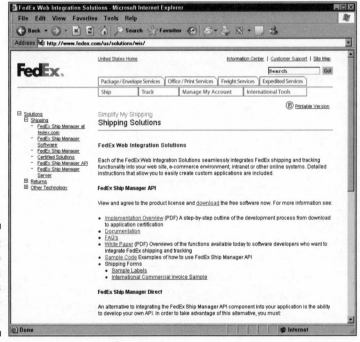

Figure 17-3:
FedEx Web Integration Solutions welcome site.

Visiting the UPS API center

Start your UPS API journey by visiting the UPS OnLine Tools center at www.ec.ups.com/ecommerce/solutions/c1.html (shown in Figure 17-4). There you find a program overview, basic program documentation, and frequently asked questions. The list of UPS OnLine Tools at the bottom of the page gives you an overview of what you can do with the UPS API.

To use the UPS API tools, follow these steps:

1. **Register with UPS and then log in.**

   The UPS API registration process can be a bit daunting, so if you want an overview of the registration process, click the Get Tools link or go to www.ec.ups.com/ecommerce/gettools/gtools_intro.html.

2. **Accept the user agreement and provide your basic contact information.**

   After you've registered with the main UPS system, the site takes you to the API documentation download page.

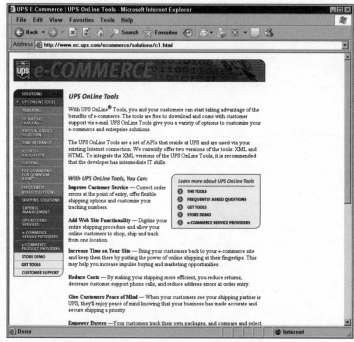

Figure 17-4:
UPS OnLine Tools welcome page.

3. **Select the tool that you want to download.**

   After you select one of the tools, UPS prompts you to register as a UPS OnLine Tools developer.

4. **Accept the end-user agreement to register with the developer program.**

   UPS e-mails you a *developer key,* which is your pass into the detailed API documentation area of the UPS API Web site. However, you still need an access key before you can begin using the API.

5. **Enter your developer key and accept yet another license agreement.**

   Finally, after all that work, UPS e-mails you the *access key.* Now you're ready to get started with the basic tools. Whew!

 When you first begin, UPS gives you access to only the basic tools. You must register separately for the premium tools: UPS Shipping and Signature Tracking. You must have a current UPS account number to access the premium tool documentation or request an access key. You also must pass the product certification process.

 To help you get started as quickly as possible, UPS offers HTML versions of the tracking tools (they're not really an API, but UPS groups the tools together with the APIs). The HTML versions don't give as much flexibility with tracking-information display, but they're the fastest way to add UPS tracking to your Web site.

Part V
The Part of Tens

The 5th Wave   By Rich Tennant

"I think the listing's claim that the car is safely submersible has proven to be a wee bit false, Edmund. Shall I compose the feedback e-mail?"

In this part . . .

Ah, the Part of Tens! No *For Dummies* book can call itself complete without a trip to this numerically obsessed section of the book.

In this particular Part of Tens, you get information about free and inexpensive resources that can simplify your quest for knowledge, quick things you can add to just about any auction without investing much time or effort, and a slew of tips for turning your About Me page and your Web site into product-selling machines. You even get some troubleshooting tips to keep things running when they look really, really broken.

Many sections in these chapters refer to other portions of the book, so you can brush up on any particular technique with just a few flips of the pages. Feel free to underline, bookmark, and generally notate what you find in here, too. After all, it's *your* book!

Chapter 18

Ten Great Resources for New eBay Programmers

*N*o matter how much experience you have with any particular topic — whether it's math, motorcycle racing, molecular biology, or meringue-making — you can always use more resources. Everybody needs them, regardless of their current skill level. Come to think of it, the "experts" I know spend an incredible amount of time identifying new resources to advance their already exceptional knowledge.

As you start your programming adventure, good resources make the trip go easier. Not only do you need *breadth* in resources — stuff that covers a wide variety of information — but you also need *depth* of resources, to uncover the hidden answers to your most challenging problems.

The Web sites, organizations, and tools in this chapter vary in their coverage and cost, but they all promise one thing: They want to simplify your life and make you more productive. Regardless of your specific informational needs, several of the resources outlined in the coming pages can expand your knowledge and help you become a better eBay developer. Good luck!

eBay Developers Program

It all starts here, at the source: eBay's official developer Web site (`developer.ebay.com`). Whether you want to start exploring the world of serious eBay programming, expand the knowledge you already have, check out some sample code, connect with fellow developers, or see who's doing what, you can find it all right here.

The site lists its main resource areas down the left side of the screen. As a new programmer, start in the *eBay API* area before getting too far into other stuff. You need a solid understanding of how the API process works before diving in too deeply here. (For the lowdown on API programming, check out Chapter 13.) Pay special attention to the other Developer Technology areas, particularly the Documentation and FAQs sections.

Avoid the marketing hype section (the one labeled *Business Benefits*) unless you want some leads and ideas of things that other developers already did. Generally speaking, you need this section's information only if you plan to sell your company on a full-scale eBay integration project or if you can't fall asleep some night.

Speaking of large-scale systems projects, spend a few minutes in the *Market Data* area to familiarize yourself with the type of data your programs can collect in there. That sales data provides a treasure trove just waiting for you to mine it.

eBay Developer Education Program

Formal training courses rank very high on my list of *positive things to do with your cash flow.* To expand your development skills in the quickest, most useful way, look into the professional training courses offered through the eBay Developer Education Program (`developer.ebay.com/education`).

The courses cover many general topics (searching, selling, opening an eBay store, and such) but also delve into more technical ones. As a developer working with the eBay environment, you need all the information available so you can really understand the eBay process and design the best applications. Best of all, the courses cost very little — usually $25 for a technical class and nothing at all for the more general courses.

To take courses in the Provider Education Program, sign up in the My Learning area (`docentnow.docenthost.com/ebaydev`); registration costs nothing. From there, you can browse the class catalog, add courses to your individual learning plan, and sign up for the sessions. You can also enter projected course completion dates to keep you focused and track your progress.

Start your educational trek with course #1, *Lifecycle of an eBay Listing*. As the title suggests, this course tracks the life of an auction listing from the perspective of the API, giving you insight on how and when various API calls fit into the process. The online course costs less than $100, which makes it a bargain considering the information it provides.

From there, eBay Provider Education offers everything from broad development sessions (#102 *Design Consideration for an Application* and #204 *Building and Maintaining a Robust eBay Application*) to more specific technology sessions (#103 *Introduction to the eBay API: XML and SOAP*). Java and .NET developers get their own sessions, too.

Completing the classes also leads you toward completing eBay's two individual certification programs: eBay Certified Engineer and eBay Certified Consultant. Companies interested in becoming eBay Certified Providers need a certain percentage of certified staff members, which makes your coursework and certification a marketable commodity. Taking the certification test costs $150, and it's well worth the money (whether or not your employer foots the bill). For more details about the Certified Provider Program, see `developer.ebay.com/certifiedprovider`.

General Language References

Learning a new programming language is a lot like learning a new natural language. You wrestle with syntax, usage, vocabulary, and the frustration of knowing what you *want* to say but having no clue precisely *how* to say it.

Other programmers walked these roads before you, and they felt the same frustrations and fought the same battles on their way to fluency in their chosen development dialect. Some of them took pity on folks just learning the languages, so they created Web sites and other online resources dedicated to making languages easier to learn and use.

Some of these sites include tutorials and discussion areas, and others focus on guides to implementing various techniques or tools. Bookmark them all for now and then flip through them as you work toward conquering your new language:

- **Dev Shed** (`www.devshed.com`) includes sections about each language, with a focus on open source options. It also offers a great section on the best application development practices, helping you turn out the best programs possible. (Look for those in the *Practices* section.)

- **SitePoint** (`www.sitepoint.com`) takes a holistic view of development, starting with everything from picking a domain name to understanding the legal and privacy issues surrounding online applications. It features an amazing Design and Layout section, which contains much-needed insights into *usability* (the art of creating programs and interfaces that people actually comprehend). It also features several development-focused blogs, plus an impressive bunch of forums.

- **DevX: Project Cool** (`www.devx.com/projectcool`) features an amazing selection of demonstrations, tutorials, and quick reference pages. Its quick reference section quickly earned a bookmark in my Web browser (particularly the sections on HTML tags and color codes because I can't remember some of those tags no matter how hard I try). For quick examples that explain great new techniques, make sure you look at the *10-Minute Solutions* section. It's great for people (like me) who learn best by seeing the code in action.

- **Builder.com** (`www.builder.com`) provides some nice basic articles for different languages as well as covers a bit of the growing .NET environment. Although its selection of other resource areas looks impressive at first glance, a few clicks reveal most of them to be little more than glorified affiliate links.

- **Webmonkey** (`webmonkey.wired.com/webmonkey`) feels kinda odd, but because it's from *Wired,* that goes with the territory. Even so, it offers a great selection of tutorials on coding, graphics, multimedia, and more. Some of its information feels a bit dated, but it still works — and that's what counts.

After you get proficient in your new language, make sure you return the favor by helping someone else learn the ropes. Teaching somebody else a language increases *your* programming skills all the faster.

Connecting with Other Developers

Although it might feel good to the ego, reinventing the wheel makes little practical sense (particularly when all the good shapes are already taken).

The same truism goes for application development. Given all the code that's floating around the planet already, the odds are good that someone else already faced whatever problem you're facing right now and figured out a particularly cool solution. Rather than spend your time beating your way through the darkness in search of the Ultimate Fix That Solves This Problem, why not save some effort by posing the question to someone else?

The development forums in Webdeveloper.com (www.webdeveloper.com) fill this need. They cover a lot of technical ground, with specific forums for all the major online programming environments, including Java, .NET, XML, and HTML, plus scripting languages such as ASP, JavaScript, and PHP. Whatever your development persuasion, you can find other people who work in your chosen language somewhere among the Webdeveloper.com forums.

Within the forums, you find discussions of current and cutting-edge programming techniques, nifty tips shared by experienced developers, and plenty of questions about the ever-shifting online programming environment. Post a question, sharpen your skills, and contribute your knowledge in these great online resource areas. You never know what you'll find out or who you might meet there!

For another great discussion area, check out Webmaster-Talk.com (www.webmaster-talk.com). It only offers discussion areas (as opposed to Webdeveloper's articles and news), but its breadth and incredibly active membership make it a great place to join, listen, and learn.

Focusing on PHP

Over the last couple of years, developers have discovered what PHP can do, and they have run with it like crazy. PHP runs on millions of Web servers all over the world, driving more applications than most undergraduates can calculate without electronic assistance. Thanks to PHP's open source background, all of that developer interest means lots of free online resources just waiting for you to discover them.

Start your quest for PHP information with a visit to the source of all things PHP: Zend (www.zend.com). Founded by the key designers of the PHP language, Zend focuses on expanding, extending, and supporting PHP in all its forms. The site includes every sort of resource a developer could want or need, from language references to community areas.

From there, a number of other resource sites beckon enticingly for your attention:

- **PHP.net** (www.php.net) includes the PHP documentation, a nice tutorial, plus a huge number of links for conferences, training sessions, user groups, and more. The download section includes both the complete PHP source code and compiled Windows versions as well as the various security fixes and patches for older PHP implementations.

- **PHP Freaks.com** (www.phpfreaks.com) focuses on tutorials, discussion forums, and lots of downloadable scripts. It's free, but it features a somewhat annoying ad atop each page. If you can get past the ad, you can find a lot to like at this site.

- **PHPBuilder.com** (www.phpbuilder.com) offers a nice collection of articles, code examples, communities, and news on PHP. The people finder stands out as a unique offering, helping connect you directly with other PHP developers around the world. And, of course, it's all free. (You've gotta love that!)

Working with PHP means getting very comfortable with MySQL as well. Because all the preceding sites include information on that popular database system, you shouldn't have any problems getting to know it.

Getting into XML

Unlike PHP, there's really no *there* when it comes to XML information. The Internet offers lots of individual development-oriented sites, but none of them carry the banner of The One True XML Information Source.

Even so, several sites definitely earn a mention for their information, discussion areas, and sample code libraries:

- **XMLMania.com** (www.xmlmania.com) provides a lot of news relating to both XML and the computer industry in general. It also includes a solid file collection of both applications and code samples. XMLMania.com also wins the award for *sort-of available in the most languages,* thanks to its integration of Google's automated translation system. (Heck, at least it tried!)

- **XMLFiles.com** (www.xmlfiles.com) hosts the strongest collection of general XML information. Beginners, advanced developers, and everybody in-between can find useful stuff here. The site also provides lots of focused explanations and samples for various XML implementations, which help you understand the many-faceted ways this language can work for you.

- ✔ **Cover Pages** (`xml.coverpages.org`) serves a dual purpose. At one level, it offers a great news service covering XML technology. It also includes an exhaustive listing of the core standards covering XML, SGML (from whence XML came), and many XML-related technologies. If you ever need to know the *real* detail on how XML works, come here.

- ✔ **XML.org** (`www.xml.org`) looks toward XML business applications instead of focusing on how XML works. It collects leads on new design ideas, links to developer organizations, and project specifications in an effort to create a central clearinghouse of XML-related application information, with the hopes of promoting XML usage throughout business, government, and nonprofit organizations.

You can find other resources with a quick romp through your favorite Web search engine, but evaluate them carefully during your visits. Lots of sites provide a thin veneer of information as a cover for promoting their for-pay services. As with all things, it pays to know where your information comes from.

Going with the Flow of Cascading Style Sheets (CSS)

The world of Web site layout and design changed mightily when Cascading Style Sheets (or CSS for short) arrived on the scene. Although developers first saw it as a tool for controlling text formats, they quickly figured out new ways to apply the amazingly flexible CSS technology. It didn't take long for CSS to go from just changing fonts to handling full-fledged page layout. Even now, developers constantly discover new tricks and techniques for squeezing greater power from CSS.

All of this interest from developers generated a wealth of online information about both the details of the technology and ways to apply it. The following sites make great places to start:

- ✔ **Cascading Style Sheets Home Page** (`www.w3.org/Style/CSS`) serves as a crossroads of information, discussion, testing, and development for CSS. It includes sections on learning to use CSS, compatible browsers, specifications, and authoring tools, plus links to CSS test sites. The site gets updated frequently, so it makes a great first stop on your information search.

- ✔ **Holy CSS, Zeldman!** (`www.dezwozhere.com/links.html`) sports just about the cutest title of any tech-oriented Web site out there, but I digress. The site focuses on resources aimed at *doing* stuff with CSS, not discussing the future of the technology or anything obtuse like that. To help you find the best resources out there, the site marks links to those items with a self-described "pukey highlight color," which really makes those links stand out. Regardless of your technical level, this site offers *lots* of stuff for you.

✔ **CSS Layout Techniques** (www.glish.com/css) provides great working examples of standard site column-oriented layouts implemented with CSS. The site displays examples of the layouts and freely offers the code that makes them work. It also includes links for other resources and CSS tutorials, making it another great stop for growing your newfound skills.

✔ **CSS Crib Sheet** (www.mezzoblue.com/css/cribsheet) does one thing, but it does that *really* well. The Crib Sheet site lists the most common issues and suggestions for troubleshooting problems with CSS. Some solutions focus on the basics (like *when in doubt, validate*), while others point out very specific issues (such as *don't rely on min-width in Internet Explorer*). The stuff in here assumes that you feel very comfortable with CSS in general, but need some insight for solving technical glitches.

✔ **CSS Zen Garden** (www.csszengarden.com) beautifully demonstrates the power behind CSS. By clicking on one of the site's design links, you apply a different style sheet to the same basic content. Immediately, the page's entire look and feel changes according to the new style sheet, yet the content remains exactly the same. Artists and developers from all over the world contribute new style sheets regularly, adding to the hundreds of examples already on the site. For a truly eye-opening experience with the power of CSS, spend some time clicking the design links and drooling over the results. Later, after honing your CSS skills, come back here and show off your talent by adding your own style sheet to the collection.

Search engines list lots of CSS-related sites, but be careful as you browse through them. Some sites lean toward the cutting-edge side of CSS level 2 (commonly referred to as *CSS2*) development — stuff that only works on a handful of Web browsers. Instead, you want to focus on the original specification, *CSS1*.

Fiddling with JavaScript

Once the absolute hot property of the programming world, JavaScript survived its brush with fame. These days, it has settled down into a useful little scripting language that's great for building self-contained gizmos on your Web site or eBay page.

Each of the following sites mixes articles with coding examples and throws in a bounty of ready-to-use scripts just for fun. None of the sites require registration to download code or read the news, although most discussion board software demands that you go through a free registration of some kind. And with that, here's your starting list of helpful JavaScript sites:

- ✔ **JavaScript Kit** (www.javascriptkit.com) really pushes tutorials, free scripts, and free Java applets. It includes a nice mixture of other tutorials as well, including both basic and advanced coverage of JavaScript along with DHTML, CSS, and generic site-building information. Its focus on doing stuff with JavaScript gives the site extra value.

- ✔ **The JavaScript Source** (javascript.internet.com) puts its resources almost entirely toward creating a huge collection of ready-to-use scripts, although it just couldn't resist adding some news headlines to the front page like everybody else. Make sure you visit the interactive Graphic Buttons Generator and prowl through the extensive script library.

- ✔ **WebReference JavaScript Articles** (webreference.com/programming/javascript) represents a corner part of the much larger WebReference.com site, but that doesn't diminish the quality of the articles found here. The more advanced articles cross-reference related topics, giving you a quick way to expand your understanding of how various Web technologies fit together.

A universe of small Web sites offers tiny tidbits of JavaScript code. No other language seems to engender so much interest from people to show what they come up with as they learn it. JavaScript devotees seem driven to display their efforts, no matter how well (or badly) things work. Still, you can learn something from almost everything you find out there (even if it's an example of how to *never ever* write a JavaScript routine).

Adding a Great Trio of Tools

Sometimes, you need something to make your life go a little faster and easier. For me, Mountain Dew makes the day go a little faster (and sometimes a little jumpier). My beloved copy of Microsoft Word combined with a portrait-oriented flat screen monitor makes my writing go easier. When you put them all together, you get a wide-eyed me writing chapters at 2 a.m., but that's beside the point. No, the point is that these things make my work go better, helping me do more and do it quickly.

As you get into application development, you probably start with the tools that you have at hand (just like Chapter 3 suggests). Those tools do a great job in the beginning, but in a short time, they start getting in the way. As your programming skill increases, you need more professional tools to stay at the top of your form.

Three of the best editing tools out there are:

- Dreamweaver MX (www.macromedia.com/software/dreamweaver)
- PrimalScript (www.sapien.com)
- Zend Studio (www.zend.com)

Depending on your development focus, any (or even all) of them make a great addition to your program collection. To make things even handier for you, we included sample versions of a couple of them on the CD in this book. Check the CD Appendix for the details.

Both PrimalScript and Dreamweaver MX handle a broad selection of languages, including HTML, PHP, JavaScript, and others. PrimalScript covers a little wider group of options than Dreamweaver MX, but Dreamweaver MX makes up for it with its in-depth support for ColdFusion and ASP.NET.

Zend Studio takes a completely different approach by focusing exclusively on PHP development. By targeting its efforts, Zend Studio creates a self-contained development environment for all your PHP work, covering everything from typing the code to debugging the results. This single-minded devotion makes a lot of sense, given that Zend is the company behind the PHP language. Still, that doesn't detract from Zend Studio's feature set or usefulness. If you want the ultimate PHP development tool (and own something else to handle the other languages), Zend Studio is your tool.

Hitting the Books

I couldn't close a chapter about programming language resources without at least one mention of the other great books contributed by my fellow *For Dummies* authors. It's a self-preservation thing — generally speaking, we all stick together. Plus we like each other's books. If we didn't think the books helped, we wouldn't recommend them. (Really — it's just how we are.)

You can split the following books into two basic categories: introductory Web site–focused titles and more advanced development books. Each one brings something unique to the programming discussion, whether its some cool ideas for using style sheets, resoundingly clear explanations of the server-centric world of PHP, or ready-to-use Web site templates.

- ✔ *HTML 4 For Dummies,* 4th Edition, by Ed Tittel and Natanya Pitts
- ✔ *Web Design For Dummies* by Lisa Lopuck
- ✔ *XHTML For Dummies* by Ed Tittel, Chelsea Valentine, and Natanya Pitts
- ✔ *Cascading Style Sheets For Dummies* by Damon Dean
- ✔ *Beginning Programming For Dummies* by Wallace Wang
- ✔ *PHP 5 For Dummies* by Janet Valade
- ✔ *PHP and MySQL For Dummies,* 2nd Edition, by Janet Valade
- ✔ *JavaScript For Dummies,* 4th Edition, by Emily A. Vander Veer
- ✔ *XML For Dummies,* 3rd Edition, by Ed Tittel
- ✔ *.NET Web Services For Dummies* by Anthony T. Mann
- ✔ *ASP.NET For Dummies* by Bill Hatfield

As with all the titles in the popular *For Dummies* line (Wiley), you can find any and all of these at your favorite independent local bookseller, your nearby book superstore, or one of those handy online bookstores.

Chapter 19

Ten Easy Enhancements for Every Auction

*E*very auction can use a little boost. (Yes, *every* one. Really.) Whether you turbocharge things with an amazingly technical solution or accomplish much the same thing by pulling something distinctly *nontechnical* out of your hat, you understand the power of the *gizmo* when it comes to online auction buyers. If you answer their questions, provide them with plenty of information, communicate what type of buying experience awaits them, and convince them about the value of your product, then eBay success definitely awaits you.

The most successful sellers automate and organize as much of their work as possible, turning their software programs into surrogate helpers that never ask for a day off and rarely take a lunch break (although they sometimes have a nervous breakdown).

This chapter looks at simple (and a few not-so-simple) things that can add dollars and creature comforts to your favorite auctions. As your technical skill increases, revisit this chapter periodically to pick up new ideas or try something a little different. Good selling to you!

Organizing for Clarity

Your customers want to know about your eBay offerings, and your auction text has the answers — if, that is, your customers can find the information buried in there! Direct your customers' attention to everything they want to know by organizing your auction listings with simple headers and plenty of white space. Point out the information they need in order to make a bidding decision. Prevent misunderstandings by highlighting your shipping fees, sale terms, and contact information. Make them salivate with a delicious portrayal of whatever you're selling and then close the deal by pointing them to the bidding box. You can do all this and more with some simple organization.

Start your organizational efforts by chopping your auction listing into segments with basic descriptive headers. Most sellers rely on a detailed main heading with a few eloquent words about the product (such as *Rare 1785 Hand-scrolled Flimsybopper*) and fill in the rest of the auction text with generic headings like *Terms* and *Shipping*. That makes your listings come together quickly while still communicating lots of information to your prospective buyer.

Put in headers for each section of your auction (including the main description), detailed explanations of an item's condition (if necessary), shipping costs, other terms of sale, your contact information, and links to other eBay products you currently offer. (Just because you're adding headings to the text doesn't mean you can get sloppy with the normal parts of the auction!)

Like the headings in this chapter, make your auction headings larger and bolder than your normal text. Luckily, the heading 1 tag, <h1>, does all that for you in a single step. Here's what the tag looks like in action:

```
<h1>Rare Victorian "Lacis" netting -- 10" square in off-
       white</h1>
<p>You're bidding on a vintage piece of handmade Victorian
       netting, a popular form of needlework during that
       period. This item measures 10" square and features
       detailed embroidery atop the netting.</p>
```

In this example, the heading appears in a large font, and the text under it comes out in normal body text size. The browser automatically pads a little extra space around the heading as well and includes its own line break at the end.

With the headers in position, add one more thing: nothing. Well, not exactly nothing — add some blank space. Folks who work in graphic design and advertising call this *white space,* and they absolutely swear by using it on the page. White space helps your buyers find, read, and understand your information. Don't drive your customers away by crushing the entire listing into an impenetrable, indecipherable block of text — spread things out a bit!

Blank space costs nothing in the online economy, so use it freely. To add some space in your auction, include extra line breaks (`<br>`) after the text in your HTML code. Just drop a line break behind the closing paragraph tag (`</p>`) in your text, as shown in the following example:

```
<h1>Rare Victorian "Lacis" netting -- 10" square in off-
        white</h1>
<p>You're bidding on a vintage piece of handmade Victorian
        netting, a popular form of needlework during that
        period. This item measures 10" square and features
        detailed embroidery atop the netting.</p><br>
```

The `<br>` tag puts an extra line of space under the descriptive text, moving it down the page a bit. The effect looks really good when combined with heading tags.

Usually a single extra tag dropped here and there does exactly what you need. You can go overboard by creating vast rolling plains of, well, plainness, so start with a little and add more from there. A little white space goes a long way.

For even better organization, throw in a full-fledged menu with anchor links that let the customer flip forward and backward through your auction listing. For more information about that, see Chapter 4.

Drawing Attention with Formatting

Thanks to the *What You See Is What You Get* (WSIWYG) display capabilities built into the Windows and Macintosh operating systems, on-screen text went from boring, dull, and monotonous to wild, funky, and beautiful. In the process, it also unfortunately went from highly readable to occasionally illegible. Granted, some of the more artistically beautiful text on the Internet really jumps off the Web page at you, but all it communicates in the process is *guess what I'm saying!*

For your eBay auction text, communication ranks way, *way* above beauty every time. Yes, you want a nice-looking listing that pleases as it informs, but to sell products, your listing *must* present information to your customers clearly and efficiently. That's why the text exists in the first place.

Why open this section with a diatribe about art versus communication? Because HTML font, size, and formatting tags give you a lot of graphical power over your text. They give you so much power, in fact, that you can get carried away with all the options and end up with an auction description that looks more like a Web-based ransom note.

The KISS principle *(Keep It Simple, Seller)* applies strongly when it comes to prettying up the text in your auction. Just because you *can* specify lots of typefaces in myriad sizes doesn't mean that you should. In fact, many top-selling auctions don't use any `<font face>` or `<font size>` commands at all — and that's not a half-bad idea. Instead of specifying various typefaces, these sellers rely on the browser's built-in settings to specify the fonts that get displayed. They spend time crafting great descriptions and then make those descriptions easy to skim by highlighting important text with **bold** HTML tags.

By carefully using simple font tags, you can guide your buyer's eyes through the description and highlight your product's (and your auction's) key benefits in the process. For instance, skim over the following paragraph. What stands out?

> You're bidding on a **vintage** piece of **handmade Victorian netting,** a popular form of needlework during that period. This item measures **10"** **square** and features **detailed embroidery** atop the netting.

In a glance, you picked up all the key parts in that description. You know what the item is, its size, some of its history, and information about its style. Without the bold text, you might barely get to the word *vintage* before you start skipping words and losing interest.

Adding the formatting requires only a few bold (`<b>`) tags, as you can see:

```
<p>You're bidding on a <b>vintage</b> piece of <b>handmade
      Victorian netting,</b> a popular form of
      needlework during that period. This item measures
      <b>10" square</b> and features <b>detailed
      embroidery</b> atop the netting.</p>
```

Notice that each bold tag includes both a starting and finishing piece to tell the browser precisely what text you want rendered in bold. Some editors use the strong tag (`<strong></strong>`) instead of bold, although it gives the same results. Use whichever tag best fits your personality.

Italic text (made with the italic tag, `<i>`) accomplishes some of the same goals as bold text, but it does so with a much lighter touch. Use italic text when you want to subtly draw attention to something but don't want that information to overpower the text around it.

Unfortunately, italic doesn't always look as great on the screen as it does on paper. Because of that, I usually rely on bold text rather than italic in my auctions. Still, it's worth trying both options for yourself to see how they work for you and your particular type of sales.

Because I already have a *warning* theme going, watch out for strange and beautiful fonts, too. Sure, *Hattingfield Modern Boingo Script Medium* looks gorgeous on your screen, but don't include any calls for it in the HTML code for your auction. Unless your auction customer's computer has its own copy of that obscure font file, the customer won't see the font you want. Instead, she gets whatever locally available font Windows selects to take its place — and Windows isn't one of the more artistic applications out there when it comes to font choices. If you simply *must* mess around with fonts in your auctions, stick to widely available ones like *Arial, Helvetica, Times New Roman,* or *Verdana.* Even then, your code always works better if you avoid font changes entirely and stick with basic formatting and heading tags like bold (`<b>`), italic (`<i>`), and Heading 1 (`<h1>`).

Going Big (Or Small) with Size Tags

There's an old saying that covers just about everything (even disparate things like ice cream and tax refunds): Bigger is better. The same rule applies to your auction text as well. Bold text stands out better than plain text, but big *and* bold text practically explodes off the screen. As with the heading tags, each person's Web browser makes its own decisions about precisely what a particular size means, but that shouldn't cause any problems for the text. Big text should still look big, and that's the whole point.

To add some new sizes to your repertoire, apply the two basic groups of HTML size tags. The first one, the `<font size>` tag, lets you specify a given size for all text appearing between the beginning and ending tags. Web browsers recognize seven sizes of text, ranging from teeny (size 1) to monstrous (size 7). Normal text appears at size 3, so the range of sizes gives you plenty of room for playing.

The `<font size>` tag looks like this in action:

```
Get your genuine<font size=5> Bag o' Rocks </font>before
          they're gone forever!
```

In this example, the name of the featured product (the ever-popular *Bag o' Rocks*) towers over the rest of the text on the line. Because the tag specifies size 5 text, customers always see whatever their browsers think that size text looks like, regardless of the size of the text around it. The browser just hits the tag, checks its notes on how big that size looks, and then formats the text accordingly.

When making a section of text bigger, watch where you put the spaces in the HTML code. It's hard to tell in the preceding example, but I put the spaces next to *Bag o' Rocks* inside the `<font size>` tags. By doing that, the browser resized the spaces to match the resized text. If you put the spaces outside of the tags so it says `genuine <font size=5>Bag o' Rocks</font> before`, then the bigger text would look a little squished in the sentence because the spaces next to it are the wrong size. It's a small thing, but the little things polish your work with an extra layer of professionalism.

The other HTML size tags, `<big>` and `<small>`, work in conjunction with the rest of the text around the tags. Instead of specifying a particular size, these tags tell the browser to either grow or shrink the enclosed text by one size. If the tags appear in a bunch of normal text (which defaults to size 3), a `<big>` tag takes the marked text to size 4, and a `<small>` tag drops it to size 2. You use these tags just like the more specific `<font size>` tag:

```
Get your genuine<big> Bag o' Rocks </big>before they're gone
          forever!
```

The `<big>` and `<small>` tags work great when you want a subtle change between the main text and the enlarged text — just something small and simple — and you want to code it quickly. Best of all, `<big>` and `<small>` give you an added bonus: Because the browser adjusts the text size relative to the text outside the tags, these tags still automatically do their thing if you enlarge or reduce the body text itself. How's that for a deal?

Highlighting Information with Color

A bed of flowers catches your eye because it's hard to ignore an explosion of color. You can get the same effect for your auction text (without the bees and the fertilizer, of course) by selectively seasoning your writing with splatters, dashes, and dots of color.

HTML gives you a couple different ways to change the color of your text. Both of the tags understand 16 basic color names: aqua, black, blue, fuchsia, gray, green, lime, maroon, navy, olive, purple, red, silver, teal, white, and yellow. Generally speaking, stick with these colors for your auction needs. They cover all the basics, and they flirt with the wacky home decorator palette as well. If you absolutely *must* put up a specific color of your choosing, you can describe it the more technical way with its six-character hexadecimal value. For instance, *red* becomes #ff0000 in hexadecimal. For more about hexadecimal color values, flip back to Chapter 4.

The first of your color options uses the `<span style>` tag. Because it works both for spot color inside your HTML document and as the power behind Cascading Style Sheets, this tag has recently replaced the older method, the `<font color>` tag (described a little later in this section).

This new `<span style>` tag gives you plenty of flexibility for changing both the foreground and background color of your text. However, unless you mix and match colors with the artistic eye of a New York fashion designer, I strongly suggest limiting your creative color impulses to the foreground text colors *only* — leave the background color alone. Thanks to the power of the `<span style>` tag, the most amazingly hideous color combinations are at your fingertips. For the sake of your sales, please don't use them!

Here's a peek at the `<span style>` tag at work. The following sample code displays a marketing sentence from an auction using the default color and then adds a touch of do-it-now red in the middle:

```
Don't miss <span style="color: red">this amazing
           antique</span>. Bid now!
Don't miss <span style="color: #ff0000">this amazing
           antique</span>. Bid now!
```

Both of these examples daub the text `this amazing antique` in the same shade of red. The first uses the color name, the second applies the hexadecimal number, and they both look the same to the buyer.

Your other option injects spot color with the `<font color>` tag. This method still works fine in eBay, but the Web programming experts out there pooh-pooh it for serious HTML work. (They prefer the style code in the preceding example or suggest using a full-fledged Cascading Style Sheet.) Still, Web browsers understand the code just fine, so if you feel like doing things the old-fashioned way, you can. (Just don't get in the habit of using this tag, okay?)

The `<font color>` tag accepts any of the 16 official color names and the weird-looking hexadecimal value that describes any color you can imagine. Here's how the tag looks in action:

```
Don't miss <font color="red">this amazing antique</font>. Bid
      now!
Don't miss <font color="#ff0000">this amazing antique</font>.
      Bid now!
```

The first example uses the color name (red) in the tag, and the second replaces that with the infinitely less friendly hexadecimal value for red. As with color specifications for the `<span style>`, both techniques deliver the same results.

To make your highlighted text stand out even more, add a bold tag (`<b>`) with the color. Put it inside the color tags, just like the following example:

```
Don't miss <span style="color: red"><b>this amazing
      antique</b></span>. Bid now!
```

The bold attribute turbocharges the color, making it practically reach out and grab your eyes. Use this combination sparingly, though. If you scatter too many colored highlights across your auction page, the poor buyer won't know where to look next! Pick out the most important "buying" words and phrases and really go to work on those. For the marginally-but-not-terribly-important words, use either bold by itself or a different highlight color. (Blue works well for that purpose, by the way.)

Cross-Selling with Links to Your Other Auctions

Nobody wants to sell your stuff quite as much as you do. Because you already spend a lot of time finding great products and writing great descriptions, why not add some links that take your customers from one auction to another within your collected listings? That way, whenever one of your auctions catches someone's eye, you get a chance to sell that person not just *one* thing but a *whole bunch* of things!

Lots of third-party auction tool companies offer this kind of service as a benefit of using their systems. If you already use a service to help post your auctions, make sure that your account uses the service's "see my other auctions" feature (or whatever it's called). You already paid the money, so you might as well get the full value from the product.

eBay understands the value of cross-selling and automatically builds a basic form of it into all your auctions. In your Seller Information box, eBay adds a lone link to View Seller's Other Items. That's a start, but more exposure never hurts.

Start your advertising quest by including at least one more copy of the View Seller's Other Items link in the body of your description. To do that, follow these steps:

1. **Open one of your current auctions in your favorite Web browser and then right-click on the View Seller's Other Items link.**

   A pop-up menu appears next to the mouse pointer.

2. **In the pop-up menu, click the item that lets you copy the URL of the link.**

   Microsoft Internet Explorer calls this option Copy Shortcut, whereas Mozilla Firefox uses the more descriptive Copy Link Location. Either way, the menu disappears after you click the appropriate option.

3. **Open your HTML auction template in your favorite editor. Paste the URL you copied in Step 2 into the template.**

   At this point, it doesn't matter where you paste the link because you're probably going to move it in just a moment.

4. **Add the appropriate HTML code to turn your just-pasted URL into a clickable link in your auction listing.**

   To do that, make the code look like the following sample but with your URL in the middle of it:

   ```
   Buy from <a
            href="http://cgi6.ebay.com/ws/eBayISAPI.dll?ViewS
            ellersOtherItems&userid=linguaplay">our other
            auctions</a> and save on combined shipping!
   ```

   The code displays the prompt text *Buy from our other auctions and save on combined shipping*. It creates a clickable link behind the words *our other auctions* and points the link at the eBay URL.

Don't worry if your finished URL looks a lot longer than this example. Your code probably contains other statements like `&include=0&since=-1&sort=3&rows-50`. You can either leave the extra stuff in your URL or cut it out — eBay's servers don't really seem to care either way.

Putting Photos Inline with Your Text

Buyers love seeing pictures of the products in your auctions. That's why eBay lets you add a free picture to every auction you post. Of course, eBay also offers you the *option* of adding a few more pictures to the auction (for a minimal fee, of course), but unfortunately every photo you include gets shoved into the same section at the very bottom of the auction — and that's not the best place for photos to go.

You can overcome that positioning problem *and* add any number of photos to your auctions at the same time by creating your own photo storage area and then including image tags (<img>) in your auction text. Although this adds an extra step to your posting process (namely, copying the photos to your online storage area), that minimal amount of work provides you with tons of flexibility, plus the ability to make a really awesome-looking auction.

First things first — you need an online home for your photos. Luckily, any Web hosting service covers this task perfectly. Even the storage space built into every AOL account (check out key word **My FTP Space**) works great! If you already have a Web site, just use a bit of space on that server. And if you always wanted to start a Web site, this makes a great excuse to start now.

Web hosts come in all shapes, sizes, and price ranges, so shop around. You can find basic hosting for as little as $2.95 per month, although *reliable* hosting usually starts in the $4.95 to $7.95 per month range. Many books and online articles tell you how to pick a hosting service, so dive into Google (or pick up a resource at your favorite bookstore) and see what you can find.

After you arrange for your Web space, find out how the host recommends transferring files from your computer to your online space. Some host companies offer a nifty Web-based tool for this, although a good FTP (File Transfer Protocol) program like Direct FTP from CoffeeCup Software (www.coffeecup.com) usually works faster, easier, and better. Check with your Web hosting company for its recommendations.

After moving your auction images up to the server, you need to add HTML code to your auctions to insert the images. Chapter 4 goes into detail on how to build the links, along with some simple tricks you can use to make the images look all the cooler.

Even though you can add pictures until your auction looks like a photo mosaic, don't get carried away. Every image you add increases the loading time for your auction, so keep the number low. Most auctions benefit from using two to three images instead of just one, but only the priciest auctions — stuff like cars, houses, priceless Ming vases, and such — require more than three pictures. If you want to use a gallery image for the auction, you still need to put one photo into the standard eBay image area.

Little Pictures, Big Pictures

Few things frustrate me more as an online auction buyer than trying to discern an item's condition when sellers post a little tiny picture (or even a bunch of little pictures) in their auctions. If you look closely, you might figure out the item's color, but postage-stamp-sized images don't do justice to a really beautiful product. Unfortunately, you can't use only huge pictures either because they throw the auction window out of whack and demand huge download times that frustrate the dial-up Internet users out there.

If only you could show a smaller image in your auction but then link to a *bigger* image outside — and do it without paying all that extra money for eBay's built-in super-sizing option, too! Once again, it's HTML to the rescue, although this time you need a handy image editing program like Paint Shop Pro or Photoshop Elements (or even Photoshop itself), plus some online image storage space (as described in the preceding section "Putting Photos Inline with Your Text").

By the way, this trick works great with the inline image concept in the preceding section. Combine the two, and you get inline thumbnail-size images that lead to big images when the buyer clicks them. Talk about a professional look!

Making these clickable uber-images means making two versions of your image: a spacious, full-size version and a small copy. Use your image editing program to shrink the photo down to a nice small (and fast-loading) picture — anything from 150 x 200 pixels to 300 x 400 pixels makes a great small size. On the flip side, don't make your big photo *too* big. A standard 600-x-800-pixel image shows more than enough detail for just about anybody. After that, save both of the images into your online storage space. Remember to change the name of the image to differentiate it from the big original! (If in doubt, just add `-thumb` onto the end of the name, like `mcpoker1-thumb.jpg`.)

With both images available in your online storage space, add the code to your auction that displays the smaller image and, in the process, turns it into a link that opens a new browser window displaying the full-size image:

```
<a href="http://www.linguaplay.com/pokerset.gif"
        target=_blank>
```

```
<img src="http://www.linguaplay.com/pokerset-thumb.gif"
          align=left border=5 hspace=15 >
</a>
```

The `<img src>` tag displays the thumbnail image, aligns it on the left side of the window (allowing text to flow around it), and formats it with a pretty border and some white space (tricks borrowed from the preceding section in this chapter). So far, so good, but what about the link? The first and last lines of code handle that. By encircling the `<img src>` tag with an anchor tag, you turn the image into a clickable link! As an added bonus, the `target=_blank` attribute in the tag tells the buyer's browser to open the photo in a new window.

You should include an explanation somewhere in your description that the buyer can click any of the images to see a full-size version of the picture in a *new browser window.* People like surprises when they shop, but the shock of clicking something that pops opens a whole new browser window might confuse some people because they think that they somehow misplaced the window containing their auction. Tell them about the feature of your auction and then tell them again elsewhere in the text.

Flash Menus Inside Auctions

Psst! Hey, you — wanna add something really spiffy to your auction? Something that makes it look more than merely professional by taking it straight into the realm of *wow?* I've got just the thing: *Flash menus.*

Ever since Macromedia (`www.macromedia.com`) introduced its amazing Flash system, Web developers all over the world have pressed it into service for everything from online slide shows to complete Web sites. For your purposes on eBay, though, you don't need most of Flash's talents. Instead, you just want it to make a very cool-looking menu — and oh, can it do that!

Thanks to some recent changes to eBay's guidelines, auctions *can* include some Flash-based components. To double-check the rules and make sure that decision still holds (because you know how eBay likes to changes its mind), go to `help.ebay.com` and search on the terms `flash content listing`.

To make a cool-looking Flash menu, you could use Macromedia's big programming tools, but that's overkill for what you plan to do (unless you already own them, that is). You can accomplish the same result with a special application designed to do this kind of thing, like CoffeeCup's *Button Factory* (from `www.coffeecup.com`). For a huge listing of similar options, search Google for `flash menu maker` — just brace yourself for the tsunami of matches!

Using your Flash menu-making program, create a gorgeous graphical menu that mirrors your auction's basic organization (from the first section of this chapter) and guides the buyer through all your informational areas. It takes only a little bit of code to accomplish all of this, mainly due to the focused programs.

Don't go hog-wild with all the options available to you in Flash programming. If you pack too many goodies into your work, your Flash menus get fat, dumpy, and slow, which delays your auction's appearance when a buyer clicks its link (and that's not good). Keep the menus simple and short so they hop helpfully into place and impress the buyer like crazy.

Most of these applications include tutorials on using the program and implementing basic Flash menu systems. If you can copy a few lines of code and run a menu-driven program, you can build a Flash menu. Good luck!

Adding a "Don't Steal This Stuff" Disclaimer

After going to all the trouble of creating some incredibly cool enhancements for your auctions — not to mention all the work you put into the descriptions and the product photos themselves — you should think about some kind of protection for your work. You can't put it under lock and key, and you can't have a security camera keep an eye on the auction in your absence. But you *can* put up a warning sign that establishes your rights and warns other sellers to leave your work alone.

If you sell products that other sellers also carry, I highly recommend adding a copyright statement to your auction. Implementing a licensing fee notice might make sense as well, particularly if you've had a problem in the past with people duplicating your images for their own auctions.

You don't need anything fancy for this or even any extra software. This doesn't use HTML or JavaScript, so it requires no programming. All you need is a little bit of plain text and some knowledge of the official eBay rules of business.

At the bottom of my auctions, I always put a copyright statement and licensing fee notice. They look like this:

```
Text and images in this auction are copyright 2004, Access
         Systems, Inc. Trademarked names and images are
              property of their respective owners.
```

```
LICENSING FEE NOTICE: If you copy the text or picture from
               our ad for your own purposes, you agree to pay us
               a $50 licensing fee per image (for photos) and per
               listed auction (for auction text). We put a lot of
               time and effort into our listings, and encourage
               you to do the same with yours.
```

The copyright statement lays my claim to the auction listing that I wrote and to the images that I made. It also makes clear that I'm not trying to usurp anybody else's copyright in the process of protecting my work. This also clearly says that I'm serious about protecting my business efforts here on eBay.

This statement goes hand-in-hand with the licensing fee notice. First, I establish ownership of my work; now, I explain what happens if someone copies it for their own use.

But you can't do that, I hear you say. *If it's in an eBay auction, then it's fair game.* Actually, no — that's a common misconception, even among long-time eBay sellers. According to the official eBay rules at pages.ebay.com/help/confidence/vero-image-text-theft.html, you can't copy *anything* from someone else's auction and then use it in your own. Even if you change it a little bit, that doesn't excuse the behavior.

My licensing fee notice warns people that if they copy my work, I plan to do something about it — and, on more than one occasion, I have, with great success. Thus far, that notice made me several hundred dollars and forced an early end to a number of auctions that illegally copied my images and text.

When I come across someone who has copied my auction text or images, I use the Ask Seller a Question link to notify them of the problem and request that they either pay my licensing fee or terminate their auction before it closes. If they refuse, then I report them to eBay for text or image theft — and eBay takes a very dim view of those actions. Most sellers comply by killing their auctions and then rewriting (or reshooting) their auctions. Others pay me the money, which gives them the right to reuse that text and image for future auctions. (After all, they *did* pay me for the rights.)

You put in a lot of effort on your auction, so why should you let someone else steal it all? You shouldn't — it's as simple as that. Add a simple copyright statement and licensing notice and then start protecting your work!

Augmenting Your Browser with the eBay Toolbar

Okay, so it doesn't technically fit in a discussion of things to enhance your auctions, but the eBay Toolbar with all its functionality goes a long way toward simplifying your broader eBay existence. Because it also guards you against password-stealing eBay spoof sites, the Toolbar also falls under the category of Security, and that's gotta count for something.

The eBay Toolbar Web site (`pages.ebay.com/ebay_toolbar`) describes the Toolbar's myriad features in some detail. To download and install the toolbar, just go to the page and click the appropriate button (it's the big one decked out in eBay Yellow, right under the picture of the toolbar in action).

As a seller, the eBay Toolbar gives you quick access to product searches, making that last-minute competitive research a breeze. For those occasional times when you bid on things (hey — it happens to me, too), the Toolbar offers up desktop alerts just before the end of an auction, giving you just enough time to place one of those auction-winning last-second bids. It also provides easy access to your Watched Items list, so you can see what's happening there.

Given the incredible rise of online scams lately (and the ever-increasing quality of the frauds), the Account Guard features come in handy. Account Guard watches for so-called *spoof* Web sites and warns you if you accidentally visit one. It also gives you an easy way to report spoof sites to eBay so it can take appropriate action against the scammer.

Best of all, you pay nothing for the eBay Toolbar — it's another of the free services offered by eBay. (Granted, eBay stands to make more money if you use it to track, snipe, and win auctions, so I suppose the Toolbar isn't *entirely* altruistic on eBay's part.)

Chapter 20

Ten Business-Building Additions for the About Me Page and Your Web Site

*I*f the three golden keys to brick-and-mortar retailing are *location, location,* and *location,* then the secrets to building your online sales must be *promotion, promotion,* and *promotion.* Retailers with a physical storefront primarily compete against the other stores in the area. In your case, "the area" means every Web browser on the planet, plus the thousands upon thousands of eBay auctions happening at any particular time. That's a lot of competition!

Building your eBay business means throwing a wide promotional net to reach as many of your potential customers as possible. It also means looking at your auctions, your About Me page, and your Web site as intake funnels, designed to not only quickly capture your prospects' interest but also draw them further into the buying process by turning their click into your sale.

This chapter suggests lots of ways to turn your auctions, your eBay About Me page, and your Web site (you *have* a Web site, right?) into powerful selling tools. Some demand very little effort, whereas others require some programming. Still, the chapter contains something for sellers at all levels of eBay business and technical sophistication. Dive in and change your business today!

Promoting Your eBay Efforts

When one of my college business advisors heard that I decided to start my own company, he offered me a simple pearl of wisdom: "Don't go anywhere without your business cards." Why? Because entrepreneurship means constant promotion. Still to this day, I leave a card or two with people everywhere I go. Over time, some of those contacts turn into new business. Others become friends and associates. Some probably lose the card (either accidentally or proactively). But regardless of the outcome, things happen because I keep handing out cards.

The same fundamental truth works with your eBay auctions. The more people you tell about your eBay business, the more eBay business you get!

Talk up your eBay sales everywhere you can — in your auctions, your About Me page, your Web site, and even your e-mail signature line. Put your Web site or your About Me address onto your business cards. Keep the drumbeat going constantly: *Find what you want in our eBay auctions.*

Auctions represent the first point of entry for your prospective buyers. Although a single item caught their interest, you want to broaden that interest into multiple purchases by showing them the rest of your wares. Do that by including several links to your About Me page throughout the auction text. In the links, entice customers into clicking by telling them why they should do it. *Save money with combined shipping* and *add another rarity to your collection* sound a lot more intriguing than *click here to visit my About Me page.*

After you get customers to the About Me page, present your products and services in an easy-to-understand way. Tell them what kinds of products your auctions usually offer and show off your expertise and convince them that you're *the expert* in this market. Give them information about your products. Promote your Web site. Whatever you do, make it interesting and useful to your buyers.

Use the same ideas with a Web site that supports your auction business. Include links to both your About Me page and your auction listings page. Tell prospective customers why buying from you makes more sense than buying from someone else. The more information you offer about your company, the more comfortable buyers feel bidding on your auctions.

Check out some of the later sections in this chapter for ideas that build on these, such as putting together an e-mail list (in the "Increasing Return Business with E-Mail Signups" section), adding news and information to your pages, promoting yourself as a product expert, and laying out your product offerings.

Cataloging Your Lines

Companies make catalogs for one simple reason: to sell more products. Why not take a page (pardon the expression) from their work by creating a simple online catalog of the wares you offer through eBay? An online catalog spurs add-ons to current sales as well as helps buyers plan future sales because they know that you can help them find particular things.

You don't need a fancy schmancy thing with tons of pictures and lengthy descriptions — if you designed them right, that's what your auctions do. No, I mean a simple listing of the types of things that you sell. If you do the list in your eBay About Me page, make sure that you limit it to the items that you sell on eBay. You can put a link there to your Web site that says something like *See our Web site for our complete product catalog,* but eBay's rules don't allow direct solicitations to purchase things outside of the auction service.

Make sure you include specific mentions of special order and seasonal products. You never know when someone might want a bunch of winter holiday decorations in the middle of the summer because they want to do a "Christmas in July" party.

To lay out your list, use either basic HTML tables or the unordered list tags (`<ul>`), as in the following example:

```
<h3>Lines we stock and sell year-round:</h3>
<ul type=disc, compact>
    <li>Dress shirts</li>
    <li>Dress slacks</li>
    <li>Casual shirts</li>
    <li>Casual slacks</li>
    <li>Socks</li>
</ul>
```

This example creates a nice bulleted list of items, topped with a brief heading. By using the bulleted list, you visually tell your customer that each of these items stands alone in your selection. (Numbered lists don't work well for this type of thing.) Add another level 3 heading (`<h3>`) if you start a new list.

Increasing Return Business with E-Mail Signups

Every time someone looks at one of your auctions, you get a brief chance to engage them and turn them into a customer. After someone buys something, you get the opportunity to make them a repeat customer — the best kind of customer of all! In both cases, communication makes all the difference. By sending a monthly e-mail to your customers, you build the perception that you're an expert and that your company knows the products.

Before you can send an e-mail newsletter, though, you need e-mail addresses for your list. More importantly, you need addresses of people who *want* to join your list. That's where things get tricky.

You automatically get the e-mail address of every person who buys a product from you, but eBay allows you to use those addresses only for eBay-specific purposes. eBay forbids sellers from adding buyer addresses (both e-mail and snail mail) to a mailing list, unless the buyers say they want to join your mailing list. (For the details of that policy, see section 5 of the eBay Privacy Policy: Your Use of Other Users' Information.) You can *invite* your trading partner to join your mailing list, but you can't sign that person up automatically.

On the other hand, eBay specifically *allows* you to put `mailto` links into your auction text (and freely include them in your About Me page). These links automatically open your customer's default e-mail program and create a new message going to the address in the link. With a little bit of HTML magic, you can also specify a subject line for the new message and some text for the message body, as the following example does:

```
For the latest news and collecting tips, join our <A
        HREF="mailto:mailinglist@linguaplay.com?Subject=Su
        bscribe?Body=Sign me up!">mailing list</A> today!
```

This link creates a new message addressed to `mailinglist@linguaplay.com`, and (if the e-mail program understands the command, which most do) fills in the subject line with `Subscribe` and the message body with `Sign me up!` To send the message, the customer just needs to click the Send button — it's that simple! When you receive one of those messages, you can safely add that person's e-mail address to your database.

Always, always, *always* give people a way to unsubscribe from your mailing list, and *always* remove addresses when people ask! You know the (ahem) *joy* of getting unsolicited e-mail and the feelings of frustration, anger, and destruction that you often wish upon the senders and their businesses. Why would you willingly generate those same feelings among your customers? You wouldn't — it makes no sense. Instead, let people off your list the first time they ask. It's just good business.

Numerous tools exist out there to automate mailing list subscriptions. If you poke around a bit, you can find free mailing list tools like Zeop (`www.zeop.com`) and Coollist (`www.coollist.com`), as well as subscription tools and formal software products that run on your Web server. If you choose to use a tool like this, read the company's end-user licensing agreement *very* closely to make sure that your customers' e-mail addresses will be safe.

For more about building your own simple tool with the filter system in your e-mail program, see Chapter 7.

Adding Profits with the eBay Affiliate Program

You already like eBay, right? You make money (or at least you want to make money) through the system. Your business either centers around eBay or owes part of its existence to the site. So why not capitalize on all that interest and open a new revenue stream for your business at the same time?

That's exactly what the eBay Affiliate Program (`affiliate.ebay.com`) does. Through its affiliate system partner, Commission Junction (`www.cj.com`), the eBay Affiliate Program offers some pretty amazing money in return for promoting eBay through banner ads, links, and even product links on your Web site.

Sadly, you can't earn commissions for referring buyers to your own auctions. It's a nice idea, but it doesn't work that way. Sorry. (I know — that's the first thought I had, too. eBay came up with it way before both of us.)

eBay pays you for two things: people who join eBay (provided the person bids or uses Buy It Now on something within 30 days of registering) and bids and Buy It Now transactions that come from one of your affiliate links. The payments come to you through Commission Junction's affiliate program. It handles the myriad little affiliate system details, letting eBay focus on what it does best.

Some companies make an entire business out of the eBay Affiliate Program. Although you probably don't want to go to that length, it's definitely worth putting some banners on your Web site or including a few links in your e-mail newsletter. After all, a little bit of free money never hurt any business!

For more about the eBay Affiliate Program, check out Chapter 6.

Anticipating Customer Questions with a FAQ

Get out a piece of paper and a pen — it's time for a quick experiment. Ready? List the top five questions you hear over and over from your customers. Write them down in any particular order. (Yes, I'll wait.)

When you finish writing down the questions, arrange them in order from most asked to least asked. Now jot down a few notes that answer each question. You don't need to go into a lot of depth, but you do need enough information so that buyers can grasp the idea and answer their question.

Congratulations — you just wrote a basic FAQ (Frequently Asked Questions document). And that's just the thing you need to take your eBay sales to the next level.

Information breeds trust from your customers. The more information you provide about your product, your company, your knowledge, your policies, and even you *personally,* the more comfortable a new buyer feels when working with you. A solid, up-to-date, informative FAQ tells customers that you think about them and that you care about them. From your perspective, a good FAQ also (hopefully) heads off lots of redundant questions by e-mail, although reality says that some people read the FAQ and then ask the same question anyway. (It's that *human* thing — sometimes life would be so much simpler if it weren't for the humans!)

Start your FAQ by looking at your business as a customer. What do you want to know about? What worries you? What would prevent you from purchasing one of your items? As you think about these things, go through the exercise at the beginning of this section. Jot down questions and answers as they come to you, and then organize them into a nicely written document. Post that document on your Web site and in your About Me page and then build links to it into your auctions. Promote the heck out of it to your customers and then watch it pay off.

For more about creating and using your FAQ, visit Chapter 6.

Looking for Something Special?

In today's wacky retail market, people want two things: price and service. Oh sure, selection hangs in there, along with product quality and the general feel of the store (online or otherwise), but it seems that most people look for price and service over anything else. By selling on eBay, you automatically feed their desire to find a great price, so why not go one step further and amaze the customers with service, too?

One very simple way to demonstrate your customer focus involves special orders. Periodically, people want something *like* the items you sell, but not exactly. Maybe it's an older model, a hard-to-find color, or just a different size. Whatever the details, special orders represent a great opportunity to pick up some extra business and turn a normal customer into a raving fan.

Include a special order page on your Web site, where you give customers the opportunity to tell you about that special something they just can't find anywhere else. Sketch a broad outline of the types of products you can help them find and the timeframe and costs involved. As the expert in your field, you should find that special orders add nicely to the bottom line without adversely impacting your time. (After all, if you can't find something, you just need to tell the customer, who still appreciates the fact that you even looked!)

Stay inside of eBay's parameters if you advertise a special order service on your About Me page. If you can get the item that your customer wants, make sure that you run the sale through an eBay transaction. A fixed-price auction works fine for this type of thing (particularly if you coordinate with the buyer on the timing).

Driving Traffic to Your Brick-and-Mortar Store

As eBay has grown over the last few years, more and more classic brick-and-mortar retailers have discovered the power of eBay as both a buying and selling tool. If you already complement your retail sales with efforts on eBay, why not work on turning your online buyers into through-the-door customers?

Promoting your store through your About Me page means adding a little description of your place of business, including all the contact information that everybody knows and loves from business cards. Make sure you put your full mailing address, phone number (both local and 800 number, if your store uses a toll-free line for distant customers), e-mail contact address, and Web site address. Putting driving directions to your store in the listing certainly doesn't hurt, either.

For extra bonus points, include a link to a map from MapQuest (`www.map quest.com`) or Expedia (`www.expedia.com`). If you use MapQuest, make sure you use the Find a Business option because that includes your store name at the top of the map. (Why turn down free advertising? Besides, it looks better and more complete if your customer prints out the map.)

When you create HTML code for the link to your map, open it in a new window to prevent your losing your customer. To do that, add the `target` tag to the end of your link, as shown near the bottom of this ridiculously long MapQuest URL:

```
See a map to <a
          href="http://www.mapquest.com/maps/map.adp?latlong
          type=internal&addtohistory=&latitude=A1n2b%2bAeoWs
          %3d&longitude=QcL3bZ7XpZQ%3d&name=More%20Than%20Ga
          mes&countryid=250&country=US&address=340%20E%20Dup
          ont%20Rd&city=Fort%20Wayne&state=IN&zipcode=46825&
          phone=260%2d497%2d8300&cat=More%20Than%20Games&spu
          rl=0&searchtype=GenSearch", target=_blank>More
          Than Games</a>. (Map opens in a new browser
          window.)
```

While you're at it, you might give your online customers an extra reason to visit your offline store by offering a discount coupon or something that they can print out and redeem when they visit. (If you feel *really* adventuresome, you can go the other direction as well by promoting your online storefront to your local customer base, but only do that if it makes good sense for your business — which it won't for most companies.)

Introducing You, the Expert!

People love buying from an expert. In fact, they love just *talking* to an expert. Why? It's ingrained in us. As kids, our parents and teachers taught us to look up to experts — after all, that's why those people are in those fields. You go to an expert for the best information and the most reliable knowledge. In the online marketplace, that's even more important because customers don't usually know the seller personally or even get to meet that person. Your expertise — your mantle of being an expert — helps sell the customer on doing business with you.

So how do you build this expertise and present it for the world to see? Start with quotes from other people in your industry. If someone introduced you at a meeting and said something nice in the process, jot it down and ask if you can use that as part of your online bio. When the local (or regional or national) media do a story about you, pull out quotes for your resume. Quotes deliver a lot of power because they aren't *you* talking about how great you are — they're someone *else* saying it. That means quite a bit, particularly if the person carries some badge of expertise himself.

Next, talk about your own experience. Mention your degrees, your years of working in the field, and your credits with products or companies out there. Did you contribute to a new product or invent one yourself? Put that in your profile. Did you win a tournament or write a book? Tell people about it. Do you own the region's largest collection of whatever-it-is or did you research some rarity in this line? All those things make great fodder to support your role as the product expert.

You can also demonstrate your knowledge in your communications, both within auction templates and when answering questions posed by your customers. Even the answers in your Frequently Asked Questions document (mentioned earlier in this chapter) help build your stature as an expert in the eyes of the customer. You anticipated the customer's questions and answered them. How cool is that?

This kind of information makes a great addition to your About Me page and to a similar sort of page (perhaps called *About Us*) on your Web site. Tell your story. Fill it with detail and colorful information, but most importantly, make sure it's accurate. People *love* a good story, and they *want* to put their trust in you (particularly if you sell cool stuff). Give them information to help them deposit that trust in you and then watch your sales numbers rise!

Offering Insights, News, and Resources

Because you sell amazing products that your customers crave, you probably know more about the market than other people, right? You spend time following the industry, getting to know the manufacturers, and becoming intimate with the product. It's all part and parcel of the business world you chose. You can put all that information to work by adding a headlines and news section to your About Me page or your Web site, where you share your depth of knowledge with your customers. Educate and entertain them, and they belong to you for life!

A simple *News and Industry Highlights* section in your About Me page goes a long way toward making this concept work. As you find interesting tidbits about your products, market, and industry as a whole, jot down a few words (even just a headline) and add it to your site or About Me page. If you feel like going all-out, include a link to the original story as well (although you don't need to go to that level if you don't want to do it). Most importantly, add a couple of sentences on why you find this news important or significant. Did someone just release a new product that you plan to carry? Did the government pass a law pertaining to your industry? Almost anything like this counts as news, provided your customers find it truly interesting and not just page-filler.

If you also collect products similar to those you sell, try building a links page populated with live hyperlinks to collector-oriented Web sites and discussion lists available online. Those resources show that you did your homework and that you know the best places to learn more. (Don't worry that links like this might lose you business. Nine times out of ten, your customers won't ever follow the links you created.)

Nevertheless, customers want to see the links there because it means that you care about both them and the industry as a whole. And because you care, you're a safe trading partner. That goes a long way toward clinching the sale right there.

Blogging for Fun and Profit

If you missed the whole Web logging (or *blogging* thing) when it took root a couple of years ago, you aren't alone — a lot of people didn't get it (heck, I still feel a bit fuzzy on the whole matter myself). Think of *blogs,* as the popular online culture dubbed them, as personal media outlets, run by, compiled by, and portraying the views of the person behind the blog. They can cover any topic you can possibly imagine, from politics to LEGO building blocks, and anything in between.

As blogs caught on during the last year or so, businesses also discovered them as a tool for communicating with their customers. Good blog software gives you a quick and easy way to post headlines and brief (or not so brief) stories about the headlines. You can include links and photos, too (although the details depend greatly on the software that you use). Most importantly, you include information that you find interesting or worthy of a stated opinion.

For a business blog, headlines, industry trends, and new product announcements make great blogging material. Posting your comments about such things enhances your reputation as an expert both inside and outside the industry, plus (if you do it well) the blog demonstrates your ongoing commitment to your chosen work. After all, it's easy to pick up a skid of some odd product and shove stuff into a few eBay auctions, but it takes a whole different level of effort and knowledge to keep up with what's new and different.

You can start and maintain your blog for free by using any one of the myriad Web-based tools out there. For starters, check out the aptly named Blogger (www.blogger.com) and LiveJournal.com (www.livejournal.com). Both services give you a good basic set of tools, so you can start your blog in no time at all. If you own space on a Web server, check with your hosting company to see if you already have access to a blogging tool. Many companies automatically install open source blogging applications like Geeklog (www.geeklog.net) as part of their basic Web site packages these days.

After you start your blog, *keep it going*. You need to post something to the blog at least every few days to make it worthwhile. Yes, this demands some of your precious time, but think of it as an investment in your business rather than a digital time sink. By posting information, news, and commentary to your Weblog, you're building that all-important résumé as an expert in the field.

Include links to your blog on your Web site, your eBay About Me page, and your auction text, too! When done right, your blog forms part of that all-important funnel for moving customers from browsing to interest and ultimately purchasing, but the blog gets to do its part only if you promote it!

Chapter 21

Ten Tricks for Troubleshooting Your Work

*W*elcome to the world of programming! Two types of programmers exist: Those who debug their programs, and those who will. Debugging involves removing all your program's bugs (some computer programmers call them "unimplemented features") so that the program works correctly every time. Novice programmers often attempt to write entire applications without testing along the way. However, as you gain experience, you'll find that it's more efficient (and results in fewer headaches) to spend a little extra time carefully debugging your program during development. Errors that crop up after you've finished development will likely take twice as long to find — and then fix.

Troubleshooting eventually becomes a way of life. You find yourself mentally debugging your programs as you write them. Some programmers prefer to write an entire section of code, methodically checking every line before running it. They live for the challenge of writing bug-free code the first time.

Others prefer to write quickly, taking time out frequently to run the program and identify bugs. Neither style is right or wrong. Choose what works for you.

Finding the elusive bugs that cause your program grief can often be aggravating and time-consuming. To help, this chapter introduces ten timesaving tips for troubleshooting your programs that make testing a breeze.

Indenting Your Code for Readability

Surprisingly enough, indenting your code consistently and dramatically decreases the number of errors you encounter. Although indenting doesn't change the program itself, it makes the code significantly easier to read.

Programming languages are structured with lines of code fitting into each other. To indent your code, add tabs or spaces to set each line of code inside each logical structure (loops, functions, if/then statements, and so on). Consider the following two examples from Chapter 17.

No indenting:

```
if ( $response <> 'VERIFIED' ) {
echo "Didn't receive a VERIFIED response!";
} else {
if ( $debug )
{
echo "Transaction VERIFIED";
}
}
```

Indented:

```
if ( $response <> 'VERIFIED' ) {

   echo "Didn't receive a VERIFIED response!";
} else {
   if ( $debug )
   {
     echo "Transaction VERIFIED";
   }
}
```

Although these two examples are functionally identical, the second example makes it easy to follow the program's logic. Even if you're not familiar with PHP's syntax, the indenting helps show the start and end of each logical structure (in this case an if statement). Each opening brace should have a closing brace at the same indent level. The indenting also helps you identify which lines of code fit within each section. Given enough time, you could work your way through the "no indenting" example to find which lines of code fit inside one another. However, indenting saves you time by making it easy to grasp the program logic at a glance.

Indenting helps not only with your main computer program but also with troubleshooting your HTML. HTML has a very structured syntax, so indenting your code helps point out problems with tag embedding.

Using a Consistent Method for Naming Variables and Functions

When you begin a new program, you can save yourself a lot of aggravation if you decide upon a consistent scheme for naming your variables and functions. You'll encounter fewer misnamed variables and spend less time scrolling through your code to track down the name of a variable or function you can't recall.

To get started, every variable should start with a lowercase letter. Then if you use a variable name with more than one word, make the starting letter of each word uppercase. For example, a variable that represents an auction's description might be called `auctionDescription`, `auctionDesc`, or `myAuctionDescription`.

Functions should start with a verb (an action word) and start with a capital letter. A function that fetches an auction's description, for example, may be named `GetAuctionDescription`, `FetchAuctionDesc`, or `LoadAuctionDescription`.

Like a programming language, naming conventions offer lots of flexibility. Some developers include a letter at the beginning of each variable that tells you what type of value it has (string, integer, and so on). The sky is the limit. You can decide what works best for you, but whichever scheme you choose, stick with it!

Adding Comments Everywhere

Nothing tests the mettle of experienced programmers more than working with a program they've never seen before or wrote more than a month ago. Keeping up with the flow of variables and functions is difficult enough when you've just written a program. But if it's been a while, you're going to have a tough time remembering what each line of the program does.

Save yourself (and others who may work with your code) a lot of grief by adding comments *everywhere*. You can add single line comments before or at the end of a line as well as large comment blocks at the beginning of a file or section. You can even go so far as to explain what every line of your program does. You'll thank yourself when you come back a year later to update your application.

Here's what a single line comment before the code looks like:

```
// Retrieve the Official eBay Time
$officialTime = getOfficialTime();
```

And here's the format for commenting every line:

```
$officialTime = getOfficialTime();    // Get eBay Time
$itemNumber   = getMyItemNumber();    // Retrieve item num
$itemPrice    = $itemCost * 1.5       // Calc item markup
```

Block comment for a section or file look like this:

```
/**********************************
 * FileName: eBayTimeAPI.php       *
 * Purpose:  Retrieve and display the *
 *           current eBay time     *
 **********************************/
```

Putting Your IDE to Work

Integrated development environments (IDEs) make life so much easier. IDEs typically allow you to run your program one line at a time. Although this functionality might not sound like a big deal, it works wonders when you're not sure where your program has gone wrong. As the IDE works its way through your application, you can pause to look at variable values and watch how the program moves through your code.

You may be surprised to find out how many times your program uses a particular function. Examining the values your variables hold at different points during the execution of your program may alarm you. A price variable may suddenly receive a value of $1,000,000,000 when a line of code multiplies the variable incorrectly. The IDE helps you find out where the problem occurred. IDEs also help development by color-coding your program, helping you avoid variable misspellings, and providing language syntax assistance.

Almost every programming language (including many Web-based languages) has IDEs available. ActiveState's Komodo PHP IDE, shown in Figure 21-1, was used to develop the examples in this book.

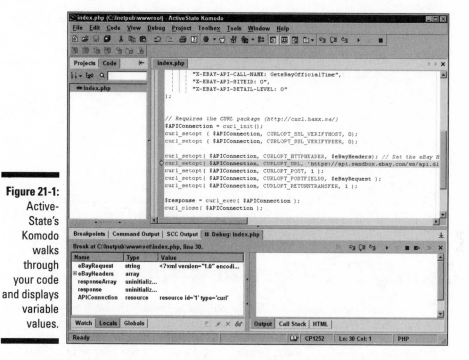

Figure 21-1:
Active-
State's
Komodo
walks
through
your code
and displays
variable
values.

Adding Debugging Outputs Everywhere

If you're not sure you want to spring for an IDE to code in, create the next best thing: a debugging code system. Because an IDE isn't available to watch the value of each variable, you want your code to do it for you. By adding statements that output the current value of a variable when you turn your debugging on, you can approximate the IDE experience (although you'll be happier with an honest to goodness IDE).

A code debugging system works a bit like the lights in your home. You include a switch in your program connected to one or more lights. When you turn the switch on, the lights all come on. To control your "lights," include a variable in your program, called a *debug flag,* that you set to ON or OFF at the beginning of your program. Then add numerous "lights" or conditional output code snippets that display the value of a variable.

This section initializes the debug flag, creating the light switch:

```
// Value of 0 turns the "lights" OFF, 1 turns "lights" ON
$debug = 0;
```

Each place you'd like to peek at the inner workings of your program, add the conditional output code (a single light) as follows:

```
// Check to see if the "lights" (debug flag) are ON
if ( $debug )
{
  // Change the variable in the output line below
  // to match the variable in your program.
  echo 'The current value of "myVar" is ' . $myVar;
}
```

Add a light for each variable you want to keep an eye on. If you're having trouble understanding what your program is doing at a particular point, add a light! Also, by making your debug outputs conditional, you can turn them off without deleting them. You'll be glad when you need them later.

Evaluating One Piece at a Time

Complex programs can be downright painful to troubleshoot. However, you can apply the old saying, "Divide and conquer." By dividing your program into bite-size pieces, you can evaluate each section at a time. When you check a section of your code, be sure that it's getting the proper inputs and then verify that the outputs look like they should. Then move on to the next section.

When all else fails, see if you can pull the code section that you're having problems with completely out of the application and drop it into a new program. Many times, you can troubleshoot a section of code more easily when it's isolated from the rest of your application.

Testing Your Program in a Different Environment

Environmental issues seem to impact Internet applications more than traditional programs. If you can't seem to track down a problem, try running your program on a different PC. With Web-based applications, you'll also want to test on a different Web browser. (If you're an Internet Explorer user, give Firefox a try at www.mozilla.org; see Figure 21-2.)

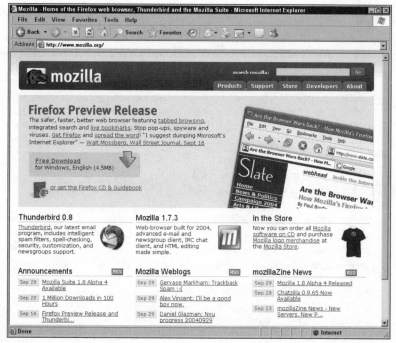

Different Web browsers handle pages differently, changing how your Web-based programs look and operate (particularly if you use client-based code like JavaScript). A different PC helps with testing your desktop-based application. You can pinpoint files you need to include when installing on a different PC as well as help to identify whether your program is causing the trouble you're facing or your PC.

Getting Other Programs Out of the Way

When developing an Internet application, be aware that programs running on your computer may cause trouble. Firewalls, pop-up blockers, and privacy protection tools all have the potential to interfere with proper communication between you and your program as well as communication between your program and the Internet. Cookie-blocking programs cause countless problems with Web-based applications that use cookies, and firewalls may block traffic (particularly when accessing special features such as an e-mail IMAP server).

To limit the trouble these utilities may cause, temporarily shut down or disable your security programs. If possible, give your application special access privileges so that you don't leave yourself open to hackers. Also, be sure to turn on your security programs immediately after you complete testing.

Because others may use your program, you'll want to develop your application in such a way that security programs don't cause trouble. If you just can't get around a particular application, be sure to document the name and version number so that your users can work around the problem, too!

Submitting Your Code for Review

When all else fails, show your code to another person. Although your best option is to walk through it with another developer, chances are good that anyone will do. It's amazing how many bugs you'll catch by explaining what your program accomplishes, line by line, to another human being.

The act of reviewing your code will bring to mind more details than you're capable of looking at when troubleshooting your code alone. It's a bizarre experience. Most likely, you'll sit down with your friend to show him your problem. As you explain the code, something will suddenly jump out at you, and you'll shout, "That's it! I found the problem!" You'll enthusiastically thank your confused friend who claims he didn't help at all.

Checking for Reserved Words or Characters

Every programming language utilizes special words or characters in the language's syntax. Be careful to use safe variable names that don't match reserved words or include forbidden characters (typically, you should stick with alphanumeric characters for variables and function names). Not sure what words your programming language holds sacred? No problem! A quick Google (`www.google.com`) search for `"PHP reserved words"` (replace `PHP` with the name of your programming language) turns up a plethora of results, detailing the many special words you should not use.

For example, you shouldn't create a variable named `class` because almost every programming language includes *class* in its reserved words list. When it comes to special characters, you also need to be careful. Just like reserved words, programming languages reserve certain characters for use only by the programming syntax. For example, PHP uses the ; character to end every line of code, the $ character before every variable name, and the ' and " characters to start string values. Using any of these characters recklessly in your code can cause all sorts of odd program behavior. You can still use most reserved characters like these in a variable value, but you may need to *escape* them with a slash (\).

For example, to include an apostrophe ('), you'd create a line of code like this:

```
$myVariable = 'Don\'t include an apostrophe without escaping
        it!';
```

Check with your programming language's documentation for details on handling special characters and escaping.

Appendix

About the CD

System Requirements

Make sure that your computer meets the minimum system requirements shown in the following list. If your computer doesn't match up to most of these requirements, you may have problems using the software and files on the CD. For the latest and greatest information, please refer to the ReadMe file located at the root of the CD-ROM.

- A PC with a Pentium or faster processor; or a Mac OS computer with a 68040 or faster processor

- Microsoft Windows 95 or later; or Mac OS system software 7.6.1 or later

- At least 32MB of total RAM installed on your computer; for best performance, we recommend at least 64MB

- A CD-ROM drive

- A monitor capable of displaying at least 256 colors or grayscale

If you need more information on the basics, check out these books published by Wiley Publishing, Inc.: *PCs For Dummies* by Dan Gookin; *Macs For Dummies* by David Pogue; *iMacs For Dummies* by David Pogue; *Windows 95 For*

Dummies, Windows 98 For Dummies, Windows 2000 Professional For Dummies, Microsoft Windows Me Millennium Edition For Dummies, and *Windows XP For Dummies,* all by Andy Rathbone.

Using the CD with Microsoft Windows

To install from the CD to your hard drive, follow these steps:

1. **Insert the CD into your computer's CD-ROM drive.**

   A window appears with the following options: HTML Interface, Browse CD, and Exit.

2. **Click the Start button and choose Run from the menu.**

3. **In the dialog box that appears, type** d:\Start.htm.

   Replace d with the proper drive letter for your CD-ROM if it uses a different letter. (If you don't know the letter, double-click My Computer on your desktop and see what letter is listed for your CD-ROM drive.)

   Your browser opens, and the license agreement is displayed. If you don't have a browser, Microsoft Internet Explorer and Netscape Communicator are included on the CD.

4. **Read through the license agreement, nod your head, and click the Agree button if you want to use the CD.**

   After you click Agree, you're taken to the Main menu, where you can browse through the contents of the CD.

5. **To navigate within the interface, click a topic of interest to take you to an explanation of the files on the CD and how to use or install them.**

6. **To install software from the CD, simply click the software name.**

   You'll see two options: to run or open the file from the current location or to save the file to your hard drive. Choose to run or open the file from its current location, and the installation procedure continues. When you finish using the interface, close your browser as usual.

Note: We have included an "easy install" in these HTML pages. If your browser supports installations from within it, go ahead and click the links of the program names you see. You'll see two options: Run the File from the Current Location and Save the File to Your Hard Drive. Choose to Run the File from the Current Location, and the installation procedure continues. A Security Warning dialog box appears. Click Yes to continue the installation.

Using the CD with Mac OS

To install items from the CD to your hard drive, follow these steps:

1. **Insert the CD into your computer's CD-ROM drive.**

   In a moment, an icon representing the CD you just inserted appears on your Mac desktop. Chances are, the icon looks like a CD-ROM.

2. **Double-click the CD icon to show the CD's contents.**

3. **Double-click** start.htm **to open your browser and display the license agreement.**

   If your browser doesn't open automatically, open it as you normally would by choosing File⇨Open File (in Internet Explorer) or File⇨ Open⇨Location in Netscape (in Netscape Navigator), and select *Developing eBay Business Tools FD*. The license agreement appears.

4. **Read through the license agreement, nod your head, and click the Accept button if you want to use the CD.**

   After you click Accept, you're taken to the Main menu. This is where you can browse through the contents of the CD.

5. **To navigate within the interface, click any topic of interest, and you're taken to an explanation of the files on the CD and how to use or install them.**

6. **To install software from the CD, simply click the software name.**

What You'll Find on the CD

The following sections are arranged by category and provide a summary of the software and other goodies you'll find on the CD. If you need help with installing the items provided on the CD, refer to the installation instructions in the preceding section.

Shareware programs are fully functional, free, trial versions of copyrighted programs. If you like particular programs, register with their authors for a nominal fee and receive licenses, enhanced versions, and technical support. *Freeware programs* are free, copyrighted games, applications, and utilities. You can copy them to as many PCs as you like — for free — but they offer no technical support. *GNU software* is governed by its own license, which is included inside the folder of the GNU software. There are no restrictions on distribution of GNU software. See the GNU license at the root of the CD for more details. *Trial, demo,* or *evaluation* versions of software are usually limited either by time or functionality (such as not letting you save a project after you create it).

Program source code

For Windows, Mac, Linux, and UNIX. All the examples provided in this book are located in the Author directory on the CD and work with Macintosh, Linux, UNIX, and Windows 9*x*/Me/XP and later computers. These files contain much of the sample code from the book. The structure of the examples directory is

```
Author/Chapter1
Author/Chapterx
```

Apache HTTP Server from The Apache Software Foundation

For Windows and Linux. Open source. To use PHP or other Web-based programming languages, you first need a Web server. Apache HTTP Server represents one of the most popular Web servers available. To find out more about the Apache Web server or to download program updates, visit The Apache Software Foundation's Apache Server Web site at httpd.apache.org.

Dreamweaver MX from Macromedia

For Windows and Mac. Trial version. Develop professional Web sites with the powerful Dreamweaver WYSIWYG (What You See Is What You Get) Web site editor. With Dreamweaver, you don't need to memorize HTML code before creating your Web site or revamping your auction template. The 30-day trial will get you going and offer a taste of Dreamweaver's many features. Visit the Macromedia Dreamweaver Web site at www.macromedia.com/dreamweaver/ for more details.

eBay Software Developers Kit (SDK)

For Windows. Freeware. Use the eBay API with the eBay SDK to power your COM or .NET application. The SDK lets your application focus on functionality, taking care of the eBay communication processes that can bog down the development process. You need to join the eBay Developers Program before using the SDK. Visit the eBay Developers Program home page at `developer.ebay.com` to download updates and join the Developers Program.

HomeSite from Macromedia

For Windows. Trial version. Give one of the most powerful hand-coding development tools a try for free for 30 days. HomeSite makes writing HTML code by hand a breeze with on-screen help, code highlighting, and plenty of shortcuts. You can also write Web applications in PHP, ColdFusion, and ASP. Visit the Macromedia HomeSite page (`www.macromedia.com/homesite`) to find out about HomeSite's many timesaving features.

HotDog Professional from Sausage Software

For Windows. Trial version. Try out HotDog Professional, a text-based HTML editor, for free for 15 days. With support for major Web-based programming languages and HTML previewing, HotDog Professional offers the tools you need to write your eBay API application or enhance your auction template. The Sausage Software Web site (`www.sausage.com`) includes updates and program details.

PHP from The PHP Group

For Windows, Linux, and Mac. Open source. PHP powers the sample code in this book. An incredibly flexible Web-based programming language, PHP gives you the power to make dynamic Web sites and integrate with the eBay API. To find out more about PHP, look up documentation, or find software for other operating systems, visit the PHP Group Web site at `www.php.net`.

PrimalScript from Sapien Technologies

For Windows. Trial version. PrimalScript, a powerful development IDE, offers support for numerous Web-based programming languages you can use to create your eBay applications. With features such as code completion, syntax coloring, and function help, you'll get more done in less time. To find out more about PrimalScript, visit the Sapien Technologies Web site at www. sapien.com.

TopStyle Lite from Bradbury Software

For Windows. Freeware. Not sure if you're ready for TopStyle Pro? No problem — the Lite version gets you started editing your style sheets without memorizing all the detailed options. When you're ready to step up to TopStyle Pro, give the Trial version on this book's CD a whirl or visit the Bradbury Software Web site at www.bradsoft.com.

TopStyle Pro from Bradbury Software

For Windows. Trial version. Without a doubt the most powerful and feature-rich style sheet editor available, TopStyle Pro makes Web development with CSS a breeze. The incredible interface includes an excellent preview tool, automated HTML updating for your old HTML tags, and more. With standards-based CSS coding taking over, you'll want to get started with TopStyle, which will save you countless hours. For a complete feature list and software updates, visit the Bradbury Software Web site at www.bradsoft.com.

Zend Studio from Zend Technologies Inc.

For Windows, Linux, and Mac. Trial version. Try out Zend Studio for free for 21 days. An excellent IDE (Integrated Development Environment) for PHP, an open source programming language, Zend Studio speeds your application development and reduces your debugging time. Zend Studio also includes PHP server components and the Apache Web Server so that you can develop PHP applications without access to an Internet Web server.

For more information and updates, visit the Zend Technologies Web site at www.zend.com.

Troubleshooting

Programs included on the CD may have higher system requirements than the general CD system requirements. If you're having difficulty with a program, check the software's home page for detailed system requirements.

The two most common problems are that you have too little computer memory (RAM) for the programs you want to use, or other programs running are affecting the installation or running of a program. If you get an error message such as Not enough memory or Setup cannot continue, try one or more of the following suggestions and then try using the software again:

- ✔ **Turn off any antivirus software running on your computer.** Installation programs sometimes mimic virus activity and may make your computer incorrectly believe that it's being infected by a virus.

- ✔ **Close all running programs.** The more programs you have running, the less memory that's available to other programs. Installation programs typically update files and programs, so if you keep other programs running, installation may not work properly.

- ✔ **Have your local computer store add more RAM to your computer.** This is, admittedly, a drastic and somewhat expensive step. However, adding more memory can really help the speed of your computer and allow more programs to run at the same time. This may include closing the CD interface and running a product's installation program from Windows Explorer.

If you have trouble with the CD-ROM, please call the Wiley Product Technical Support phone number at 800-762-2974. Outside the United States, call 317-572-3994. You can also contact Wiley Product Technical Support at www.wiley.com/techsupport. John Wiley & Sons will provide technical support only for installation and other general quality control items. For technical support on the applications themselves, consult the program's vendor or author.

To place additional orders or to request information about other Wiley products, please call 877-762-2974.

Index

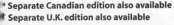

SPORTS, FITNESS, PARENTING, RELIGION & SPIRITUALITY

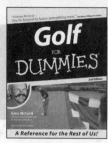
0-7645-5146-9

0-7645-5418-2

Also available:

Adoption For Dummies
0-7645-5488-3

Basketball For Dummies
0-7645-5248-1

The Bible For Dummies
0-7645-5296-1

Buddhism For Dummies
0-7645-5359-3

Catholicism For Dummies
0-7645-5391-7

Hockey For Dummies
0-7645-5228-7

Judaism For Dummies
0-7645-5299-6

Martial Arts For Dummies
0-7645-5358-5

Pilates For Dummies
0-7645-5397-6

Religion For Dummies
0-7645-5264-3

Teaching Kids to Read For Dummies
0-7645-4043-2

Weight Training For Dummies
0-7645-5168-X

Yoga For Dummies
0-7645-5117-5

TRAVEL

0-7645-5438-7

0-7645-5453-0

Also available:

Alaska For Dummies
0-7645-1761-9

Arizona For Dummies
0-7645-6938-4

Cancún and the Yucatán For Dummies
0-7645-2437-2

Cruise Vacations For Dummies
0-7645-6941-4

Europe For Dummies
0-7645-5456-5

Ireland For Dummies
0-7645-5455-7

Las Vegas For Dummies
0-7645-5448-4

London For Dummies
0-7645-4277-X

New York City For Dummies
0-7645-6945-7

Paris For Dummies
0-7645-5494-8

RV Vacations For Dummies
0-7645-5443-3

Walt Disney World & Orlando For Dummies
0-7645-6943-0

GRAPHICS, DESIGN & WEB DEVELOPMENT

0-7645-4345-8

0-7645-5589-8

Also available:

Adobe Acrobat 6 PDF For Dummies
0-7645-3760-1

Building a Web Site For Dummies
0-7645-7144-3

Dreamweaver MX 2004 For Dummies
0-7645-4342-3

FrontPage 2003 For Dummies
0-7645-3882-9

HTML 4 For Dummies
0-7645-1995-6

Illustrator CS For Dummies
0-7645-4084-X

Macromedia Flash MX 2004 For Dummies
0-7645-4358-X

Photoshop 7 All-in-One Desk
Reference For Dummies
0-7645-1667-1

Photoshop CS Timesaving Techniques
For Dummies
0-7645-6782-9

PHP 5 For Dummies
0-7645-4166-8

PowerPoint 2003 For Dummies
0-7645-3908-6

QuarkXPress 6 For Dummies
0-7645-2593-X

NETWORKING, SECURITY, PROGRAMMING & DATABASES

0-7645-6852-3

0-7645-5784-X

Also available:

A+ Certification For Dummies
0-7645-4187-0

Access 2003 All-in-One Desk
Reference For Dummies
0-7645-3988-4

Beginning Programming For Dummies
0-7645-4997-9

C For Dummies
0-7645-7068-4

Firewalls For Dummies
0-7645-4048-3

Home Networking For Dummies
0-7645-42796

Network Security For Dummies
0-7645-1679-5

Networking For Dummies
0-7645-1677-9

TCP/IP For Dummies
0-7645-1760-0

VBA For Dummies
0-7645-3989-2

Wireless All In-One Desk Reference
For Dummies
0-7645-7496-5

Wireless Home Networking For Dummies
0-7645-3910-8